MCSE Windows NT
For Dummies

M000224373

Intel Hardware Minimums

124MB free hard disk space

12MB RAM (Intel processors)

486/25 Intel processor

VGA adapter

CD-ROM (not required for installation from network)

Windows NT Setup Options

/B	Install without creating boot floppies
/OX	Create boot floppies without starting installation
/S	Source file location, such as /S:\\MainServer\NTSetup
/U	Unattended install (requires /S switch)
/C	Don't check for free disk space
/F	Don't verify files

WINNT and WINNT32 Versions

There are two files that must be used in order to begin the installation of Windows NT: WINNT and WINNT32. Which one you use depends on whether you are upgrading your previous version of Windows NT or not.

- Use WINNT to install Windows NT on a machine that does not have a version of Windows NT.

- Use WINNT32 to upgrade a previous version of Windows NT.

Disk Configurations

Name	Configuration	Hardware Minimum	Fault Tolerance
Disk Striping (w/o parity)	Data divided into 64k blocks and spread across the disks	Two disks	None
Disk Striping with parity	Similar to disk striping, but parity information is spread across disks in addition to the data	Three disks (one for parity)	Reconstruct a failed drive
Disk Mirroring	Duplicate partitions on separate disks; disks share controller	One controller, two disks	Access duplicate partition; vulnerable to controller failure
Disk Duplexing	Duplicate partitions on separate disks; includes spare controller	Two controllers, two disks	Access duplicate partition; less vulnerable to a controller failure
Volume Set	Consolidates data from multiple areas of free space into one drive letter	One to thirty-two disks	None

COMPUTER BOOK SERIES FROM IDG

MCSE Windows NT® Server 4 For Dummies®

Cheat Sheet

REGEDIT or REGEDT32 ?

There are two utilities for editing the Windows NT 4.0 Registry: REGEDIT and REGEDT32.

When searching for values (located on the right-hand pane), use REGEDIT, which closely resembles the Windows 95 Registry editor. REGEDT32, native to Windows NT, has more security features than REGEDIT, such as the ability to set permissions on certain keys in the Registry. REGEDT32 does not let you search for values as REGEDIT does.

Tuning server settings

Minimize Memory Used	Up to 10 network connections
Balance	Up to approximately 64 connections (default)
Maximize Throughput for File Sharing	Maximum memory for file sharing
Maximize Throughput for Network Applications	Optimizes memory for applications

Moving and copying on NTFS partitions

- ✔ If you are copying within a partition, the file will inherit the target folders permissions.

- ✔ If you are moving within a partition, the file will retain its original permission.

- ✔ If you are moving across a partition, the file will inherit the target folder's permissions.

Name resolution

Domain Name Service (DNS)	Resolves host names to IP addresses
Windows Internet Naming Service (WINS)	Resolves NetBIOS names to IP addresses dynamically
HOSTS	Static text file to resolve host names to IP addresses
LMHOSTS	Static text file to resolve NetBIOS names to IP addresses

System or Boot partition?

It sounds backwards, but

- ✔ Boot files are on the system partition.
- ✔ System files are on the boot partition.

ARC naming convention

The ARC naming convention is used in the boot.ini file to specify the disks and partitions your operating systems are located on. It will look similar to this: multi(0)disk(0)rdisk(0)partition(1).

multi(x)	SCSI controller with BIOS **enabled**
scsi(x)	SCSI controller with BIOS **disabled**
disk(x)	SCSI disk with system files. (This is 0 when multi is used.)
rdisk(x)	Physical disk with system files
partition(x)	Partition with system files

Server roles

- ✔ You must reinstall Windows NT to change a PDC or BDC.

- ✔ You must promote a BDC to a PDC.

- ✔ A member server can change domains without reinstalling Windows NT.

IDG BOOKS WORLDWIDE

...For Dummies: #1 Computer Book Series for Beginners

MCSE WINDOWS NT® SERVER 4 FOR DUMMIES®

by Ken Majors, MCSE, and
Brandon McTague, MCSE

Foreword by
Eckhart Boehme, Marketing Manager,
Certification and Skills Assessment, Microsoft Corporation

IDG BOOKS WORLDWIDE™

IDG Books Worldwide, Inc.
An International Data Group Company

Foster City, CA ♦ Chicago, IL ♦ Indianapolis, IN ♦ New York, NY

MCSE Windows NT® Server 4 For Dummies®

Published by
IDG Books Worldwide, Inc.
An International Data Group Company
919 E. Hillsdale Blvd.
Suite 400
Foster City, CA 94404
www.idgbooks.com (IDG Books Worldwide Web site)
www.dummies.com (Dummies Press Web site)

Library of Congress Catalog Card No.: 98-85838

ISBN: 0-7645-0400-2

Printed in the United States of America

10 9 8 7 6 5 4 3 2 1

1E/RU/QX/ZY/IN

Distributed in the United States by IDG Books Worldwide, Inc.

Distributed by Macmillan Canada for Canada; by Transworld Publishers Limited in the United Kingdom; by IDG Norge Books for Norway; by IDG Sweden Books for Sweden; by Woodslane Pty. Ltd. for Australia; by Woodslane (NZ) Ltd. for New Zealand; by Addison Wesley Longman Singapore Pte Ltd. for Singapore, Malaysia, Thailand, Indonesia and Korea; by Norma Comunicaciones S.A. for Colombia; by Intersoft for South Africa; by International Thomson Publishing for Germany, Austria and Switzerland; by Toppan Company Ltd. for Japan; by Distribuidora Cuspide for Argentina; by Livraria Cultura for Brazil; by Ediciencia S.A. for Ecuador; by Ediciones ZETA S.C.R. Ltda. for Peru; by WS Computer Publishing Corporation, Inc., for the Philippines; by Unalis Corporation for Taiwan; by Contemporanea de Ediciones for Venezuela; by Computer Book & Magazine Store for Puerto Rico; by Express Computer Distributors for the Caribbean and West Indies. Authorized Sales Agent: Anthony Rudkin Associates for the Middle East and North Africa.

For general information on IDG Books Worldwide's books in the U.S., please call our Consumer Customer Service department at 800-762-2974. For reseller information, including discounts and premium sales, please call our Reseller Customer Service department at 800-434-3422.

For information on where to purchase IDG Books Worldwide's books outside the U.S., please contact our International Sales department at 650-655-3200 or fax 650-655-3297.

For information on foreign language translations, please contact our Foreign & Subsidiary Rights department at 650-655-3021 or fax 650-655-3281.

For sales inquiries and special prices for bulk quantities, please contact our Sales department at 650-655-3200 or write to the address above.

For information on using IDG Books Worldwide's books in the classroom or for ordering examination copies, please contact our Educational Sales department at 800-434-2086 or fax 317-596-5499.

For press review copies, author interviews, or other publicity information, please contact our Public Relations department at 650-655-3000 or fax 650-655-3299.

For authorization to photocopy items for corporate, personal, or educational use, please contact Copyright Clearance Center, 222 Rosewood Drive, Danvers, MA 01923, or fax 978-750-4470.

About the Authors

Kenneth Majors is currently working as a Senior Network Engineer for Levi, Ray, & Shoup, Inc in Kansas City. He has designed and deployed Windows NT enterprises for large companies and municipalities in the Midwest. Ken has been an MCSE since 1996. He can be reached via e-mail at kmajors@sound.net or kmajors@lrs.com. You can also find him on the Web at www.sound.net/~kmajors or www.lrs.com.

Brandon McTague is a senior systems engineer with the Global Financial Services division of Perot Systems Corporation. He currently manages an NT engineering team for the investment division of a major European bank. Brendan received his MCSE in July, 1995 with electives in Microsoft TCP/IP and Systems Management Server. He completed the requirements for the NT 4.0 MCSE certification track in October, 1997.

Syngress Media creates books and software for Information Technology professionals seeking skill enhancement and career advancement. Its products are designed to comply with vendor and industry standard course curricula and are optimized for certification exam preparation.

About the Contributors

Matthew Hull is a MCSE, and also holds a MCP + Internet certification, and has a Masters in Telecommunications. Matthew is an IT Specialist in Systems Management for IBM Global Services.

Paul Shields is a MCSE. He is currently working as advisor for Desktop Computing and Support Strategies at a major telecommunications firm.

Steve Vaughn runs a small consulting firm in upstate New York. Specializing in PC management and internetworking, Steve Vaughn Consulting, Inc. provides research, prototyping and integration services to large enterprises. You can contact Steve Vaughn at svaughn@frontiernet.net.

Robert Aschermann, MCP, MCSE, MCT, MBA has been an IS professional for nearly ten years. During his career, he has worked in technical support, systems design, consulting, and training. Mr. Aschermann has been an MCSE for almost three years and has passed 15 Microsoft certification exams.

Bradley John Schaufenbuel is a consultant on the Internet Architecture team, which is a part of the Technology Infrastructure Services group at Arthur Andersen Technology Solutions in Chicago, Illinois.

Jeffrey Ferris is an MCSE in the Kansas City area, currently employed as an NT Systems Integrator for one of the Big Three long distance providers. Jeffrey has been working with computers since just after leaning to walk, focusing on TCP/IP technologies and Windows NT for the past three years.

Angie Nash currently lives in Raleigh, North Carolina, with her husband Jason (who is also a CNE, MCSE, and MCT) and their two cats. Angie works for EDS as a Systems Administrator and Trainer.

Michael Cross is an MCSE, MCP Specialist: Internet, and has spent the past 17 years glued to a computer. He is a computer programmer, network support specialist, and an instructor at local private colleges. Michael also runs his own business (consulting, programming, Web page design, hardware, networking, and freelance writing). He lives in London, Ontario Canada with his lovely fiance, Jennifer, and two spaz cats.

Author's Acknowledgments

We would like to thank the people at IDG Books who worked to bring this book to market. They include Diane Steele, Jill Pisoni, Mary Corder, Mary Bednarek, Pat O'Brien, and Phil Worthington.

ABOUT IDG BOOKS WORLDWIDE

Welcome to the world of IDG Books Worldwide.

IDG Books Worldwide, Inc., is a subsidiary of International Data Group, the world's largest publisher of computer-related information and the leading global provider of information services on information technology. IDG was founded more than 25 years ago and now employs more than 8,500 people worldwide. IDG publishes more than 275 computer publications in over 75 countries (see listing below). More than 90 million people read one or more IDG publications each month.

Launched in 1990, IDG Books Worldwide is today the #1 publisher of best-selling computer books in the United States. We are proud to have received eight awards from the Computer Press Association in recognition of editorial excellence and three from *Computer Currents'* First Annual Readers' Choice Awards. Our best-selling *...For Dummies*® series has more than 50 million copies in print with translations in 38 languages. IDG Books Worldwide, through a joint venture with IDG's Hi-Tech Beijing, became the first U.S. publisher to publish a computer book in the People's Republic of China. In record time, IDG Books Worldwide has become the first choice for millions of readers around the world who want to learn how to better manage their businesses.

Our mission is simple: Every one of our books is designed to bring extra value and skill-building instructions to the reader. Our books are written by experts who understand and care about our readers. The knowledge base of our editorial staff comes from years of experience in publishing, education, and journalism — experience we use to produce books for the '90s. In short, we care about books, so we attract the best people. We devote special attention to details such as audience, interior design, use of icons, and illustrations. And because we use an efficient process of authoring, editing, and desktop publishing our books electronically, we can spend more time ensuring superior content and spend less time on the technicalities of making books.

You can count on our commitment to deliver high-quality books at competitive prices on topics you want to read about. At IDG Books Worldwide, we continue in the IDG tradition of delivering quality for more than 25 years. You'll find no better book on a subject than one from IDG Books Worldwide.

John Kilcullen
CEO
IDG Books Worldwide, Inc.

Steven Berkowitz
President and Publisher
IDG Books Worldwide, Inc.

Eighth Annual
Computer Press
Awards ≥1992

Ninth Annual
Computer Press
Awards ≥1993

Tenth Annual
Computer Press
Awards ≥1994

Eleventh Annual
Computer Press
Awards ≥1995

Publisher's Acknowledgments

We're proud of this book; please register your comments through our IDG Books Worldwide Online Registration Form located at http://my2cents.dummies.com.

Some of the people who helped bring this book to market include the following:

Acquisitions, Editorial, and Media Development

Project Editor: Pat O'Brien

Acquisitions Editor: Jill Pisoni

Copy Editor: Phil Worthington

Technical Editors: Greg Frankenfield, Mark Kory

CD-ROM Exam Reviewers: Joe Wagner, MCSE, Systems Engineer, ST Labs, Inc.; Steven A. Frare, MCP, Network Engineer, ST Labs, Inc.

Media Development Editors: Marita Ellixson, Joell Smith

Associate Permissions Editor: Carmen Krikorian

Media Development Coordinator: Megan Roney

Editorial Manager: Mary C. Corder

Media Development Manager: Heather Heath Dismore

Editorial Assistant: Darren Meiss

Production

Project Coordinator: Karen York

Layout and Graphics: Lou Boudreau, Linda Boyer, J. Tyler Connor, Maridee V. Ennis, Angela F. Hunckler, Jane E. Martin, Heather N. Pearson, Anna Rohrer, Brent Savage, Kathie Schutte, Janet Seib, Kate Snell, Michael A. Sullivan

Proofreaders: Christine Berman, Kelli Botta, Laura L. Bowman, Michelle Croninger, Rebecca Senninger, Janet M. Withers

Indexer: Christine Spina

Special Help

Publication Services, Inc.; development of the QuickLearn game by André LaMothe of Xtreme Games, LLC; CD-ROM Exam authored by Barbara A. Nahquoddy; Sandy Blackthorn, Sherry Gomoll, Dwight Ramsey, Kelly Ewing, Barry Pruett

---

General and Administrative

IDG Books Worldwide, Inc.: John Kilcullen, CEO; Steven Berkowitz, President and Publisher

IDG Books Technology Publishing: Brenda McLaughlin, Senior Vice President and Group Publisher

Dummies Technology Press and Dummies Editorial: Diane Graves Steele, Vice President and Associate Publisher; Mary Bednarek, Director of Acquisitions and Product Development; Kristin A. Cocks, Editorial Director

Dummies Trade Press: Kathleen A. Welton, Vice President and Publisher; Kevin Thornton, Acquisitions Manager

IDG Books Production for Dummies Press: Michael R. Britton, Vice President of Production and Creative Services; Beth Jenkins Roberts, Production Director; Cindy L. Phipps, Manager of Project Coordination, Production Proofreading, and Indexing; Kathie S. Schutte, Supervisor of Page Layout; Shelley Lea, Supervisor of Graphics and Design; Debbie J. Gates, Production Systems Specialist; Robert Springer, Supervisor of Proofreading; Debbie Stailey, Special Projects Coordinator; Tony Augsburger, Supervisor of Reprints and Bluelines

Dummies Packaging and Book Design: Robin Seaman, Creative Director; Jocelyn Kelaita, Product Packaging Coordinator; Kavish + Kavish, Cover Design

◆

The publisher would like to give special thanks to Patrick J. McGovern, without whom this book would not have been possible.

◆

Contents at a Glance

Cartoons at a Glance

By Rich Tennant

page 267

page 423

page 307

page 7

page 413

page 27

page 173

page 353

page 107

Fax: 978-546-7747 • E-mail: the5wave@tiac.net

Table of Contents

Part V: Resources

Sometimes, network users act like second graders fighting over the kickball and an extra glass of juice. When you master Part V, you can prove you have the skills to help everyone play safely.

Part VI: Connectivity

Hey, this NT Server thing wasn't here first! Part VI guides you through what you need to know about NetWare servers and the Remote Access Service (RAS).

Part VII: Monitoring, Optimization, and Troubleshooting

Yeah, maintenance always comes last. Prevention, troubleshooting, and recovery are detailed in Part VII.

Part VIII: The Part of Tens

I've sliced and diced the most helpful exam tips into tasty tidbits. Enjoy!

Part IX: Appendixes

Appendixes A and B are complete practice exams that show you whether you're ready for the Big Game. If you find out you're still second-string, every answer tells you exactly what you need to review.

Appendix C explains what's on the CD-ROM, which is packed with powerful study aids and valuable resources.

Studying Chapters

MCSE Windows NT Server 4 For Dummies is a self-paced method of preparing for the exam. But you don't have to guess what to study. Every chapter that covers exam objectives guides you with

- ✔ Preview questions
- ✔ Detailed coverage
- ✔ Review questions

This step-by-step structure identifies what you need to study, gives you all the facts, and rechecks what you know. Here's how it works.

First page

Each chapter starts with a preview of what's to come, including

- ✔ Exam objectives
- ✔ Study subjects

Not sure you know all about the objectives and the subjects in the chapter? Keep going.

Quick Assessment questions

The opening checks whether you already know about the exam objectives. The questions are grouped by objectives. If you miss a question, the answer tells you which section to review in the chapter.

- ✔ In a hurry? Just study sections for the questions you miss.
- ✔ Get every one? Jump to the end of the chapter and try the practice exam questions.

Study subjects

When you study a chapter, carefully read through it just like any book. Each subject is introduced — very briefly — and then you see what you need to know for the exam.

MCSE Windows NT Server 4 For Dummies doesn't just recite the dry facts. As you study, special features show you how to apply everything in the chapter to the exam.

Labs

Labs guide you through the steps of using the product and solving problems. Step-by-step exercises walk you through skills that are likely areas of focus on the exam.

I simplify each lab step to better convey the ideas of the process at the same level that the exam tests them, like this:

Lab 15-4	Setting Up an Export Server

1. **Run Services from the Control Panel.**

2. **Choose the Directory Replicator service.**

   Set Startup to Automatic. Set Log On As to the replicator account for that domain. Enter the Password for the replicator account.

3. **Run Server Manager and select the export server.**

4. **Choose Computer⇨Properties.**

5. **Select Replication.**

6. **Click OK.**

Icons

Special graphics mark paragraphs that are worth a second look.

Time Shaver helps you manage and save time while taking the exam or studying.

Instant Answer identifies correct and incorrect exam answers at a glance.

Remember highlights important capabilities and advantages of the technology.

Warning points out problems and limitations of the technology that may appear on the exam.

Tip paragraphs won't help your test score, but they may save your life, like this: *Take your special someone out to dinner after you pass the exam and reintroduce yourself.*

Tables

Sometimes, you need just the facts. In such cases, tables are a simple way to present everything at a glance, like this:

Table 16-1	RAS Server Configuration Options
Option	*Function*
Dial-out protocols	Select dial-out protocols.
Server settings	Configure dial-in protocols.
Encryption settings	Set the authentication level required for logon.

Prep Tests

You finish the chapter with Prep Test questions that mimic the sort of questions you can expect on the exam. Each question gauges your understanding of an aspect of the chapter. If you miss a question, the answer tells you which section of the chapter to review.

As on the exam, Prep Test questions have circles to mark when only one answer is right. When questions can have more than one answer, the answers have squares to mark.

What's Next?

MCSE Windows NT Server 4 For Dummies takes the anxiety out of studying for the exam. Just turn the page and dig in.

It's time to start!

Part I
Getting Testy

The 5th Wave — By Rich Tennant

"This part of the test tells us whether you're personally suited to the job of network administrator."

In this part . . .

1 tell you exactly what to expect on the Server exam, such as number of questions, format, items being tested . . . yeah, that kind of info. I introduce what all the exam tests and give examples of how the exam presents test questions. I also throw out some study tips and suggestions here, as well as give you the lowdown on requirements and additional resources for obtaining that MCSE certification.

Chapter 1

The NT Server 4.0 Exam

*T*est taking is very difficult for some people, but it won't be stressful for you. You will walk into the testing center confidently to take your Server exam. Why? Because you will be totally prepared. Believe me, that is a great feeling. And passing the exam is an even better feeling. Everything I learned in the Server exam was applicable to the Enterprise exam you may find yourself taking next. Most of what I have learned while studying for the Server exam is also applicable to the Workstation exam.

Becoming certified was the greatest career move I ever made. I knew that passing computer industry certifications was hot, but I had no idea how in demand I would be.

Certification doesn't mean you are master of all Microsoft networking, it just proves you have knowledge of Windows NT and the related technology, as well as the desire to work towards accomplishing a goal. By studying for these exams, you are going to learn how to use the product that will transcend your certification into proven experience.

Exam Blueprint

The first step toward confidence is familiarity, so I'm starting with the big picture. Here's what the NT Server exam looks like.

Objectives

The certification exam tests your abilities to plan, implement, administer, and troubleshoot Windows NT Server in a simple computing environment. The following are the Microsoft exam objectives.

Planning

- ✔ Choosing a file system
- ✔ Choosing a fault-tolerance method
- ✔ Choose a protocol for various situations

Installation and Configuration

- ✔ Install Windows NT Server on Intel-based platforms
- ✔ Install Windows NT Server to perform various server roles
- ✔ Install Windows NT Server by using various methods
- ✔ Configure protocols and protocol bindings
- ✔ Configure network adapters
- ✔ Configure Windows NT Server core services
- ✔ Configure peripherals and devices
- ✔ Configure hard disks to meet various requirements
- ✔ Configure printers
- ✔ Configure a Windows NT Server computer for various types of client computers

Managing Resources

- ✔ Manage user and group accounts
- ✔ Create and manage policies and profiles for various situations
- ✔ Administer remote servers from various types of client computers
- ✔ Manage disk resources

Connectivity

- ✔ Configure Windows NT Server for interoperability with NetWare servers by using various tools
- ✔ Install and configure Remote Access Service (RAS)

Monitoring and Optimization

- ✔ Monitor performance of various functions by using Performance Monitor
- ✔ Identify performance bottlenecks

Troubleshooting

- ✔ Choose the appropriate course of action to take to resolve installation failures
- ✔ Choose the appropriate course of action to take to resolve boot failures
- ✔ Choose the appropriate course of action to take to resolve configuration errors
- ✔ Choose the appropriate course of action to take to resolve printer problems
- ✔ Choose the appropriate course of action to take to resolve RAS problems
- ✔ Choose the appropriate course of action to take to resolve connectivity problems
- ✔ Choose the appropriate course of action to take to resolve resource access problems and permission problems
- ✔ Choose the appropriate course of action to take to resolve fault-tolerance failures

Questions

You will receive between 50 and 65 multiple-choice questions on this exam. Each test is randomly selected from a database of questions. The questions are constructed to test both

- ✔ Your mastery of basic facts
- ✔ Your ability to evaluate a set of circumstances and requirements

Multiple answers

Some of the questions will have more than one correct answer, so read through all of the possible answers. The questions that allow you to choose more than one answer have square *check boxes* instead of round *radio buttons*.

Check boxes don't mean there *must* be more than one correct answer. Radio buttons mean there is *only* one correct answer.

If you answer every question and you still have some time left, recheck to be sure you have selected the correct number of answers for each question.

Several questions may look alike, but one or two words may be different. Read each question carefully, no matter how familiar it seems.

If you find yourself unsure about an exam question, click the *Mark* check box. That makes it easy to come back later in the exam.

Illustrations

Many of the questions contain an *exhibit* (a diagram or screen shot that provides information). Exhibits can include

- ✔ Network diagrams
- ✔ Dialog boxes
- ✔ Geographic layouts

If you have spent time working with Windows NT, the figures with actual NT dialog boxes are easy to answer. The questions on real-life scenarios with network diagrams and geographic layouts have tons of information.

Exam time

You will be given about 90 minutes for the exam. There will be a countdown clock on the screen for a reminder. If you are prepared for the exam, you should have plenty of time.

Don't rush. There are no bonus points for finishing early. I don't know anyone who has failed to answer all the questions in the allotted time.

Success from Start to Finish

Ready to schedule your test? Slow down. Take the time to understand what you need to do and how long you need to do it.

Preparation

You should study until you are confident in your ability to take the test. This depends on your experience and study time. In general, if you have no experience with Windows NT Server, access to necessary resources and equipment, and plenty of time to study, you should be ready to take the certification exam in four weeks.

The Introduction of this book explains how to prepare by working through this book from cover to cover.

If you have experience with previous Windows NT Server versions and can devote a couple of hours a day for brushing up with this book, you could be ready in a week or two.

When you pass two practice exams in a row, you're ready to try the real exam.

Exam day

The first thing you will do when arriving to take your exam will be to sign in with the Testing Coordinator. You need two forms of identification, one of which must be a photo ID. You aren't allowed to carry anything into the testing area, including

- ✔ Books
- ✔ Bags
- ✔ Papers
- ✔ Cell phones
- ✔ Pagers

Starting with a smile

You're escorted into a closed room and shown to a testing station. Each station contains a computer and is separated from the others by partitions. You're furnished with scratch paper and a pen or pencil or a thin whiteboard and an erasable marker instead. All materials should be returned at the end of the exam.

Testing rooms are monitored by sight and sound. Any questions of the integrity of your exam will result in termination of that exam.

Keeping your cool

The most important advice anyone can give you about taking a Microsoft certification test — and that includes the Server exam — is *read each question carefully and completely*. Questions test your problem-solving skills as aggressively as they test your product knowledge.

- ✔ Only one or two words may be different in two exam questions.
- ✔ Terminology may be cited in a very precise manner.
- ✔ Some questions are deliberately ambiguous.

The best method of test taking is to make three passes through the exam from start to finish:

1. First, answer questions you recognize instantly.

2. On the second pass, answer questions you can solve with a little work.

3. Finally, answer questions that require a lot of analysis.

The testing software makes skipping questions easy. Just click the *Mark* check box on all the questions you have not yet answered. You can go back to all the marked questions as many times as you want.

Finishing with a bang

If you finish the test early, go back and review the answers you marked. Use as much of the remaining time as you need to recheck your answers. If you change an answer, be sure you really have a better choice.

Don't leave any questions unanswered. If you don't know the answer, guess. There is no penalty for wrong answers. If you leave it blank, you miss it.

Leaving with the results

The exam program stops automatically when your time is up. (If you decide to quit before the end of the allotted time, click the *End Exam* button.) Your test is graded immediately and the results appear on the screen. The results are printed for you, too. The Testing Coordinator notarizes the printout and stamps it.

The notarized printout is your official report. Don't lose it!

If you pass, the testing organization sends the results to Microsoft. Congratulations! Your MCP kit will arrive in a few weeks!

If you come close but fail, don't feel too bad. These tests are *tough.* I don't know any MCSE who passed every exam on the first try. If you missed by a hair, review your weak areas and try again. You will know your weak areas by the percentage you score for each category on the exam report.

Chapter 2

Exam Prep Roadmap: Windows NT Server Basics

- -

In This Chapter

▶ Windows NT Executive and Kernel

▶ The Windows NT security model

▶ Working with other operating systems

▶ Minimum requirements

- -

*H*aven't spent quality time with Server 4.0? Just a little rusty? Aren't sure? This chapter discusses the basics of NT Server 4.0 and gives you a handle on which features you need to know well for the exam.

Windows NT Server Overview

Windows NT was designed as a whole new operating system. The designer kept the Windows interface and designed a modular architecture for the core of the operating system. The design model also supported 32-bit processing, to target the high-end workstation and server markets, and connected both servers and desktops to a common operating system.

The Microsoft Windows NT Server operating system has become an established multipurpose network operating system. NT Server combines:

- ✔ Application server
- ✔ File and print server
- ✔ Communications server
- ✔ Internet/intranet server

Compared to products with similar features and performance, Windows NT Server is especially manageable, usable, and, scaleable.

With Windows NT 4.0, the user interface changed to match Windows 95. Better tools for sharing data connect users around the corner, or around the world.

Windows NT and Windows 95

Although the user interfaces look similar, Windows NT and Windows 95 share little on the same computer. You cannot upgrade from Windows 95 to Windows NT. If you require a dual boot, you must perform a new installation of Windows NT, because the formats of the Registries are completely different.

Applications that must be shared on dual boot systems must be installed twice, once for each operating system. The separate installations register the application into each operating system's Registry. You can do these installations in the same directory; separate copies of the application aren't required.

Windows NT Server contains support for both Windows NT Workstation and Windows 95 clients for network management.

✔ Windows 95 can function as a diskless workstation that boots from a Windows NT Server.

✔ Windows 95 desktops can function as clients for all Windows NT Servers.

✔ The NT Installation CD includes server management tools for both Windows NT Workstation and Windows 95.

Windows NT Feature Set

Besides the features of the previous versions of Windows NT Server, version 4.0 adds the following:

✔ **Common user interface and management**

- Windows 95 interface

- Remote booting of Windows 95 desktops

- Remote administration

✔ **Advanced Internet support**

- Internet Explorer 3.0

- Internet Information Server (IIS)

- DirectX support

✔ **Advanced messaging**

- Exchange
- Telephony API

✔ **Better networking**

- Enhanced TCP/IP protocol
- DNS server
- Multiprotocol routing
- Connectivity with Novell NetWare 4.*x* servers running NDS

Windows NT kernel

The microkernel is the heart of the operating system. It schedules activities for the processor and synchronizes multiple processors. Windows NT 4.0 gives the microkernel greater functionality. Figure 2-1 shows the Windows NT architecture model.

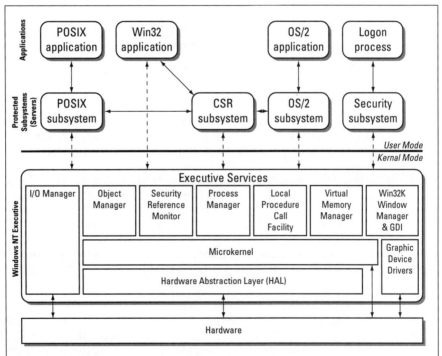

Figure 2-1:
The Windows NT architecture.

The scheduled activities are known as *threads,* the most basic scheduling entity in the system. Every process has at least one thread. A *multithreaded* application can use multiple processors to increase performance.

Threads define

- ✔ The context of a process that represents an address space
- ✔ A set of objects visible to the process
- ✔ A set of threads that runs in the context of a process

The microkernel is the only way that software can interface with hardware in Windows NT. The microkernel communicating with the HAL (Hardware Abstraction Layer) manages all hardware.

Security

Windows NT security is provided by its Security subsystem. Figure 2-2 shows the process flow for security.

Windows NT was designed to meet the National Computer Security Center (NCSC) C2 rating so NT includes

- ✔ **Mandatory logon:** For accountability.
- ✔ **Discretionary access control:** For an enforceable security policy.
- ✔ **Auditing:** Accountability again.

Fault tolerance

Windows NT supports fault tolerance in many ways. The most popular and apparent are the *RAID file systems.* Windows NT supports the RAID 0, 1, and 5 file systems. I discuss these RAID file systems in more detail in Chapter 6.

The NTFS file system supports a hot-fix feature, in which NTFS constantly monitors its disk areas and automatically moves data written to a bad sector to a good sector then removes the bad sector from service. NTFS also provides a log file to restore files in the event of a disk failure.

Symmetric multiprocessing provides redundancy in case of a processor failure. This is rare; multiple processors normally just enhance performance.

Preemptive multitasking

Preemptive multitasking is the capability of the operating system to take control of the processor without the task's cooperation. (A task also can relinquish control of the processor, as in cooperative multitasking.) Taking control away from a task is called *preemption.* Windows NT uses preemptive multitasking for all processes except 16-bit Windows 3.1 programs — a Windows 3.1 application uses cooperative multitasking.

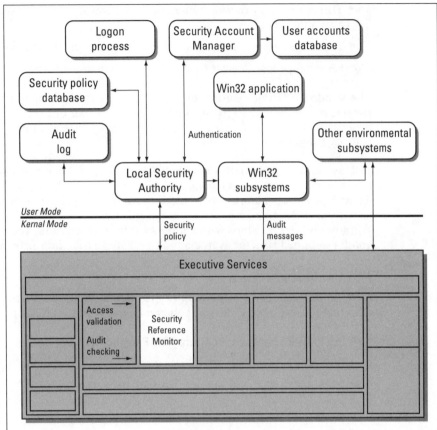

Figure 2-2:
The
Windows
NT Security
subsystem.

Preempting a process can make multiple tasks seem to operate at the same time. It also prevents a badly written application from locking up the processor. Preempting also allows you to prioritize tasks. A preemptive operating system can take control of the processor away from a task in two ways:

- ✔ **A task's time *quantum* (or *time slice*) runs out.** Each task has control for a set amount of time.

- ✔ **A task that has higher priority is ready to run.** The currently running task loses control of the processor whenever a task that has higher priority becomes ready to run.

Symmetric multiprocessing

The Windows NT microkernel takes maximum advantage of multiprocessor configurations by implementing *symmetric multiprocessing* (SMP):

> ✔ Threads of any process, including the operating system, can run on any available processor.
>
> ✔ Threads of a process run on different processors at the same time.
>
> ✔ Server processes can respond to more than one client at a time.

The Windows NT microkernel allows processors to share memory and assigns ready threads to the next available processor or processors. No processor is ever idle or executes a lower priority thread when a higher priority thread is ready to run.

SMP systems provide better *load balancing* and *fault tolerance*. Because the operating system threads run on any processor, a CPU bottleneck is less likely. A processor failure only reduces the computing capacity of the system.

Windows NT Server ships with support for four processors. You need a vendor-supplied HAL for systems that have more than four processors.

Platform independence

Platform independence, or *portability,* means that Windows NT runs on more than just one type of processor. You can install Windows NT Server 4.0 on

> ✔ Intel 80486, Pentium, Pentium Pro, Pentium II
>
> ✔ DEC Alpha AXP RISC
>
> ✔ MIPS R4000 RISC (except with Service Pack 3)
>
> ✔ PowerPC (except with Service Pack 3)

Windows NT file system (NTFS)

You have two file system choices for Windows NT:

> ✔ FAT (File Allocation Table)
> ✔ NTFS (NT File System)

Although FAT has a lower overhead, it isn't good for a server because it lacks security and recoverability. Also, NTFS supports larger partitions than a FAT file system does. You can convert a partition from FAT to NTFS without losing data.

On a RISC-based machine, you need to have a 5MB FAT partition for boot purposes. You can format all other partitions as NTFS. Only computers running Windows NT can access an NTFS partition directly; network users can access files on an NTFS partition as long as they have the access permission to do so.

Reliability

The NTFS file system protects from loss of data by using

- ✔ **Lazy write:** Protects NTFS systems from a disk failure because transactions are logged before they're carried out.
- ✔ **Hot fix:** Takes damaged disk areas out of service and moves the data to a good sector. NTFS constantly monitors its disk areas for damage. The process is invisible to all applications, users, and other processes.

Security

File security involves two main areas:

- ✔ Controlling access to the file
- ✔ Protecting the integrity of the file

NTFS lets you control user access at both the folder and file level. You can give a person Full Access to a folder but No Access to all the files within it, or vice versa. Table 2-1 lists the standard permissions for folders. The individual file attributes are

- ✔ Read (R)
- ✔ Write (W)
- ✔ Execute (X)
- ✔ Delete (D)
- ✔ Change Permissions (P)
- ✔ Take Ownership (O)

You set permissions from the Security tab for the given file or folder properties. Figure 2-3 shows the File Permissions security page for a file.

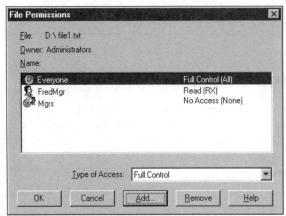

Figure 2-3:
The File
Permissions
page.

You need to know the various permissions and what a user can do with each type. The exam has many questions that pertain to permissions. The big key is that No Access means no access. It overrides all other permissions.

Tables 2-1 and 2-2 list standard user permission for folder and files.

Table 2-1	Standard User Permissions for Folders
Folder Permission	*Access*
Full Control (All) (All)	Change permissions for the folder and its contents; take ownership of the folder and its contents; add, change, and read files.
Change (RWXD) (RWXD)	Add, change, and read files.
Add & Read (RWX) (RX)	Add and read files, but cannot change them.
Read (RX) (RX)	Read files and run applications in the folder.
List (RX) (Not Specified)	List files and subfolders. No access to files created by other users.
Add (WX) (Not Specified)	Add files to the folder, but no access to the files after they are in the folder.
No Access (None) (None)	No user access, even if a user belongs to a group with Full Access.

Table 2-2	Standard User Permissions for Files
File Permissions	*Explanation*
Full Control (All)	Set permission, take ownership, read, change, and delete the file.
Change (RWXD)	Read, change, and delete the file.
Read (RX)	Read file, including applications.
No Access (None)	No access to the file, even if a user is a member of a group that has Full Access.

Networking services

Communication across a network is essential for Windows NT Server. You set up all network functions from the Network applet in the Control Panel. Figure 2-4 shows the Network Services tab.

Protocol support

Windows NT Server comes with protocols for connectivity to other computer systems:

✔ Network Basic Input/Output System (NetBIOS)

✔ NetBIOS Extended User Interface (NetBEUI)

✔ Transmission Control Protocol/Internet Protocol (TCP/IP)

✔ NWLink Internetwork Packet Exchange/Sequenced Packet Exchange (IPX/SPX)

✔ Data Link Control (DLC)

✔ AppleTalk

Vendors also provide other protocols for Windows NT. You load them via the Networks applet on the Control Panel.

Multiple clients

Windows NT Server offers support for several network clients:

✔ MS-DOS

✔ Windows 3.1*x*

✔ Windows 95

✔ Windows NT

✔ Macintosh

✔ NetWare

Figure 2-4:
The
Network
Services
tab.

These clients are supported by the included network services. You load these services via the Network applet in the Control Panel:

- Services for Microsoft
- Services for NetWare
- Services for Macintosh

You can add other services by loading drivers from the network vendor.

Windows NT allows an unlimited number of connected users access to shared resources. You use the Sharing tab of the folders Properties box.

Windows NT versus Other Servers

Windows NT Server is a multipurpose operating system that offers a robust set of tools, utilities, and network protocols to integrate into a heterogeneous environment. Windows NT Server's support for multiple client types makes it a good choice if you're adding to existing networks. The following sections compare the Windows NT Server operating system to other network operating systems.

Novell NetWare

Windows NT Server provides the necessary tools to seamlessly integrate with existing NetWare 2.*x*, 3.*x*, and 4.*x* servers:

- Client Services for NetWare
- Gateway Service for NetWare
- NWLink
- Migration Tool for NetWare

Available utilities enhance the integration of Windows NT Server and NetWare: File and Print Services for NetWare and Directory Service Manager for NetWare.

UNIX

Windows NT Server is easily integrated into a UNIX environment. Several utilities allow complete integration with, or migration from, a legacy system. POSIX-compliance and TCP/IP protocols allow for interoperability with UNIX clients and servers.

Macintosh

The built-in Services for Macintosh and AppleTalk network protocols
provide support for Macintosh clients. Macintosh and Windows clients can
collaborate and share files on the Windows NT Server. The Macintosh
doesn't need any specialized software to access the Windows NT Server
resources: All the proper allowances occur at the server level. Machintosh
users may not even know they're accessing a Windows NT Server.

Windows NT Hardware Requirements

Windows NT needs a computer that can provide optimum performance and
accessibility to clients.

Microprocessor

The microprocessor is the heart of the server. Windows NT Server runs
on many processor types, but you should go with an Intel pentium or
Digital Alpha if you can. If you plan a high-usage server, consider multiple
processors.

Memory

The more memory, the better. Factors to consider when figuring out how
much memory to add include

- ✔ Number of users
- ✔ Type of applications
- ✔ Required performance levels

Disk space

Windows NT Server with a few options takes up about 200MB of disk space.
When you start adding users and applications, a disk drive can fill up
surprisingly fast. The exact amount of storage depends on your specific
needs.

Peripherals

Additional things that you need on your Windows NT Server include

- A VGA display is the minimum — and it's good enough, unless you intend to spend a lot of time working at the server.

- Floppy disk — either a high density $5^1/_4$ or $3^1/_2$ inches. You may need to use floppies for the setup disks to get started. Windows NT Server comes with $3^1/_2$-inch setup floppies in the box.

- A 4X or better CD-ROM is required for RISC-based computers and recommended for x86 servers.

- A network adapter is required to configure any of the networking components.

- A mouse or other type of pointing device is recommended.

Part II
Planning

The 5th Wave   By Rich Tennant

WHITEY'S
21-HOUR STORE

"Einstein over there didn't know it would take three hours a day to replicate the inventory system."

In this part . . .

*H*ere's where I begin breaking down the actual process of studying for the exam. I guide you in beginning a usage study and help you review disk drive configurations to fit various requirements. I cover choosing file systems and fault tolerance methods according to specific requirements. And I discuss planning issues and preparing to choose a network protocol.

Chapter 3

Usage Survey

· ·

Exam Objectives

▶ Planning the network
▶ Choosing network type
▶ Utilizing NT Server in the network

· ·

*Y*ou need to have a firm fundamental grasp of the usage survey for questions on the exam that cover planning an NT Server installation. The exam may not require you to list the elements of the survey, but questions on planning do assume a fundamental understanding of the process.

The exam questions that call for knowledge of the usage survey test your ability to gauge both the current and future requirements of your network.

The first step in planning a network is a *survey*. Knowing the requirements of a network enables you to devise a network that meets those requirements. Planning a network is like planning a trip:

✔ Determine your point of origin.

✔ Define your destination.

✔ Map the steps from beginning to end.

Keep in mind two key questions as you study for usage survey questions:

✔ Is Windows NT the appropriate operating system for the network that I'm planning? Be prepared for determining if Windows 95 may be more appropriate.

✔ What data must I have to begin a successful installation of Windows NT Server?

Quick Assessment

Planning the Network

1   _____ is an appropriate operating system choice when security isn't a major concern.

2   A domain requires one _____ to authenticate users, and can have additional _____.

3   Which client operating system do you use on networks that require a high level of security? _____.

4   You often use _____ when working with legacy hardware or with Plug and Play hardware.

Choosing Network Type

5   _____ are often placed at different sides of a WAN to reduce domain logon traffic across the WAN.

6   If you have a small network, a cheaper alternative worth considering is per _____ licensing.

7   If you only have two servers in your domain, you should have a _____ and a _____ for fault tolerance.

Utilizing NT Server in the Network

8   Microsoft allows for two security models, the _____ model and the _____ model.

9   _____ are servers that validate domain logons and maintain the user account database.

10 The _____ file system is the most secure file system.

Answers

1 *Windows 95.* Review "Choosing the network operating system."

2 *PDC, BDCs.* Review "Windows NT Server Roles."

3 *Windows NT Workstation.* Review "Windows NT Workstation."

4 *Windows 95.* Review "Windows 95."

5 *Backup domain controllers.* Review "Windows NT Server Roles."

6 *Server.* Review "Licensing: Is That Marriage or Hunting?"

7 *PDC, BDC.* Review "Windows NT Server Roles."

8 *Workgroup; Domain.* Review "Network Security Models."

9 *Primary domain controllers.* Review "Network Security Models."

10 *NTFS.* Review "Windows NT Workstation."

Planning the Network

When you review for the NT Server 4.0 exam, you need to recognize when Windows 95 may be the better operating system choice.

✔ Windows 95 uses share level security when sharing resources.

✔ Windows 95 works with a wide variety of hardware, including a variety of Plug and Play devices.

✔ Windows 95 can run software that requires direct access to the hardware.

The following characteristics of NT Server may make NT the appropriate operating system choice:

✔ NT Workstation provides a higher degree of network security.

✔ NT Workstation maintains a user account database.

✔ NT Workstation uses share level security and requires client users to have a valid username and password when sharing resources.

You need to determine your server's role on the network as part of your usage survey. Each of the four server roles depends on participation in the workgroup or domain security model:

✔ **Primary domain controllers (PDCs)** validate domain logons and maintain the user account database.

✔ **Backup domain controllers (BDCs)** assist the PDC with logon validation. Network administrators often place backup domain controllers at different sides of a WAN to reduce domain logon traffic across the WAN.

✔ **Member servers** are members of the domain but provide no logon validation.

✔ **Stand-alone servers** function in the workgroup environment.

You often see examples of each of these server types on a single network.

Conducting a Survey

Conducting a survey often turns into a complicated, drawn-out process involving many people and departments within your organization. Thankfully, *the exam provides you with data and asks you to draw conclusions.*

Expect to see questions that involve variations on the following key elements of any good network planning survey:

- ✔ Current and future number of users and computers
- ✔ Current and future models and makes of computers
- ✔ Peripherals, particularly legacy devices
- ✔ WANs currently in use (including Internet Services)
- ✔ LANs currently in use (including subsystems of the planned network)
- ✔ Software in use
- ✔ Security requirements

Planning Network Requirements

When you build a network after you complete your survey, you translate needs into practical network requirements. The exam focuses on your ability to successfully plan, maintain, and optimize a network.

Choosing the network operating system

The exam has scenario-type questions that list a set of network requirements and ask you to determine the appropriate operating system. Be familiar with the factors that affect the operating system selection:

- ✔ Available hardware
- ✔ Security requirements
- ✔ User needs

A good understanding of these three factors should see you through most network requirement questions.

Although Microsoft does provide several choices for network operating systems (including DOS and Windows for Workgroups), when the exam focuses on choosing the right operating system, the answer nearly always comes down to Windows 95 or Windows NT.

Windows 95

Windows 95 commonly serves as either a stand-alone operating system or as a client network operating system. You use a stand-alone operating system on computers not connected to other computers. You use a client network operating system for computers that will connect to other computers, and for computers that request the services of a server.

6 Your network has offices in New York and Los Angeles. The domain controllers for the single domain are located in Los Angeles. Users in New York are complaining about the slow logon times.

Requirement: Reduce logon traffic across the WAN.

Optional Results:

Allow New York to manage its own resources.

Allow users in Los Angeles to access resources in New York.

Proposed solution: Place a BDC in New York. Grant permissions to the resources in New York to users in Los Angeles.

The solution does which of the following?

A ○ Meets the requirement and both desired conditions.

B ○ Meets the requirement and one desired condition.

C ○ Meets the requirements and no desired condition.

D ○ Does not meet the requirements.

7 Domain A trusts Domain B in a one-way trust. How should you grant users from Domain B access to resources in Domain A.

A ○ Create a global group in Domain A. Place the user accounts from Domain B into the global group. Place the global group from Domain B into a local group on Domain A. Grant permission to the local group.

B ○ Create a global group in Domain B. Place the user accounts from Domain B into the global group. Place the global group from Domain B into a local group on Domain A. Grant permission to the local group.

C ○ Grant permission to the users' domain accounts from Domain B.

D ○ You can't grant permission to resources on Domain A to users on Domain B.

8 Which type of server can become a PDC without reinstalling NT Server?

A ○ Backup domain controllers

B ○ Stand-alone

C ○ Member

Answers

1 *C.* Promote a BDC and then promote the older PDC to the new PDC when it is back online. Promoting the original PDC back up to PDC when it comes online again will make sure this computer can once again function as PDC. *Review "Windows NT Server Roles."*

2 *B.* Users can be restricted to files and folders. With the NTFS file system, you can assign permission right down to the file level. Only users or groups that you specify will be granted access. *Review "Windows NT Workstation."*

3 *D.* Domain, because one user needs to maintain the accounts. Even though there is a small number of users, the domain model should be used because one person needs central control of maintaining the accounts. *Review "Network Security Models."*

4 *A.* Windows 95 is the best choice. It provides support for the Plug and Play devices, works well on older hardware, and can automatically detect docked configurations. *Review "Windows 95."*

5 *D.* FAT file system provides optimal performance on drives smaller than 500MB. *Review "Windows NT Workstation."*

6 *B.* This solution does meet the required result because the BDC now will validate the users. The optional result of allowing users in Los Angeles to access resources in New York has been satisfied. However, the PDC remains in Los Angeles and no resource domain has been created for New York, so the Los Angeles domain continues to manage those resources. *Review "Primary domain controller" and "Backup domain controllers."*

7 *B.* You have to create the global group from user accounts on the local domain. You then add the global group to local groups on the resource domain and grant permission to the local group. *Review "User accounts, local groups, and global groups."*

8 *A.* You can simply convert a BDC to a PDC. To make a member server or a stand-alone server a PDC, however, you have to reinstall NT Server. *Review "Windows NT Server Roles."*

Chapter 4

Hardware Selection

Exam Objectives
▶ Hardware detection tools
▶ Types of hardware devices
▶ Types of servers

*I*n this chapter, I discuss various server configurations and I show you selecting the different hardware pieces that comprise your Windows NT Server. Windows NT Server offers support for almost all current technologies and I discuss the performance features of many types of common components. The exam doesn't test you on individual components, but it does present situational questions on setup, troubleshooting, and performance tuning.

Quick Assessment

Hardware
Detection
Tools

1 The definitive resource for Windows NT hardware is the _____.

2 At boot up, _____ modifies the Windows NT Registry.

Types of
Servers

3 You can use the _____ tool to check troublesome SCSI devices.

Hardware
Devices

4 Windows NT supports three levels of RAID: RAID _____, RAID _____, and RAID _____.

5 File and print servers require _____ amounts of storage.

6 Windows NT Server supports several major processors, including _____, _____, _____, and _____.

7 The type of multiprocessing that Windows NT supports is called _____.

8 Increasing the amount of cache memory generally _____ performance.

9 Windows NT supports two major types of disk interface: _____ and _____.

10 The most common media for backup is _____.

Answers

1   *Hardware Compatibility List (HCL).* Check out "Hardware Overview."

2   *Ntdetect.com.* Read "Hardware Overview."

3   *SCSI Investigator.* Review "Hardware Overview."

4   *0; 1; 5.* Check out "RAID."

5   *large.* Read "File and print servers" for information.

6   *Intel 486 and above; Digital Alpha; MIPS; PowerPC.* Review "Selecting a Microprocessor."

7   *Symmetric Multi-Processing (SMP).* Check out "Multiprocessing."

8   *increases.* Review "Cache."

9   *IDE; SCSI.* Review "Hard disks, soft shoulders."

10   *tape.* See "Tape device drivers: Duct or duck?"

Hardware Overview

Hardware is the stuff that makes up your server. Windows NT Server supports most all major technologies for hardware. You have many choices available for each component. Each component offers specific features for different situations.

Although you may get a few specific questions on the exam about hardware, most exam questions deal with hardware in a more general sense. Having at least some knowledge of the various technologies can help you make hardware choices when answering tricky questions.

Three utilities in particular can help you determine the compatibility of your hardware configuration:

- ✔ **NT Hardware Qualifier (NTHQ):** Helps you determine the compatibility status of your hardware and produces a report of the configuration it finds.

- ✔ **Ntdetect.com:** Runs every time Windows NT Server starts up. It looks for any changes to the hardware and makes the appropriate change in the Registry.

- ✔ **SCSI Investigator:** Aids in determining SCSI devices on your system and generates a report similar to that which NTHQ produces.

Lab 4-1 creates a DOS bootable floppy disk that will run the NTHQ utility.

Lab 4-1   Using the NTHQ

1. **Load the Windows NT Server CD-ROM.**

2. **Run a file called Makedisk.bat (located in the \Support\Hqtool folder).**

3. **Insert the floppy disk when prompted.**

4. **Reboot the server.**

This floppy made in the lab is a DOS-bootable floppy and will run NTHQ automatically. NTHQ produces a report to document the configuration it finds. You also can use it to troubleshoot a failing installation if the problems stem from the hardware. NTHQ also shows all the hardware that it detects.

File and print servers

The file and print server is a mainstay of the server world. File and print servers require high availability and storage capacity.

When you design a file and print server, emphasize storage and reliability. To accommodate all users requiring access to the server simultaneously, you need increased network bandwidth. Generally, the processor and memory of a file and print server isn't heavily utilized, other than for buffering data and processing print jobs. Additional printer ports may be required if network printers are not utilized.

All NT Servers can be file servers, print servers, or both.

Application servers

When you design an application server, you want to emphasize multiple processors, large memories, and large bandwidth network adapters. Unless you plan to store files on an application server, you don't need to worry much about disk storage space — you just need to make sure that you have enough disk space for temporary storage and page files.

Internet and intranet servers

The Internet and intranets are designed to provide information to a large number of users. These servers hold files, run applications, and process data. If you have a large site, you may use one or more servers to provide these services.

When you design an Internet or intranet server, emphasize high bandwidth network adapters, disk storage and memory, and processing performance. A large number of requests requires even greater processing power. If information is held mainly in static pages, memory and storage assumes greater importance.

Messaging servers

Messaging servers are a critical server in most IT organizations. Users can tolerate almost any type of delay except loss of their e-mail.

The nature of these servers requires high availability, large storage capacities, and high bandwidth. When you design a messaging server, you want to emphasize redundant power supplies, large RAID arrays, high speed network cards, large memories, and tape backup.

Remote Access Services (RAS) servers

There may be a question about connecting a small office to the corporate network with RAS and ISDN. You can share an ISDN line among a group of users with RAS.

RAS servers enable users to connect from the outside world into the company network. RAS servers require multiple serial ports. Windows NT Server can support 256 remote access connections. To support this many connections, you need a modem pool or other type of terminal server equipment. You can speed response time by using high speed network cards to move the data from multiple users to the company network. Reasonable-sized memories can support many remote access users. If you expect users to process data on the RAS server, you need to increase disk storage and processor performance, as well.

Selecting a Microprocessor

Windows NT Server supports several types of processors. Each processor type has individual features and limitations.

Intel

Windows NT Server supports all versions of the Intel X86 family, from the 80486/25 to the latest Pentium, Pentium Pro, and the Pentium II processors. Many applications are available for these processors, including both single- and multiple-processor platforms.

Most of the questions on the exam are for Intel-based servers.

RISC

The Digital Alpha RISC processor boasts the highest processor speed of any Windows NT processor. This processor currently comes in speeds ranging from 225 MHz to 500 MHz and is specifically designed for 64-bit applications. This family of processors has a long list of applications and the list is growing. The Alpha scales well into multiprocessor platforms. Although available for workstations, the primary market of this processor is for high-end servers. This is the second most popular processor for Windows NT servers. There may be some questions on the exam regarding RISC processors.

MIPS

MIPS is an abbreviation for Microprocessor without Interlocked Pipeline Stages. It's a RISC architecture processor where no interlocks occur between pipeline stages. Well-known MIPS implementations are the R3000, R4000, R6000, and R10000. The R10000 implementation boasts over 200 MHz speed and has 64K of on-chip cache. It can execute four instructions per cycle and is marketed for high-end desktops and servers.

Windows NT Server 4.0 ceased to support this platform at Service Pack 3. The MIPS processor is finding a place in the market running Windows CE.

PowerPC

PowerPC processors support fewer instructions but process individual instructions faster. The physical size of the chip is about the same as a thumbtack. Reduced power consumption is another plus. The PowerPC chip can process up to three instructions per clock cycle.

The PowerPC processor was the newest RISC processor to have Windows NT ported to it. Microsoft dropped NT Server 4.0 support for the PowerPC at Service Pack 3.

Multiprocessing

Multiprocessing offers higher throughput of data and a fault redundancy on processors. The real reason to choose a multiprocessing system is for the performance gain.

Multiprocessing allows multiple CPUs to share the workload within the computing system. A similar concept is *multitasking,* which allows the simultaneous execution of multiple application tasks.

Symmetric multiprocessing (SMP) refers to the operating system's capability to schedule sections (or threads) of code for execution on the first available CPU. An idle CPU always receives the next piece of code, causing all CPUs to execute close to the same amount of code.

Selecting a Motherboard

The motherboard that you select effectively determines many of the other hardware choices that you must make, such as what peripheral bus to use, the number and types of processors to support, the amount of memory to support, and the amount of cache memory available.

Cache

Cache memory is a special high-speed memory designed to accelerate processing of CPU memory instructions. The CPU can access instructions and data located in cache memory much faster than it can access instructions and data located in main memory. Types of cache memory include *primary cache* (also known as Level 1 [L1] cache) and *secondary cache* (also known as Level 2 [L2] cache). Cache can also come in two different types: *Internal cache* is built into the computer's CPU and *external cache* is located outside the CPU.

Primary cache is the cache located closest to the CPU. Usually, primary cache is internal and secondary cache is external. Some early-model personal computers have CPU chips that don't contain internal cache. In these cases, the external cache, if present, actually acts as the primary (L1) cache.

Cache refers to where the processor stores information that it may need or information on which it is currently working. Systems typically come with 256K, 512K, or 1MB of cache memory.

Peripheral bus

There are several styles of peripheral bus. Most motherboards today support at least one or more of the common types. Each type has particular features associated with it. You should select the type of peripheral bus that fits with the types of add-on cards you require.

Most of the information in the Peripheral Bus section is not on the exam. If you are familiar with the types of peripheral buses, skip this section.

Industry Standard Architecture (ISA)

The 8-bit version came on the original PC and the AT, but the AT uses an extension to make it 16-bit. It has a maximum data transfer rate of about 8 Mbps on an AT, which actually is well above the capability of disk drives, and of most network and video cards. The average data throughput runs at approximately 2 Mbps. The design of the ISA peripheral bus complicates mixing 8- and 16-bit RAM or ROM within the same 128K block of upper memory. An 8-bit VGA card can force all cards in the same address range to use 8 bits — a common source of crashes with 16-bit network cards.

Extended Industry Standard Architecture (EISA)

EISA is an evolution of ISA and (theoretically) backward-compatible with it, including the speed (8 MHz). The increased data throughput owes mainly to the bus doubling in size, but you must use EISA expansion cards. It possesses its own DMA arrangements, which can use the complete address space. One advantage of EISA is the ease with which you can set up expansion cards: You just plug them in and run the configuration software, which automatically detects their settings.

Micro Channel Architecture (MCA)

A proprietary standard established by IBM to take over from ISA, and, therefore, incompatible with anything else. It comes in two versions, 16- and 32-bit and, in practical terms, can transfer around 20 Mbps.

Peripheral Component Interconnect (PCI)

A mezzanine bus, divorced from the CPU. It has some independence and the capability to cope with more devices, more suited to cross-platform work. It is *time-multiplexed,* meaning that address and data lines share connections. It has its own burst mode that allows 1 address cycle to be followed by as many data cycles as system overheads allow. It can operate up to 33 MHz (or 66 MHz with PCI 2.1) and can transfer data at 32 bits per clock cycle, so you can get up to 132MB/sec (or 264MB/sec with 2.1).

Each PCI card can perform up to eight functions, and you can have more than one busmastering card on the bus. It is part of the Plug and Play, so it is auto configuring (although some cards use jumpers instead of storing information in a chip); cards also share interrupts in the same way. The PCI chipset handles transactions between cards and the rest of the system, and allows other buses to be bridged to the PCI bus (typically an ISA bus that allows older cards to be used). Not all PCI buses are equal, though; certain features may be absent. The connector may vary according to the voltage the card uses.

Memory

There are several types of memory to store running program segments and current data before writing to disk. Pulling information from memory is always faster than getting it from the disk drive.

Integrated peripherals

Many motherboards are starting to integrate peripheral controllers. Everything from mouse and keyboard controllers to communication and printer ports to video and IDE or SCSI bus controllers are now integrated into the motherboard. Integrated peripherals provide the basic services required for the server without taking up a slot on the peripheral bus. The drawback to this design shows up when you need to upgrade to newer or different controllers, which isn't possible with some integrated designs.

BIOS

BIOS stands for Basic Input Output System. All computer hardware has to work with software through an interface. The BIOS gives the computer a built-in starter kit to run the rest of the software from floppy disks and hard disks. The BIOS boots the computer by providing a basic set of instructions. It performs all the tasks that need to be done at start-up time: POST (Power-On Self Test, booting an operating system from floppy or hard disk). Furthermore, it provides an interface to the underlying hardware for the operating system, in the form of a library of interrupt handlers. For instance, each time a key is pressed, the CPU (Central Processing Unit) performs an interrupt to read that key. This interface is similar for other input/output devices (serial and parallel ports, video cards, sound cards, hard disk controllers, and so on).

Storage Devices

Windows NT Server supports many types of storage devices straight from the box. Additional drivers are available from the manufacturer or are available from Microsoft via TechNet, the Microsoft Web site, or the MSDN library.

Storage devices range from the basic hard drives to RAID arrays with support for many types of tape drives, removable media, WORM drives, and CD recorders. You can use almost any storage device with Windows NT Server.

Hard disks, soft shoulders

Today's hard drives use either SCSI (small computer systems interface) or IDE (integrated drive electronics) drives.

Multiple physical disks

Multiple disk drives are supported on every type of drive interface. Some support more than two drives per interface. The type of disk interface you install on your server has a direct effect on the server's performance and capabilities.

Specific speed and performance requirements for servers usually dictate the utilization of SCSI disk drives. That said, however, a small server with IDE disk drives can still be a suitable server.

Configuration of multiple drives ranges from a master/slave setting on an IDE interface to addressing on an SCSI. Each type of interface has its own rules for multiple drive support.

SCSI devices

The Small Computer Systems Interface (SCSI) drive has a built-in smart bus and allows you to connect up to seven SCSI devices. Before you can use an SCSI device, you must install an SCSI adapter on the computer.

SCSI drives come in three types: SCSI I, SCSI II, and SCSI III. SCSI devices all have different SCSI numbers (1 through 7). SCSI devices are daisy-chained, and the device at the end of the chain contains a terminating resistor.

You can use the SCSI Investigator tool to find out what SCSI resources are available and determine their compatibility with Windows NT Server. To create the SCSI utility disk, run Makedisk.bat from the installation CD-ROM (Makedisk.bat is located in \Support\Scsitool\). Running this program creates a DOS bootable floppy and autoruns the SCSI Investigator. The SCSI Investigator tool generates a report that lists all SCSI devices that it detects.

IDE

The controller of an Integrated Drive Electronics (IDE) drive is built into the electronics of the hard drive. The advent of IDE drives enabled disk manufacturers to create onboard programs that are capable of active error checking, zone recording, higher disk rotation speeds, and drive remapping. If you have an IDE drive and you connect another hard drive to your system's controller, you configure a master/slave relationship between the two drives. If you add another drive, you probably will need to set a dip switch on the new drive to define its role in the PC.

RAID

Redundant Array of Inexpensive Disks (RAID) is a logical joining of smaller disk drives to form a larger, and in some cases fault tolerant, *logical* drive.

Windows NT Server supports RAID categories 0, 1, and 5:

- **RAID 0:** Called *striping*. Data is written across all drives in the set. Two drives are required for a RAID 0 set. This set is not fault tolerant. Figure 4-1 shows RAID 0.

- **RAID 1:** Called *mirroring*. All the data from one drive is written on the mirrored drive. If the primary drive fails, the mirror can be used to continue working. This configuration requires at least two drives. Figure 4-2 depicts an example of RAID 1.

- **RAID 5:** Called *striping with parity*. This configuration requires a minimum of three drives. Data is written to two drives and parity is written to the third. Data and parity are intermingled across all three drives. Figure 4-3 shows how RAID 5 distributes the data and parity.

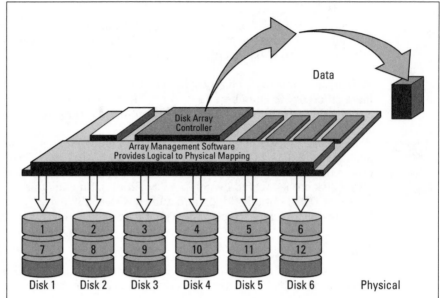

Figure 4-1:
RAID 0.

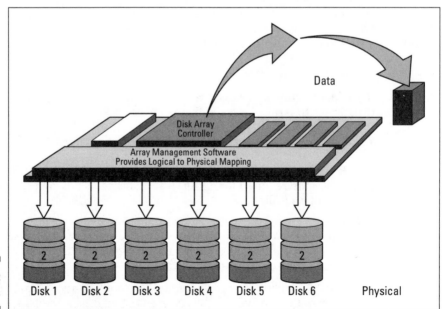

Figure 4-2:
RAID 1.

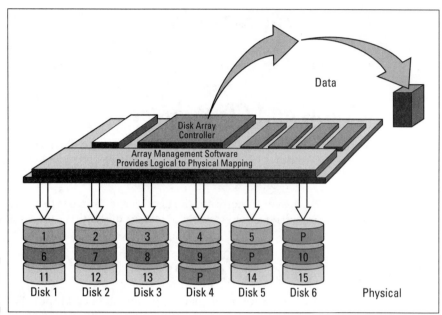

Figure 4-3:
RAID 5.

Controller cards that perform the RAID management for the operating system are available. These cards improve the performance of the server and offer support for *hot swapping* disk drives. Hot swapping refers to changing the disk drive while the server is still powered up and running.

Tape device drivers: Duct or duck?

The most common medium for backups, the one that Windows NT Backup uses, is magnetic tape. Tape is popular because it offers great capacity at low cost. The primary tape drive types used for server backup include quarter-inch cartridge (QIC), digital audio tape (DAT), and 8-mm cassette. High-capacity, high-performance tape drives generally use SCSI controllers.

Ideally, a tape drive should have more than enough capacity to back up your largest server. It should also provide error detection and correction during backup and restore.

CD-ROM

You must have a CD-ROM for installation on RISC-based servers. CD-ROM speeds range from 1X to 30X on current drives. A minimum speed of 4X is desired for a server. CD-ROM drives are supported in both SCSI and IDE interfaces.

Removable hard disks

Removable hard disks drivers come from the hardware manufacturer. A variety of styles and types of removable media are available.

WORM and CD-R drives

Write Once Read Many (WORM) and CD-Recorder (CD-R) drives are supported by Windows NT Server. These type drives give the server access to data that does not change but is required to be online.

Windows NT Server directly supports drives for some types of these devices but requires a driver from the manufacturer of the drive for other types.

Interfaces and Adapters

Windows NT Server supports many different style and topologies of networks. You can implement nearly any major variety of network. When you choose a Network Interface Card (NIC), be sure to know the existing topology and speed of the network to which you aim to connect.

It's all in the cards: Network adapters

The *network interface card* serves to connect your PC to the local area network (LAN). There are many types of network design and topologies. The type of NIC to use depends on your site's topology. You usually connect the NIC to the LAN in one of three ways, depending on the type of cabling. You may see up to three different connectors on some network cards.

The most common type of connection is the *RJ-45,* which looks like a large telephone jack. You see this type of connector on 10BaseT networks. The cable looks like ordinary telephone line. The workstations are usually connected to hubs. The maximum length of wire is 100 meters.

The next most common type of connection is a *BNC connector.* You see this type of connector on thin Ethernet cable (sometimes called *thinnet*), which you generally see configured in a bus topology, connected to each PC. The cable is terminated at both ends by a 50-ohm terminating resistor.

The third type of connector that you may find on an NIC is the *AUI port.* This connector looks like a joystick port and connects the drop-down cables from thick Ethernet networks.

Modems

Modems come in two basic types: internal or external models for desktop systems or PCMCIA cards for laptop computers. The internal models are usually 8-bit ISA cards, and the external models connect via a serial cable to an existing serial port on the computer.

You may be eager to run out and purchase the fastest modem available, but remember that the actual connection speed is controlled by the *slowest* modem. If you have a 56 Kbps modem and dial up a 14.4 Kbps modem, your connection speed cannot be faster than 14.4 Kbps. Another factor that affects the speed of a connection is the quality of the phone line.

Most modern modems also can send and receive faxes. Some of the more expensive modems also can convert your computer into a voice mail answering system, and some support simultaneous voice and data transmissions.

Video

The video card, or *video display adapter,* controls the computer monitor. In some systems, this adapter is integrated into the motherboard. In other systems, you find the display adapter in an expansion slot on the motherboard. Most of these adapters contain a VGA connector.

Most video display adapters are SVGA cards. These cards come in various bus designs, from the standard 16-bit ISA to 64-bit PCI configurations. You find a wide variety of memory configurations on these cards.

Video memory improves the speed of the video card and determines the colors and the resolutions the card can display. For servers, high performance video is less of a concern.

Prep Test

1 You have been given an assortment of components with which to assemble a server for Windows NT Server. What resource can you use to verify compatibility so that only a minimum of configuration problems occur?

A ○ Hardware Resource Guide

B ○ Hardware Configuration List

C ○ Hardware Compatibility List

D ○ Hardware Resource List

2 Which RAID level is commonly referred to as disk striping?

A ○ RAID 0

B ○ RAID 1

C ○ RAID 3

D ○ RAID 5

3 The NT Hardware Qualifier tool reports which of the following? (Choose all that apply.)

A ❑ All hardware that it detects.

B ❑ Compatibility with Windows NT.

C ❑ The nearest Windows NT Server.

D ❑ All network servers that it can detect.

4 What program updates changes to the server hardware in the Registry?

A ○ Nthq.com

B ○ Ntdetect.com

C ○ Ntldr.exe

D ○ Ntoskrnl.com

5 Windows NT Server supports disk drives with ____ interfaces. (Choose all that apply.)

A ❑ SCSI

B ❑ MCA

C ❑ PCI

D ❑ ISA

6 Windows NT supports tape drives with which of the following formats? (Choose all that apply.)

A ❑ DAT

B ❑ QIC

C ❑ 8MM

D ❑ DLT

7 You are the administrator of a Windows NT Server with a PowerPC processor. You have the most current service pack loaded. Which service pack do you have?

A ○ 1

B ○ 2

C ○ 3

D ○ 4

8 What is the minimum number of disk drives required to support RAID 5?

A ○ 1

B ○ 2

C ○ 3

D ○ 4

9 Increasing the L2 cache on a motherboard will most likely _____ performance of the processor.

A ○ Improve

B ○ Impair

C ○ Not affect

10 Windows NT supports which types of peripheral bus? (Choose all that apply.)

A ❑ PCI

B ❑ MCA

C ❑ EISA

D ❑ SCSI

Answers

1 *C.* Hardware Compatibility List (HCL). The best resource for hardware issues. *See the "Hardware Overview" section.*

2 *A.* RAID 0 is just striping. *Refer to "RAID."*

3 *A and B.* NTHQ reports all the hardware it detects and check its compatibility with Windows NT. *Refer to "Hardware Overview."*

4 *B.* Ntdetect.com checks the status for the hardware every time Windows NT boots up. *See "Hardware Overview."*

5 *A.* SCSI is the only disk interface listed. Don't let the question fool you. Choosing all that apply doesn't mean more than one is correct. *See "SCSI Devices."*

6 *A, B, C, and D.* All these tape formats are supported. *Recheck "Tape device drivers: Duct or duck?"*

7 *B.* The PowerPC was supported only up to Service Pack 2. *Restudy "Selecting a Microprocessor."*

8 *C.* You must have three disk drives for RAID 5. *Look again at "RAID."*

9 *A.* Improve performance. Cache is a fast storage spot for the processor. *Reread "Cache."*

10 *A, B, and C.* SCSI is not a peripheral bus architecture. *Check "Peripheral Bus."*

Chapter 5

Storage

● ●

Exam Objectives

▶ Planning the disk drive configuration for various requirements

▶ Understanding fault tolerance

▶ Allocating disk space capacity

▶ Improving performance

▶ Recovering from failures

● ●

*T*he Windows NT Server exam tests your knowledge of all the storage options available. It presents both direct questions and situational questions. The first half of this chapter talks about the types of file systems and their features. The second part discusses the more advanced features of disk administration, fault tolerance, and replication.

The exam tests your knowledge of file systems and backups in a number of ways. It asks direct questions about volumes and volume sets. It also throws many situational questions at you, generally listing a configuration and calling on you to choose the best way to accomplish the given task.

The exam also includes questions on setting up and recovering from failed drives in fault tolerant volume sets. You need to get familiar with the different backup strategies. You're bound to have at least one question about replication and you can expect several questions to demand knowledge about rights and access privileges. Don't worry: I cover all of this material in this chapter.

Quick Assessment

1 You must have _____ in terms of hardware configuration before you can take advantage of disk duplexing.

2 You want to protect a Windows NT server from failure, and you have more than three disk drives. The most efficient method of fault tolerance to implement in this case is _____.

3 You have a Windows NT Server with the boot partition mirrored. The primary partition fails. What happens?

4 Your Windows NT Server has a RAID 0 volume set with four 500MB disk drives. The usable size of this volume is _____.

5 The administrator of a Windows NT server needs to create a fault toler ant disk volume set. He has available two drives with 350MB of free space and one with 150MB of free space. What is the largest fault toler ant volume set he can make?

6 You are using disk duplexing for the boot and system partitions. The controller fails on the primary device. You need to edit the _____ file so that the system boots using the duplexed drive.

7 A common use for replication is _____.

8 BobJ is a member of the Backup Operators group. Which files and folders can BobJ back up on the Windows NT server?

9 JoeS wants to back up all his files so that he can use them at home. He needs all his files but wants them backed up on the regular incremental backup. He should use the _____ backup method.

10 When Sara backed up her project files she selected to back up the security as well as the files. If the project files need to be restored. Who can restore these files?

Answers

1 *matching disk drives and 2 controllers.* See "Duplexing."

2 *RAID 5 (Stripe set with parity).* See "Fault Tolerance."

3 *2GB.* Review "Partitions and Volumes."

4 *350MB.* Review "Mirroring," "Duplexing," and "Striping with parity."

5 *Nothing.* See "Mirroring."

6 *Boot.ini.* See "Duplexing."

7 *Replicating login scripts to domain controllers.* Review "Server replication."

8 *Any and all files on the server.* Check out "Tape backup."

9 *Copy.* Review "Tape backup."

10 *A member of the Backup Operators or Administrators group.* Review "Tape backup."

Storage Strategies

File storage is a hot topic for the Server exam! Windows NT offers several options concerning what file system to use on a server. You need to know how all these options work so that you don't get tricked.

Disk space

You can use FAT, NTFS, or a combination of the two on an NT Server configuration. You can run multiple operating systems, which means that you can use all of the respective features that each operating system offers.

Storage options

The two basic options for storage are

- **FAT:** *File allocation table.*
- **NTFS:** *New technology file system.*

The other file system type to mention is CDFS (compact disk file system). CDFS is for CD-ROM use. You cannot format a disk drive with CDFS.

Windows NT 4.0 does not support the HPFS or FAT32 file systems.

Choosing a File System

Choosing a file system for Windows NT Server is a major decision. Understand your options and the reasons you would choose one. Several questions on the exam involve the file system type.

Dual-boot systems

If you need to boot more than one operating system on this server, use a FAT file system on the boot partition. You can have other NTFS partitions, but they're invisible when you use the alternate operating system.

NTFS

The NTFS file system incorporates significant improvements and changes. Files remain organized in directories, called *folders*. Unlike FAT, NTFS partition size is unlimited, and root directories require no special treatment.

Only the Windows NT operating system can access NTFS volumes. NTFS is more advanced than FAT in three ways:

- ✔ NTFS offers enhanced security
- ✔ NTFS manages large volumes more efficiently
- ✔ NTFS is a recoverable file system

The four components of the NTFS structure are:

- ✔ **Partition Boot Sector:** Contains the information that tells NTFS whether the disk is bootable.
- ✔ **Master File Table:** Keeps records of the 16 NTFS system files that comprise the NTFS file system structure.
- ✔ **System Files:** Contains the 16 NTFS system files.
- ✔ **File Area:** Contains your data.

The exam does not question you about the specifics of the NTFS file structure, so I go no farther with it here. Table 5-1 shows the default cluster size and sectors per cluster for a given partition size.

Table 5-1	NTFS Default Cluster Size	
Partition Size	*Sectors Per Cluster*	*Cluster Size*
512MB or less	1	512 bytes
513MB to 1024MB	2	1K
1025MB to 2048MB	4	2K
2049MB to 4096MB	8	4K
4097MB to 8192MB	16	8K
8193MB to 16,384MB	32	16K
16,385MB to 32,768MB	64	32K
> 32,768MB	128	64K

Fault tolerance

Both NTFS fault tolerance methods controlled by the operating system; no user interaction is necessary.

✔ **Transaction logging:** Combines lazy-writes and a volume recovery technique. Transaction logging typically only takes a second to verify an NTFS volume. NTFS automatically checks your SCSI disks for bad sectors each time it reads and writes with cluster remapping.

✔ **Cluster remapping:** If Windows NT tells the NTFS that it's writing to a bad sector, NTFS finds a new sector to write the data. NTFS stores the address of the bad sector so that it cannot be used again. If Windows NT informs NTFS that it's reading from a bad sector, NTFS stores the address of the bad sector but the data in that sector is lost.

Security

The exam usually poses several questions about various aspects of NTFS security. Unlike FAT, NTFS allows you to set permissions on folders and individual files. FAT only lets you add permissions to a share; any subdirectories and files within that share all contain the same permissions. NTFS lets you assign different permissions to each file in the share.

The flexibility of NTFS for assigning permissions is convenient when you want to give someone access to a file or folder without creating a new share for it.

When you choose to restrict everyone from a file, you still have access to it, because you are the Creator or Owner of the file.

You can set different security levels in NTFS. Folder permissions are separate from share permissions. If you do not assign specific permissions to a file, it inherits the permissions of the folder where it resides.

Note that the FAT permissions are still available to NTFS. If a file or folder is assigned Full Control but you set the Read-Only flag on the properties page for that file or folder, then the file or folder is Read-Only.

The No Access permission is final with NTFS, and the exam tries to trip you up. If you get a question that asks what rights someone has to an NTFS file or folder, *read the question carefully*. When you use NTFS permissions, no member of any group that has been granted No Access to a file or folder has any access to that file or folder, regardless of whether the individual's user account does give permission to access that file or folder.

File and partition sizes

I didn't have any questions that dealt directly with file and partition sizes on my exam. NTFS can support up to a 2-terabyte (a *terabyte* is 2^{41} bytes) partition size using today's industry standard 512K cluster size. Theoretically, NTFS can support up to a 16-exabyte (an *exabyte* is 2^{64} bytes) partition.

Owing to today's hardware limitations, the maximum possible NTFS file size runs between 4 gigabytes (GB) and 64GB. NTFS is not recommended on small partitions because it takes more overhead than FAT. Currently, NTFS is recommended on partitions over 400MB.

File compression

You will see questions on NTFS compression. NTFS to compresses a file, directory, or even a volume. The process generally compresses text files about 50 percent and executable files about 40 percent.

You need to know whether a file keeps its compression attribute when you move or copy it. Remember the following list of different scenarios and you're set! Here's how NTFS file compression works:

- ✔ If you copy a compressed file to an uncompressed folder on the same partition, the file ends up uncompressed.

- ✔ If you move a compressed file to an uncompressed folder on the same partition, the file ends up compressed.

- ✔ If you copy or move an uncompressed file to a compressed folder on the same partition, the file ends up compressed.

- ✔ If you copy or move a file from a compressed partition to an uncompressed folder on a different partition, the file ends up uncompressed.

- ✔ If you copy or move a file from an uncompressed partition to a compressed folder on a different partition, the file ends up compressed.

You can compress files from Windows Explorer by selecting the file, directory, or partition and then choosing Properties, or you can run Compact.exe from the command line. Table 5-2 lists the switches for Compact.exe.

Table 5-2	Command Line Switches for Compact.exe
Switch	*Description*
/c	Compresses the specified files. Compressed directories compress any files that you add to them.
/u	Uncompresses the specified files. Directories do not compress files that you add to them later.
/s	Compresses files in the given directory, as well as any and all of its subdirectories.
/a	Shows files with Hidden or System attributes.
/l	Continues running Compact.exe even after errors occur.
/f	Forces compression on all specified files, even previously compressed files.
/q	Shows you summary information.

You cannot compress an open file with Windows Explorer or Compact.exe.

FAT

FAT (File Allocation Table), originally designed for small disks, is the "other" main file system that Windows NT supports. In fact, a wide variety of operating systems support FAT. Here are FAT's five main components:

- ✔ **Partition Boot Sector:** Contains the information that lets FAT know whether the disk is bootable.

- ✔ **FAT1:** Keeps information on clusters, including

  - Unused clusters

  - Clusters in use by files

  - Bad clusters

  - Last clusters in files

- ✔ **FAT2:** Serves as a duplicate of FAT1.

- ✔ **Root folder:** Contains an entry for each folder and all files that reside in the root directory.

- ✔ **Other files and folders:** Contains entries for all of the other files and folders on the partition.

One difference between the root folder and other files and folders is that the root folder can handle only 512 entries. Table 5-3 shows the default cluster size and sectors per cluster for partition sizes. I have not encountered this information on any exams, but I include it here in case you do.

Table 5-3	FAT Default Cluster Size	
Partition Size	*Sectors Per Cluster*	*Cluster Size*
0MB to 32MB	1	512 bytes
33MB to 64MB	2	1K
65MB to 128MB	4	2K
129MB to 255MB	8	4K
256MB to 511MB	16	8K
512MB to 1023MB	32	16K
1024MB to 2047MB	64	32K
2048MB to 4095MB	128	64K

Be ready for questions about FAT volumes. _The only operating system that recognizes NTFS is Windows NT._

FAT versus VFAT

The version of FAT that Windows NT 4.0 implements is the _VFAT_ system. VFAT allows for the use of long filenames. The VFAT file system still maintains a traditional 8.3 filename. When a client cannot recognize the long filename, VFAT presents a truncated 8.3 name.

Although I didn't get any questions about VFAT (Virtual File Allocation Table), I cover it here just in case. VFAT is the Windows 95 version of FAT. The difference rests in the use of a 32-bit VFAT driver instead of the 16-bit SMARTDrive driver used with MS-DOS. The VFAT driver offers increased performance over the SMARTDrive driver for multitasking and disk I/O.

VFAT is what provides the capability to create long filenames in Windows 95. When you create a long filename, VFAT creates an 8.3 alias to that filename; for example, VFAT might give Longfilename.doc an 8.3 alias of Longfi~1.doc. It creates this 8.3 alias so that the file can remain available to MS-DOS applications. Windows NT doesn't use the VFAT driver; however, it does use the same algorithms and creates filename aliases on FAT partitions so that MS-DOS users can still view the files.

FAT features

FAT is the most widely accepted file system; it's compatible with Windows NT, Windows 95, MS-DOS, and OS/2. If you get any questions that talk about a dual boot with Windows NT and another operating system, therefore, you know the other operating system has to reside on a FAT partition.

If questions ask about FAT32, an updated version of FAT on Windows 95 (OSR2), know that FAT32 is _not_ compatible with Windows NT.

Security

The only security features on a FAT file system are the traditional _RASH_ (Read-Only, Archive, System, and Hidden) permissions. Regular NTFS permissions are available to shared folders on a FAT partition. That's important, because many exam questions deal with the permissions and access as they relate to shares and FAT partitions.

Partitions and Volumes

You can arrange physical disks into *logical partitions*. You format each
partition for a file system as a volume and assign it a drive letter. Your tool
for partitioning disks is the *Disk Administrator,* shown in Figure 5-1.

Disk Administrator
Partition Fault Tolerance Tools View Options Help

Disk 0 2014 MB	C: NTFS 2012 MB	Free Space 2 MB
Disk 1 2441 MB	D: NTFS 2441 MB	
CD-ROM 0	E:	

☐ Primary partition

Partitions

Partitions are grouped into two types:

- ✔ **Primary:** The operating system uses these partitions.

- ✔ **Extended:** You can subdivide extended partitions into logical drives.
  You also can use the free space on extended partitions to create volume
  sets or RAID volumes.

On RISC-based computers, the primary partition boot partition must be FAT.

Master Boot Record

The Master Boot Record (MBR) is a bootstrap routine that the BIOS in your
computer uses. It looks at the active partition on your disk drive to find the
startup for the operating system.

You may get a question on the exam pertaining to how to correct a corrupted MBR. You need to boot from a system floppy for DOS 6.0 or higher and run FDISK /MBR to recreate the Master Boot Record.

The only other question that I've seen asks how you mark an active partition. The only way that you can mark a partition as active is by using the Disk Administrator tool, and then you can mark primary partitions only.

Partition table

The *partition table* describes a disk's physical layout and arrangement. It identifies the system partition by a marker pointing to the boot sector of the *active* partition.

The *system* partition holds the boot files, Ntldr, Boot.ini, and Ntdetect.com. The *boot* partition holds the Windows NT system files, Ntoskrnl.exe, among others. Don't be confused by this. The Windows NT system partition must be on the active partition. You can place the Windows NT boot partition on any recognized partition on any disk drive in the computer.

Volumes

Volumes and *volume sets* are how Windows NT deals with partitioned disk drives and multiple disk drives partitioned and joined together to look like a single disk drive. A *volume* is just a single partition on a disk drive. A *volume set* is one or more partitions connected in one of four methods:

- Mirrored (RAID 1) duplicate data written to separate partitions on different disk drives
- Extended separate partitions on the same or different disk drives acting as a single partition on a single disk drive
- Striped (RAID 0) 2 to 32 partitions exactly the same size on different disk drives writing data across all drives at the same time
- Striped with parity (RAID 5) 3 to 32 partitions of exactly the same size on different disk drives writing data and parity across all drives at the same time

You use the Disk Manager to create and manage volumes. Know how to create and manage each type. (See Chapter 6 for more about Disk Manager.) Several exam questions cover creating and extending volume sets.

Drive letters

You assign drive letters to volumes and volume sets. You can change which letters are assigned to a volume or volume set by using the Tools menu in Disk Manager. You can assign any drive letter from A to Z. Technically, however, A and B are reserved for floppy drives. That leaves only 24 for Windows NT to use. The operating system assumes that at least one multiple disk volume set must be utilized in any implementation that involves more than 24 volumes.

Volume sets

Joining two or more partitions on the same or different physical disk drives creates a volume set. Simple volume sets consists of two or more partitions on the same or different physical disk drives. You typically assign such a volume set just one drive letter. They are not fault tolerant but you can extend them if necessary. The size of this type of volume set is the sum of the sizes of all partitions included in the set.

Stripe sets

Stripe sets (RAID 0) consist of 2 to 32 physical disk drives that have exactly matching partitions. Data is written across all partitions at the same time. Using a stripe set provides a performance gain over using a plain volume set. The size of this type of volume set is the size of the partition times the number of disk drives participating in the set.

Stripe set configurations also provide no fault tolerance. If a drive fails, the stripe set fails, too; you must rebuild it from Disk Manager. You have to reload the data from backup. This type of configuration is good for situations where speed and performance are more important than fault tolerance.

Stripe sets with parity

A stripe set with parity (RAID 5) is the best configuration for fault tolerance. Like the stripe set, all participating partitions must be exactly the same size. The main difference between the two is that stripe sets with parity require a minimum of three disk drives. Sizing is calculated according to the following formula, where n represents the number of partitions:

Size = $(n-1) \times$ partition size

Data and parity is written at random across all participating drives. No one drive holds all parity or all data. When a disk fails, the system has either all the data or most of the data and parity. If all the data is present, the system checks it by figuring the parity. If most of the data is present, Windows NT can figure out the missing pieces of data by using the parity. This arrangement can tolerate one missing disk drive.

After you replace the failing disk drive, you can regenerate the failed portion by choosing Tools⇨Regenerate. This method offers a good choice for both performance and fault tolerance, and constitutes the best choice for mission critical data and servers.

Fault Tolerance

Fault tolerance covers a broad area, including several methods that range from RAID volume sets to tape backup and disaster recovery. This section covers some of the more important methods. The exam has a few questions covering each area.

Tape backup

Windows NT has a built-in tape backup facility. Ntbackup.exe installs with Windows NT, but you must install the drivers for your tape drive before you can use it. The exam has only a couple questions regarding the backup utility.

Members of the Administrators group and the Backup Operators group can back up any and all data on a server. Members of the Owner group for a file or folder can back up their files or folders. Expect at least one question about permissions on the exam.

Tape backup systems

Windows NT looks for tape devices during startup. Windows NT includes built-in support for QIC, 4mm DAT, and 8mm.

You may get a question about backing up without a tape drive. If so, just remember that you can use the BACKUP or XCOPY command to back up to floppy or disk. These commands resemble their DOS cousins.

Local tape backup

Using the Ntbackup.exe utility performs a local tape backup. You select the drives, directories, or files you want to back up. You need to know that in order to back up the Registry, you must have at least one other file on the same volume selected.

The same rule applies when you restore the Registry from tape — at least one other file must be selected.

Networked tape backup

You perform network backups by connecting to the *administrative share* (C$, D$, and so on) of the networked drive, then backing up the connected drive. Here are the key points to know about network backups:

- ✔ Registries and event logs of the remote computers are not backed up.
- ✔ Network backups take longer because of network speeds.
- ✔ Typically, a batch script serves to connect and disconnect the shares.
- ✔ You use the AT command if you want to schedule the backup to run at a specific time.
- ✔ You need to know some of the switches for Ntbackup.exe, and I list these for you in Table 5-4.

Table 5-4	Ntbackup.exe Switches
Switch	*Description*
/a	Appends the backup set to the end of the existing backup set.
/b	Backs up the local Registry.
/e	Logs exceptions; similar to a summary log.
/l filename	Assigns a log filename.
/r	Limits the rights of the backup to the Administrators, Backup Operators, or Owners of the data.
/t{normal / copy / incrimental / differental / daily}	Specifies the type of backup to perform.
/v	Verifies the backup.
/hc:{on|off}	Turns on hardware compression (if the tape drive supports it).
Cmd /c net use x	Connects to a remote share.
Cmd /c net use x /delete	Disconnects from remote shares.

Backup types

A typical exam question concerning backup types: The exam gives you a situation and asks you to choose the appropriate type of backup. Memorize this list of the five types of backup and you can fly through these sorts of questions!

- ✔ **Normal:** Backs up all selected files and folders and marks all backed up files.

- ✔ **Copy:** Backs up all selected files and folders; does not mark backed up files.

- ✔ **Differential:** Backs up selected files and folders that have changed since the last backup; does not mark backed up files.

- ✔ **Incremental:** Backs up selected files and folders that have changed since the last incremental backup; does not mark backed up files.

- ✔ **Daily:** Backs up files and folders that have changed that day; does not mark backed up files.

Mirroring

Disk mirroring creates an exact replica of the primary drive on another drive. Both the original and the replica (mirror) are attached to the same controller. If the original fails, you don't lose any data. If the original drive fails, the system automatically switches over to the mirror. If you do experience a drive failure, you need to reboot the system and edit the the Boot.ini file to change the ARC name to point to the mirrored partition.

Lab 5-1 steps you through the process of recovering a mirrored set.

Lab 5-1	Recovering a Mirrored Partition

1. **Edit the Boot.ini file to point to the mirrored drive.**
2. **Boot the system off the mirrored drive.**
3. **Use Disk Administrator to break the mirror.**
4. **Replace the failing drive.**
5. **Use Disk Administrator to re-create the mirror set.**

Duplexing

Duplexing is like mirroring, except that you keep the drives on separate controllers to eliminate a single point of failure. Duplexing also removes the performance with one data twice controller.

Recovery of a failed duplexed set is the same as for a mirrored set.

Striping with parity

Striping with parity is where you join multiple physical drives with exactly matching partitions in a volume set. Data is written across all drives with parity so that the failure of any one drive cannot cause the volume set to fail. Because the data and parity is randomly written across all the drives in the set, the remaining drives either have all the data and no parity or most of the data and the parity to regenerate the missing data.

This configuration requires at least 3 drives and supports up to 32 drives.

Striping with parity is the preferred method for fault tolerance in Windows NT. You cannot, however, include the system partition in a striped set with parity.

The exam does not take hardware RAID controllers into consideration. All questions about striping with parity assume that the Windows NT software performs the function.

Lab 5-2 shows you the procedure to recover a RAID 5 volume set. It's easy.

Lab 5-2	Recovering from a Drive Failure

1. **Replace the failing drive.**
2. **Use Disk Administrator to regenerate the volume set.**

RAID

RAID stands for *Redundant Array of Inexpensive Disks*. It's a method of joining groups of smaller inexpensive drives together to form larger storage devices. Windows NT supports three of the several types of RAID.

The exam includes questions about these three levels of RAID. Be familiar with them and know how to figure the aggregate capacity of each level.

RAID levels

✓ **RAID 0:** Striping without parity. Provides no fault tolerance, but is fast and requires only two disk drives. You calculate logical drive size by adding the partition sizes of all participating drives:

Logical_drive_size = partition size × number of drives

- **RAID 1:** Disk mirroring. Provides reasonable protection but comes with performance considerations. Duplexing relieves the performance issues but the cost is high because the mirror requires two drives. Figure the logical drive size by looking at the size of one of the partitions:

  Logical drive size = partition size of original drive

  The mirror does not increase the available storage of the logical drive.

- **RAID 5:** Striping with parity. Provides the highest level of protection. Results in only a modest performance loss at a more reasonable overhead cost. You calculate the size of a RAID 5 set by multiplying the size of the partition by one less than the number of drives:

  Logical drive size = partition size × (number of drives – 1)

Server replication

Replication lets you maintain specific, identical sets of files and directories on different servers. Updates to the files or directories on one server are periodically replicated to the other servers. All participating servers must run the Replicator service. Use the Server Manager to configure replication.

Export servers can replicate directory trees that involve as many as 32 subdirectories, with up to 1,000 files per directory.

For the exam, the main use for replication is to maintain a set of identical logon scripts on servers that process logon requests in a domain.

By default, the replication folders are in the Winnt\system32\repl folder, in the \import and \export subdirectories, respectively.

Prep Test

1 You're the administrator of a Windows NT Server network. You have a server that includes five 1GB disk drives on two controllers. You have been instructed to develop a fault tolerant strategy for maximum protection and maximum storage. What do you do?

A ○ Build a RAID 5 volume with all 5 drives.

B ○ Build a duplexed set for the system drive and a striped set with parity for the data drives.

C ○ Build a RAID 0 set for the system drive and a RAID 1 set for the data drives.

D ○ Mirror the system drives and build a stripe set for the data drives.

2 Which type of backup strategy do you use to back up selected files and folders and mark them as backed up?

A ○ Copy

B ○ Daily

C ○ Differential

D ○ Normal

D ○ Full

3 Who can back up files and folders on a Windows NT Server? (Select all that are correct.)

A ❑ Users

B ❑ Owners

C ❑ Backup Operators

D ❑ Power Users

4 You are loading Windows NT Server on to a machine previously loaded with Windows 95. Setup tells you that it cannot find a suitable partition on which to load Windows NT Server. What's a possible reason?

A ○ An old version of DOS has formatted this disk.

B ○ Windows 95 formatted the disk with a FAT32 file system.

C ○ Windows NT Server needs an HPFS file system to load.

D ○ Windows 95 has placed a VFAT file system on the disk.

5 To ensure that all the domain controllers use the same login scripts, use server _____ among all participating servers.

A ○ Domain trusts

B ○ Replication

C ○ Synchronization

D ○ Dynamic allocation

6 Which file systems does Windows NT Server support? (Select all those that do *not* apply.)

A ❑ FAT

B ❑ CDFS

C ❑ NTFS

D ❑ HPFS

7 You should use a batch file to perform a network backup on many Windows NT Servers. A line in the batch file to back up the remote server, Accounting, would look like:

A ○ net use X: \\accounting\c$

    ntbackup backup X: /a /b /l accounting.log /t normal

B ○ net use X: \\accounting\c$

    ntbackup backup X: /a /l accounting.log /t normal

C ○ net use X: \\accounting\c$

    ntbackup backup X: /b /l accounting.log

D ○ net use Z: \\accounting\c$ ntbackup backup Z: /r /l accounting.log /t normal /hc:on

8 You can set permissions for files and folders on an NTFS volume at what level?

A ○ Only at the folder level

B ○ At both the folder and file level

C ○ Only at the file level

D ○ At no level, because you can't set individual file or folder permissions on NTFS volumes

9 If you build a stripe set with parity on two 800MB drives, what is the total size of the volume set?

A ○ 800MB

B ○ 1600MB

C ○ 2400MB

D ○ None of the above

10 You are the administrator of a Windows NT Server. All volumes are formatted with NTFS. Users from the Engineering group are complaining that they can't write into a particular folder. You check the folder and find that the Engineering group has Full Control of the folder. What might be wrong?

A ○ The users are not the Owners of the data.

B ○ The FAT permissions are set to Read-Only.

C ○ The Everyone group has no permissions to the folder.

D ○ The users are using Windows 95 on their workstations.

Answers

1 *B.* A duplexed set for the system partition guards against a single point of failure and a striped set with parity protects the data drive. Windows NT does not support a RAID 5 set on the system drive. You either cannot do the other answers or they do not provide fault tolerance across all volumes. *Review "Duplexing."*

2 *D.* The others do not back up all files or do not mark them as backed up. *Review "Tape backup."*

3 *B and C.* Owners, Backup Operators, and Administrators may back up files and folders. *Review "NTFS."*

4 *B.* Windows NT Server does not recognize FAT32 file systems. *Review "Dual-boot systems."*

5 *B.* Replication is the correct answer. *Review "Server replication."*

6 *D.* Windows NT Server no longer supports HPFS. Make sure you read the questions fully. Review *"Choosing a File System."*

7 *B.* The others want to back up the local Registry or restrict access. *Review "Tape backup."*

8 *B.* Files and folders on an NTFS volume can have different permissions set. *Review "NTFS."*

9 *D.* It takes three drives, minimum, for a striped set with parity. They do ask tricky questions sometimes. *Review "Volumes."*

10 *B.* FAT permissions are available on NTFS volumes and take precedence over NTFS permissions. *Review "Dual-boot systems."*

Chapter 6

Administration

· ·

Exam Objectives

▶ Creating and deleting partitions

▶ Extending volume sets

▶ Creating and recovering fault tolerant volume sets

▶ Creating and updating an Emergency Repair Disk

▶ Performing backups and restoring data

· ·

*A*dministration of storage resources is a key part of the exam. Disk administration tasks you are tested on include:

✔ Creating partitions

✔ Formatting partitions

✔ Deleting partitions

You also need to know how to create and recover fault tolerant volumes. Questions with illustrating pictures are identified by an Exhibit button on the question page. Virtually all questions regarding storage include an exhibit of a Disk Administrator screen. Get familiar with this screen.

This chapter covers these functions and the Disk Administrator tool so that you can prepare for storage and administration questions.

Quick Assessment

Creating and
Recovering
Fault
Tolerant
Volume Sets

1 You are the administrator of a Windows NT server that has three disk drives. The free spaces in the extended partitions are 100MB on the first drive, 150MB on the second, and 50MB on the third. Creating a volume set with this free space would yield _____ of new storage.

Performing
Backups and
Restoring
Data

2 To recover a failed stripe set, you use the _____ utility.

3 You must edit the _____ file before you can boot from the mirrored partition in a mirrored set.

4 To back up the local Registry on a Windows NT Server, you must check the _____ option and you must select at least one other file or folder on the _____.

Creating and
Updating an
Emergency
Repair Disk

5 You use the _____ utility to create an Emergency Repair Disk.

6 What do you do if you need to recover from a corrupted Windows NT system?

Creating and
Deleting
Partitions

7 The active partition points to the _____.

8 You use the _____ service to schedule backup jobs.

9 The only users who can back up and restore data are those who are members of the _____, _____, and _____ groups.

Extending
Volume Sets

10 You use the CONVERT.EXE utility to convert file systems from _____ to _____.

Answers

1 *300MB.* Review "Creating and deleting volumes and volume sets."

2 *NTBACKUP.EXE.* See "Backing up a volume."

3 *Boot.ini.* See "Mirror Sets."

4 *Backup Local Registry; system partition.* See "Backing up a volume."

5 *RDISK.EXE.* See "Using RDISK."

6 *Boot up using the NT startup disks, then use the ERD.* See "Using RDISK."

7 *system partition.* Review "Defining active partitions."

8 *Schedule.* See "Scheduling jobs."

9 *Owners; Backup Operators; and Administrators.* See "Restoring data."

10 *FAT; NTFS.* See "Formatting volumes."

Disk Administrator

The Disk Administrator, shown in Figure 6-1, is the primary tool for all storage-related functions.

With the Disk Administrator, you can

- ✔ Create partitions
- ✔ Delete partitions
- ✔ Format partitions
- ✔ Create Volume Sets
- ✔ Recover from fault tolerant volume sets

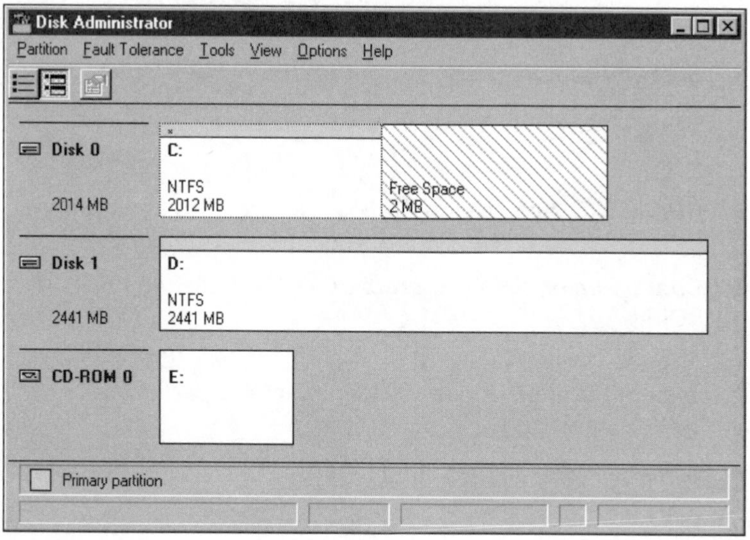

Figure 6-1:
The Disk
Administrator.

Creating and deleting partitions

Disk drives today can hold very large amounts of data. There are many times you may want to separate or partition a disk drive into separate smaller sections. A single hard drive can appear as multiple logical drives. There are some basic rules for dealing with partitions.

- ✔ A hard drive can have from 1 to 32 separate partitions, but must have at least one partition before it can be used.
- ✔ A partition can contain one or more file systems.
- ✔ If you attempt to change a partition, you lose any underlying data.

✔ You can partition any free unpartitioned space on a hard drive without harming the data on the other partitions.

✔ Deleting any partition doesn't affect the other partitions.

Windows NT supports only the FAT and NTFS file systems. File system types other than FAT and NTFS can reside on a Windows NT machine; they're just invisible to Windows NT.

In Lab 6-1 you create a partition.

Lab 6-1	Creating a Partition

1. **Open Disk Administrator (choose Start⇨Programs⇨Administrative Tools⇨Disk Administrator).**

2. **Select the unpartitioned space.**

3. **Choose Partition. Then choose Create, or Create Extended, from the menu.**

   Windows NT creates the partition and asks you to commit the changes.

4. **Choose Partition⇨Commit Changes Now from the menu.**

Now that you have created a partition, it is time to delete one. Lab 6-2 demonstrates how to delete a partition. Once a partition is deleted, the data is gone.

Lab 6-2	Deleting a Partition

1. **Open Disk Administrator.**

2. **Select the desired partition.**

3. **Choose Partition⇨Delete.**

   A warning box informs you of the consequence of your action.

4. **Choose OK.**

   Another dialog box prompts you to commit the changes.

5. **Choose Partition⇨Commit Changes Now.**

Primary and extended partitions

There are some specific rules you need to know about partitions.

✔ Each disk drive can have as many as three primary partitions and one extended partition.

✔ An extended partition can be subdivided further into multiple logical drives.

✔ The total number of primary partitions and logical drives cannot exceed 32 on any one physical hard disk.

Defining active partitions

The partitions that contain the startup and operating system files are commonly called the *system partition* and the *boot partition,* respectively.

The *system partition* for Windows NT is the volume that contains the hardware-specific files for loading Windows NT. A primary partition must be

✔ Marked as active

✔ Located on the disk that the computer accesses when it starts up

You can have no more than one active partition at a time. To use another operating system, you must mark its system partition as active and then restart the computer.

The active partition, typically on the C: partition (but always check first anyway), is the one that has an asterisk (*) on its color bar. Notice the asterisk on the C partition back in Figure 6-1.

The system partition is the one that has the boot files, and the boot partition is the one that has the system files.

Lab 6-3 demonstrates how to mark a partition as active. Be sure to take note of which partition is active at the beginning of the lab. When you are finished be sure to set the active partition back to the original partition. If you forget, your computer won't reboot correctly.

Lab 6-3	Marking a Partition Active

1. **Open Disk Administrator.**

2. **Select the partition to make active.**

3. **Choose Partition⇨Mark Active.**

   A warning box tells you about the consequence of your action.

4. **Choose OK.**

   A dialog box prompts you to commit the changes.

5. **Choose Partition⇨Commit Changes Now.**

   The asterisk moves to the other partition.

Creating and deleting volumes and volume sets

Most exam questions on administration and storage focus on creating volumes and volume sets. You need to know how the Disk Administrator

- Creates volumes and volume sets
- Deletes volumes and volume sets
- Extends volume sets

What is the difference between a volume and a volume set? The answer is in the numbers. A volume is an organizational structure upon one or more partitions that supports file storage. If you select one or more partitions on a physical disk drive and format them, the result is a volume. A volume set is a volume made up of more than one partition.

Each volume set can include up to 32 areas of free space from one or more physical disks. When you create a volume set, you can make the free space an unallocated area within an extended partition or you can make it an unpartitioned area elsewhere on the disk. Figure 6-1 shows a volume set E, which consists of two areas in the extended partition on disk 0. Figure 6-1 also shows the two types of free space. The free space between drives E and L is unallocated space in an extended partition. This can be used to create another logical drive or extend a volume set. The free space at the right side of Figure 6-1 is unpartitioned space. A partition must be created in this space before it can be used.

You cannot use volume sets to bypass the limit of four partitions on a disk drive. For example, Figure 6-1 shows

- Three primary partitions
    - Drive C
    - Drive D
    - Drive L
- One Extended Partition with
    - Logical drive I
    - Logical drive K
    - Volume set E
    - 4MB of unallocated space
- 43MB of unpartitioned space

The free space between the second part of volume set E and the primary partition L is part of the extended partition. This free space can create one or more logical drives in the extended partition. The free space to the right of primary partition L is wasted disk space, however, because you have already met the limit of three primary partitions and an extended partition.

You can tell whether free space is unallocated space in an extended partition or is unpartitioned space. The diagonal lines slant to the left on unpartitioned space and to the right on unallocated space. Notice the extended partition I shown in Figure 6-2.

Extending volume sets

You can extend NTFS volumes and volume sets by adding free space. Disk Administrator forces the system to restart after you quit and save your changes and formats the new area without affecting files on the original volume or volume set. Lab 6-4 shows how to extend the volume set.

Lab 6-4   Extending a Volume Set

1. **Open Disk Administrator.**

2. **Select an existing volume or volume set and one or more areas of free space.**

3. **Choose Partition⇨Extend Volume Set.**

   A dialog box displays the minimum and maximum sizes for the volume set.

4. **In the Create Extended Volume Set dialog box, indicate a desired size for the volume set you're creating.**

5. **Choose OK.**

   Disk Administrator determines how much space to use, then restarts your server, formats the free space and adds it to the volume set. Throughout it all, Disk Administrator never touches the existing data.

The exam has at least one question about how to add space to a volume without having to reload the drive. The answer is to *extend the volume set.*

Creating stripe sets

You create stripe sets like volume sets, but more restrictions apply:

- ✔ Each member of a stripe set must be on a different physical disk drive.

- ✔ The minimum number of disk drives is two (the maximum is still 32).

- ✔ The partitions for the striped set must be the same size.

A stripe set offers high performance, but is not fault tolerant. If one of the drives fails, you must rebuild and reload the whole volume. If you have a dual-boot system, most other operating systems cannot recognize a stripe set.

If you put a share on a stripe set, any client user who can connect to the share can use it to the extent of their permissions.

Labs 6-5 and 6-6 cover stripe sets. If you are working with a computer that doesn't have the required number of disk drives, just work your way through the menu selections and take note of the procedures.

Lab 6-5	Creating a Stripe Set

1. **Select two or more areas of free space on 2 to 32 disk drives by clicking the first partition and holding the Ctrl key as you click the free space on the remaining disk drives.**

2. **Choose Partition⇨Create Stripe Set.**

   Disk Administrator displays the maximum and minimum sizes for the stripe set.

3. **In the Create Stripe Set dialog box, type the size you want for the stripe set and choose OK.**

   Disk Administrator divides the total size among the selected disks and assigns a single drive letter to the stripe set.

Lab 6-6   Deleting a Stripe Set

1. **Select the stripe set to delete.**

2. **Choose Partition⇨Delete.**

   A message box pops up, warning you about the loss of data and prompting you to confirm.

3. **Choose Yes.**

Stripe sets with parity

A *stripe set with parity* data writes to one of the drives in the volume set. If a disk fails there is enough information to re-create the missing piece of data.

You create stripe sets with parity in almost the same way that you create stripe sets. The difference is that you must use at least three disk drives to create this type of stripe set. Why? A stripe set with parity needs an additional drive to write the parity for the striped data.

You can expect an exam question that calls on you to figure the size of both striped sets and striped sets with parity. Don't forget that you use the following formula to figure the size of a striped set with parity:

```
partition_size * (number_of_drives - 1)
```

In Labs 6-7 and 6-8, you create a Stripe Set with Parity.

Lab 6-7   Creating a Stripe Set with Parity

1. **Select three or more areas of free space on 2 to 32 disk drives.**

   You select by clicking the first partition and holding the Ctrl key down while you click the free space on the remaining disk drives.

2. **Choose Fault Tolerance⇨Create Stripe Set with Parity.**

   Disk Administrator displays the maximum and minimum sizes for the stripe set.

3. **In the Create Stripe Set dialog box, type the size you want for the stripe set and choose OK.**

   Disk Administrator divides the total size among the selected disks and assigns a single drive letter to the stripe set with parity.

Lab 6-8   Deleting a Stripe Set with Parity

1. **Select the stripe set with parity that you want to delete.**

2. **Choose Partition⇨Delete.**

A message box warns you about the loss of data.

3. Choose Yes to confirm.

Creating mirror sets

Disk mirroring is the only type of fault tolerance that you can give the system partition. You establish disk mirroring by maintaining a complete copy of one partition on another partition on another disk drive. You use the same drive letter for both partitions.

The exam may have a question about how to set up disk duplexing. Disk duplexing is like a mirrored set, but it uses two controllers. Duplexing also increases performance over a standard mirror set.

Labs 6-9 and 6-10 show you how to create and break a mirrored set. Pay particular attention to the steps involved. Some of the questions ask the procedure for building and breaking mirrored sets. If your computer does not have the available resources for the labs, you still want to read through them and find all the menu items.

Lab 6-9	Creating a Mirror Set

1. Select the partition to mirror and an area of free space at least the same size on another disk drive.

You make the selection by clicking the first partition and holding the Ctrl key down as you click the free space on the other disk drive.

2. Choose Fault Tolerance⇨Establish Mirror.

Disk Administrator creates an equal-sized partition in the free space and assigns the drive letter to the mirrored set.

Lab 6-10	Breaking a Mirror Set

1. Select the mirror set to break.

2. Choose Fault Tolerance⇨Break Mirror.

A message box appears, warning you of the imminent doom of the mirrored relationship and prompting you to confirm.

3. Choose Yes to confirm.

After breaking a Mirrored Set you may need to recover the disk space for another purpose. Lab 6-11 goes through the process of converting the broken mirrored partition back to general free space.

Lab 6-11	Converting the Unmirrored Partition to Free Space

1. **Select the unmirrored partition that you no longer need.**

2. **Choose Partition⇨Delete.**

   A message warns you about the loss of data and asks you to confirm.

3. **Choose Yes to confirm.**

Assigning drive letters

A volume on a Windows NT Server needs a drive letter before you can access it. Windows NT supports up to 32 disk drives, so its makers anticipated the spanning of logical disks across multiple hard drives. Letters A and B are for floppies, which leaves 24 available letters, C though Z, to assign volumes.

Windows NT assigns the next available letter to each new volume you create. You can change the drive letter by using Tools⇨Assign Drive Letter, which invokes the Assign Drive Letter dialog box, shown in Figure 6-3.

Figure 6-3:
The Assign
Drive Letter
dialog box.

The exam may pose a question on how to change the drive letter for the CD-ROM drive. Just use the Tools⇨Assign Drive Letter option in Disk Administrator.

Formatting volumes

You must format a newly created volume before you can use it. The two types of format that you can use with Windows NT Server are FAT and NTFS. Lab 6-12 shows you how to create volumes.

We've seen only one question about formatting with the NTFS file system (the advanced file system that works with all volume types). Just remember that for a dual-boot system or a RISC-based computer, you must format the system partition as FAT.

Lab 6-12   Formatting and Labeling a Volume

1. Select the newly created partition or partition set.

2. Choose Partition⇨Commit Changes Now.

3. Choose Tools⇨Format.

The Format dialog box appears, as shown in Figure 6-4.

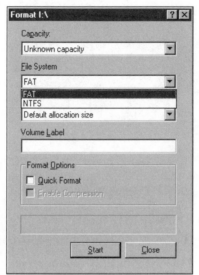

4. Select the desired file system type and enter a label for the drive in the dialog box.

5. Choose OK to begin the format process.

A confirmation box appears.

6. Select Yes.

A progress box appears.

To convert a FAT file system to NTFS, use the CONVERT.EXE utility from the command prompt. The format of the command is

```
convert <drive_letter>: /fs:ntfs
```

A message says that the drive will be converted the next time the system boots. This conversion is a one-way operation. You cannot convert from FAT to any file system other than NTFS, and you cannot convert an NTFS file system to FAT. This conversion does not affect the data on the drive.

Using RDISK

RDISK, shown in Figure 6-5, makes and updates the Emergency Repair Disk (ERD). Anytime you make changes to the system, run RDISK to update your ERD. During installation of Windows NT you are asked to create an Emergency Repair Disk. If you elect not to build the ERD at installation, or if the ERD has been lost, you can create a new one with the RDISK utility.

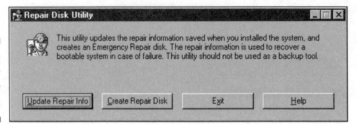

Figure 6-5:
The Repair
Disk Utility
dialog box.

Executing RDISK /S from the Run dialog box (choose Start⇨Run) saves the current Registry to \Winnt\System32\Config and prompts you for a formatted disk. The ERD contains the following Registry Keys and files:

- ✔ SYSTEM._HKEY_LOCAL_MACHINE\SYSTEM compressed
- ✔ SOFTWARE_HKEY_LOCAL_MACHINE\SOFTWARE compressed
- ✔ SECURITY._HKEY_LOCAL_MACHINE\SECURITY compressed
- ✔ SAM._HKEY_LOCAL_MACHINE\SAM compressed
- ✔ NTUSER.DA_Default profile, compressed
- ✔ AUTOEXEC.NT %winntroot%system32\autoexec.nt
- ✔ CONFIG.NT %winntroot%system32\config.nt
- ✔ SETUP.LOG a list of installed files and their checksums
- ✔ DEFAULT._KHET_USERS\DEFAULT compressed

The ERD doesn't contain the entire Registry, just enough to fix most common errors.

You cannot boot from the ERD. To use the ERD, you must use the Windows NT Setup floppies 1 and 2. Select R for repair, deselect any items you don't want to perform, and then insert disk 3 and the ERD as prompted.

Fault recovery

The exam tests your knowledge of recovering from faults. The two types of fault tolerant volumes are the mirror set and the stripe set with parity.

Mirror sets

Recovering from a failed mirror set is easier than it seems. When a member of a mirror set experiences a problem, Windows NT automatically uses the good drive and orphans the failing one. You need to perform the steps in Lab 6-13 in order to replace the failing drive and regain your fault protection.

Lab 6-13	Recovering from a Failed Mirror Set

1. **Choose Fault Tolerance⇨Break Mirror.**

2. **Reassign the drive letter to the good member.**

3. **Replace the failing drive.**

4. **Re-create the mirror set (refer to Lab 6-9).**

A boot floppy will be required to boot the system so you can run Disk Administrator if

✔ The mirrored partition contains a boot partition

✔ The failing drive was the original member of that set

You must create an up-to-date boot floppy for the system to access it. The files on this floppy will point to the other partition in the mirror set. Lab 6-14 tells you how to create this boot floppy. It is a good idea to do this when you create the mirror set and keep the boot floppy near the computer for which it was created. This procedure can also be used to create a boot floppy for troubleshooting boot problems. Just don't edit the Boot.ini file.

Lab 6-14	Creating a Boot Floppy

1. **Format a floppy using Windows NT.**

2. **Copy Boot.ini, Ntldr, and Ntdect.com.**

3. **If your system uses an SCSI controller with BIOS translation disabled, copy Ntbootdd.sys.**

4. **If you need to boot into MS-DOS or another operating system, copy Bootsect.dos.**

5. **Edit Boot.ini to match the new parameters and new locations of the boot and system partitions.**

The exam always asks at least one question that calls on you to know about ARC naming conventions. You can find examples of ARC naming conventions in the Boot.ini file. It will look something like this:

```
[Boot loader]
timeout=30
default=multi(0)disk(0)rdisk(0)partition(1)\Winnt

[operating systems]
multi(0)disk(0)rdisk(0)partition(1)\Winnt="Windows NT
        Version 4.0"
multi(0)disk(0)rdisk(0)partition(1)\Winnt="Windows NT Ver-
        sion 4.0 [VGA mode]" /basevideo /sos
```

To answer any ARC naming conventions, remember the following values:

multi(x) = adapter number, starts at zero

disk(x) = SCSI bus number, starts at zero

rdisk(x) = disk on adapter, starts at zero

partition(x) = partition on the disk, starts at one

So multi(0)disk(0)rdisk(0)partition(1) describes the first adapter, the first SCSI bus on that adapter, the first disk on the SCSI bus, and the first partition on that disk. You are asked to choose which ARC naming description will point to a specific partition on a disk drive.

Stripe set with parity

Recovering from a failure on a stripe set with parity is easy. The system can rebuild the data on-the-fly from parity information stored on the still operational drives. To master the process, try Lab 6-15.

Lab 6-15   Rebuilding a Striped Set with Parity

1. **Replace the failing drive.**

2. **Select an area of free space on the new drive.**

3. **Choose Fault Tolerance⇨Regenerate.**

4. **Exit Disk Administrator and reboot.**

   The regeneration process takes place in the background.

Backup

Backing up critical data is an important task for any network administrator. Windows NT ships with a backup utility called NTBACKUP.EXE. The storage medium with NTBACKUP is the tape drive. Even though NTBACKUP offers support for several tape types, you must install the drivers for the specific type of tape before you can use the backup utility.

Backing up a volume

To launch NTBACKUP, you choose Start⇨Programs, Administrative Tools⇨ NTBackup. The Backup dialog box opens, as shown in Figure 6-6. The Backup utility

- ✔ Looks for tape drives
- ✔ Reports the status of all tape drives

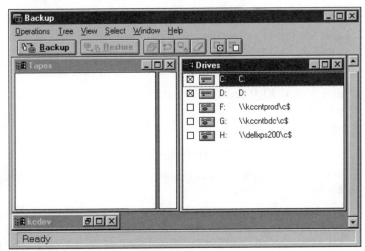

Figure 6-6: The Backup dialog box.

Lab 6-16 steps you through the process. If you do not have a tape drive attached to your computer you will not be allowed to do a backup, but you can still see the disk drives and go through most of the menus.

Lab 6-16	Backing Up

1. Start NTBACKUP.EXE and a list of available drives appears.

2. Select files for backup

To back up an entire drive, click the box next to the drive letter. An X appears in the box next to the drive letter.

3. **Make sure you have a tape in the tape drive and then click the Backup button.**

4. **Select the different backup options.**

5. **Choose OK.**

The default name for the backup log file is BACKUP.LOG. It's in the \systemroot folder. To get a list of skipped files, select the FULL DETAIL logging option.

Restoring data

You restore data like you perform backups, as you see through Lab 6-17. Place the tape that contains the backup set that you want to restore in the tape drive and start NTBACKUP. The left pane includes a tape icon with information about the tape itself. The right pane lists the tape contents.

Lab 6-17	Restoring Data

1. **Start NTBACKUP.EXE.**

2. **Load the tape to view the catalog, to see which files and folders are available for restoring.**

3. **To create a catalog simply choose Operations⇨Catalog.**

4. **After NTBACKUP creates the catalog, select the file and folders to restore.**

5. **Click the Restore button.**

6. **Select a location for the restored files and folders.**

Only Administrators, Backup Operators, and Owners can back up or restore data.

7. **Select the different restore options; refer to Chapter 5. Remember, to restore the registry you must click the Restore Local Registry check box and select at least one file or folder from the tape catalog.**

8. **Choose OK.**

Remember that before you can back up or restore the local Registry, you must select at least one other file for backup or restore. A summary log lists the failures in a restore operation.

Scheduling jobs

You can schedule backups by writing a batch file and using the AT.EXE command to schedule when the batch file runs. The AT command uses the Schedule service in Windows NT. This service must be running on the machine running the scheduled batch job. The syntax for the AT.EXE command is

```
AT [\\computername] [id] [/delete] time [interactive]
        [/every:date[….]]|next: date[….]] "command"
```

Prep Test

√**1** The Windows NT server fails to boot. You use a boot floppy, then start the Disk Administrator. What might you see on the display?

A ○ Wrong Active Partition

B ○ Failed drive on the stripe set without parity

C ○ Too many logical drives in the extended partition

D ○ You need to create a stripe set on the boot partition

2 When a disk fails in a stripe set with parity, what utility recovers it?

A ○ NTBACKUP.EXE

B ○ Disk Administrator

C ○ FDISK.EXE

D ○ REGEDT32.EXE

3 Members of which of the following groups cannot restore data into a different directory than it was backed up from? (Choose all that apply.)

A ❑ Server Operators

B ❑ Account Operators

C ❑ Backup Operators

D ❑ Administrators

4 After running a backup job, a message tells you 25 files were not backed up. The list of files that were not backed up are contained in _____.

A ○ BACKUP.LOG

B ○ BADLIST.TXT

C ○ ERROR.LOG

D ○ SKIPFILE.TXT

5 You are the administrator of a Windows NT Server that has five disk drives. The free space on each is as follows: Drive 1 has 200MB. Drive 2 has 100MB. Drive 3 has 0MB. Drive 4 has 300MB. Drive 5 has 250MB. You want to create a stripe set with parity that has 400MB. Which drives do you use?

A ○ 1, 5

B ○ 2, 4, 3

C ○ 1, 4, 5

D ○ 2, 4, 5

6 You are the Administrator of a Windows NT Server that has five disk drives. The free space on each is as follows: Drive 1 has 200MB. Drive 2 has 100MB. Drive 3 has 0MB. Drive 4 has 300MB. Drive 5 has 250MB. You want to create a mirror set that has 250MB. Which drives do you use?

A ○ 1, 2

B ○ 5, 3

C ○ 1, 5

D ○ 4, 5

√**7** Running RDISK.EXE /S copies the current Registry settings to which folder?

A ○ \winnt\system\registry\

B ○ \winnt\system32\sam\   *P6. 98*

C ○ \winnt\system32\config\

D ○ \winnt\system\repl

√**8** To create a boot floppy for Windows NT server, you must have a Windows NT-formatted floppy with which files? (Choose all that apply.)

A ❑ Boot.ini

B ❑ NTOSKRNL.COM   *pg. 99*

C ❑ NTLDR

D ❑ NTDETECT.COM

9 The system partition of a RISC computer must have a(n) _____ file system.

A ○ NTFS

B ○ FAT

C ○ HPFS

D ○ FFS

√**10** What must you do to catalog a tape when you use NTBACKUP.EXE?

A ○ Choose Tools⇨Catalog.

B ○ Choose Restore and then click the Catalog check box.

C ○ Choose Operations⇨Catalog.

D ○ You cannot catalog a tape with NTBACKUP.EXE.

P6 102

Answers

1 *A.* The wrong active partition will cause the BIOS to look at the wrong partition for bootstrap information. An asterisk in the color bar of the partition marks the active partition. *Review the "Defining active partitions" section for more information.*

2 *B.* You use Disk Administrator to regenerate a stripe set with parity. *See the "Stripe sets with parity" section under "Fault Recovery."*

3 *A, B.* Read the questions carefully. The ones that *cannot* restore data to a server are the Server Operators and Account Operators. *See the "Restoring data" section for more information.*

4 *A.* BACKUP.LOG is the file that lists the skipped files. (But only if you specified a full log for the backup.) *BACKUP.LOG is covered in the "Backing up a volume" section.*

5 *C.* You need a minimum of three drives for a stripe set with parity. One partition is used for parity and does not count for storage size. The only three partitions with enough free space are drives 1, 4, and 5. *See "Stripe sets with parity" under "Creating stripe sets."*

6 *D.* The only two drives with enough free space are drives 4 and 5. *See "Stripe sets with parity" under "Creating stripe sets."*

7 *C.* The location of the Registry files is \winnt\system32\config. *See "Using RDISK."*

8 *A, C, D.* These three files are the boot files on the system partition. They must be on the floppy to point to the boot partition for Windows NT. *The section "Using RDISK" describes the process of creating boot floppies.*

9 *B.* A RISC computer must have a FAT system partition. You also must use a FAT system if you want to have a dual boot computer. *See "Formatting volumes" for more information.*

10 *C.* You can catalog a tape from the Operations menu of NTBACKUP.EXE. *See "Backing up a volume."*

Part III
Installation

"One of the first things you want to do before installing NT Server is fog the users to keep them calm during the procedure."

In this part . . .

I cover lots of information in this section. I help you study the install process on Intel-based platforms, as well as the requirements for RISC-based systems, using the various methods that Windows NT Server supports.

I cover the Control Panel (what I call the system administrator's second best friend) and I discuss some of the tools you can use to configure an NT 4.0 Server. In addition, I cover all the protocols necessary to know for passing the exam, including NetBIOS, TCP/IP, NWLink, and NetBEUI.

Chapter 7

Installation Methods

Exam Objectives

▶ Installing Windows NT Server on Intel-based platforms

▶ Installing Windows NT Server to perform various server roles

▶ Installing Windows NT Server by using various methods

• •

*E*ven though installation is one of the five areas that Exam 70-67 covers, don't expect more than a handful of questions on the topic. Of the 70 or so questions on the Server exam, only about five involved installation.

In general, the questions come in three flavors:

✔ What's the best installation method for a certain situation?

✔ How does the installation method work?

✔ How do you get rid of an installed file system?

Quick Assessment

Installing
Windows
NT Server
by Using
Various
Methods

1 The _____ installation switch creates three boot floppies, but does not install.

2 If you want to change the length of time that the system waits before it starts up the operating system, adjust the _____ line in the Boot.ini file. PG 123-124

3 Operating systems that require the _____ file system cannot recognize partitions formatted with the NTFS file system.

4 If you install Windows NT Server from DOS, you must go to the drive letter where the CD-ROM is located and issue the _____ command.

5 The _____ switch installs NT without requiring the setup disks.

6 If you're performing an upgrade to NT 4, you use the _____ command.

Installing
Windows
NT Server
to Perform
Various
Server
Roles

7 To achieve fault tolerance on your network, you can install your Windows NT Server as a _____.

8 If you install a server that is not part of your domain, it will be designated a _____ (also called a _____).

Installing
Windows NT
Server on
Intel-based
Platforms

9 The minimum requirement for hard disk space is _____MB for Intel PCs and _____MB for RISC-based PCs.

PG
112

Answers

1 *⁄OX.* Check out Table 7-2 and the section "Installing from CD-ROM."

2 *timeout=.* Read "Changing the boot operating system."

3 *FAT.* Check out "Booting multiple operating systems."

4 *WINNT.* Review "Winnt and Winnt32."

5 *⁄B.* Review "Beginning setup from another operating system."

6 *WINNT32.EXE.* Read "Winnt and Winnt32."

7 *BDC.* Read "Backup domain controller."

8 *Stand-alone server; member server.* Check out "Member servers and stand-alone servers."

9 *124 and 158.* Check out Table 7-1 for all the Microsoft hardware requirements.

Hardware Preparation

Almost all MCSE exams emphasize knowing default system settings. You need to know the minimum requirements for Windows NT Server for the various processor architectures, such as Intel and RISC.

Memorize the general hardware requirements for installing NT Server, given here in Table 7-1, and you may get a couple of easy questions!

Table 7-1	Minimum Hardware Requirements for Windows NT Server 4
Item	*Requirement*
Processor	Intel 486/25 or higher or a RISC, such as Alpha, MIPS, or PowerPC
Memory	12MB RAM (Intel); 16MB RAM (RISC)
Hard disk space	124MB (Intel); 158MB (RISC)
Monitor	VGA or higher monitor
Disk drive	$3^1/_2$ floppy drive
CD-ROM drive	CD-ROM drive or access to CD-ROM drive over network
Mouse	Mouse or other pointing device
Network card	Not required, but recommended

Booting multiple operating systems

You need to know how NT Server interacts with other operating systems such as Windows 3.*x*, Windows 95, and Windows NT Workstation when installed on the same computer. You need to know how to save your current desktop settings and program groups if you install Windows NT Server over another operating system. You also need to know which operating systems Windows NT Server cannot coexist with and still maintain your original settings; that is, know which operating systems you cannot install Windows NT in the same directory as.

The following is a list of important facts about installing Windows NT Server that you should memorize for the exam:

   ✔ If you install NT Server after the existing operating system, Windows NT will automatically add an entry to the startup menu for the existing operating system. To start NT Server, select it from the startup menu.

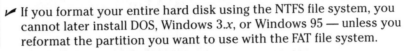

>
>
> ✔ If you install an operating system other than Windows NT *after* you install Windows NT, you will lose the startup menu, because the other operating system overwrites the boot sector that contains the Windows NT startup file. You must update your system using an emergency repair disk that you created during installation; if you didn't create one, you have to use the RDISK utility to update the startup menu.
>
> ✔ Operating systems that require the FAT file system cannot recognize partitions formatted with the NTFS file system. To ensure that all operating systems on the computer can access certain information, store that info on a FAT file system partition.
>
> ✔ If you format your entire hard disk using the NTFS file system, you cannot later install DOS, Windows 3.*x*, or Windows 95 — unless you reformat the partition you want to use with the FAT file system.

Windows 95

If Windows 95 was installed before you installed Windows NT, a menu option is automatically created for Windows 95. You don't need to select the MS-DOS menu option on the startup menu and then issue a specific command to enter Windows 95; you can simply create a separate entry for Windows 95.

Windows 3.x

Because Windows 3.*x* requires DOS, you can select it by choosing MS-DOS from the startup menu and then issuing the command to start Windows.

DOS

To boot to DOS, select the MS-DOS option from the Windows NT startup menu. You can only boot to DOS if you have formatted the partition with the FAT file system. If DOS was installed before you installed Windows NT, assume that you already have a FAT file system partition on the computer.

Installation Methods of the Stars

There are many different ways to install NT Server. For the exam, focus on the major installation methods, such as CD-ROM and network installs.

Don't worry about the unattended installations for the NT Server exam.

The following four questions help determine the course of action you take during installation and how to deal with certain exam scenarios:

> ✔ Do I have a CD-ROM?
>
> ✔ Do I already have an operating system installed?

✔ Can I install over the network?

✔ Is this an upgrade?

Installing from CD-ROM

When you install from a CD-ROM, you have two installation options:

✔ Beginning setup from another operating system

✔ Using a boot disk with CD-ROM drivers

Beginning setup from another operating system

Beginning Windows NT setup from another operating system is the easiest installation method. You get questions about the switches used during installation.

Insert the Windows NT Server CD-ROM while in the current operating system (your CD-ROM drive needs to be running in the current operating system). We are using Windows 95/NT, as evident by the reference to the Start menu. You need to use the Run dialog box (choose Start⇨Run), because you have to specify the /b switch. Here's the command to type:

```
D:\winnt32 /b
```

The /b switch skips the default creation of the three boot floppies, saving plenty of time.

If you install NT Server from DOS, you choose the CD-ROM drive and issue the WINNT command. (Not the Winnt32 command — don't be fooled!)

You can use the three installation floppy disks that came with NT Server. If you don't have these floppies (for example, you lost them), you can create them with the NT Server CD-ROM. Drop in the CD and switch to the CD-ROM drive. Type this command:

```
D:\i386\winnt /ox
```

Using the /ox switch lets you create the boot floppies without installing NT. After you finish creating the floppies, place the first floppy in the disk drive of the computer that you want to install Windows NT Server on and restart the computer.

Learn which executables to use for installing NT in situations. Table 7-2 points out the switches you're most likely to encounter on the exam.

The most important installation switches are /b, which enables you to skip creating boot floppies during installation, and /ox, which lets you create the boot floppies without having to perform the installation right then.

Table 7-2	The Server Installation Switches Most Likely to Show Up on the Exam
Switch	**Purpose**
/OX	Only creates three boot floppies; does not install.
/B	Installs NT without requiring the setup disks.
/S:<source path>	Specifies the source to the Windows NT source files.
/T:<temp drive>	Specifies the drive to hold the installation temp files.
/I:<inffile>	Specifies the name of the setup file.
/U	Unattended installation. The /S switch must also be present.
/F	Does not verify files.
/C	Skips free disk space check.

The /b and /ox setup switches are great candidates to memorize for the test. You can memorize the /b switch more easily if you think of "boot" floppy. Try this: **B**ig **S**tuff **I**s **T**oo **C**omplex **F**or **U**ntrained **O**perators.

Using a boot disk with CD-ROM drivers

You can install DOS and then your CD-ROM drivers, giving you access to the CD-ROM so that you can begin the install, or you can create a boot floppy that loads your CD-ROM drivers. Here are the downfalls of the two installation methods:

- ✔ It takes time either way to install DOS or to create a boot disk that loads the CD-ROM drivers.
- ✔ Either way, you must have your CD-ROM drivers disk handy.
- ✔ When you create the boot floppy that loads your CD-ROM drivers, you have to know how to make the configuration files look back on the floppy for the drivers.

Installing from the network

In addition to CD-ROM installations, Microsoft lists network installs as one of the exam objectives for Server. Network install questions can cover the process (for example, a "you have a networked computer without an operating system installed . . ." type of scenario) or Network Client Administrator. Don't expect to see any questions on unattended installations or the Uniqueness Database File.

Network administrators usually have a network share on a server that contains the files necessary for installation. You do not have to copy the entire CD-ROM to the network, just the source files for your processor architecture — probably located in the i386 directory. This installation method is cool because you can access the share and begin installing from anywhere on the network. You also use this method when you can't find the *NT Server* CD-ROM.

With installation files saved on the network, you can access the share and begin installing from anywhere on the network. You also use this method when you can't find the *NT Server* CD-ROM or when a computer lacks a CD-ROM drive.

When you install from the network, you have a number of options for how to begin and carry out the NT Server installation. If you see an installation question that references installing on two or more computers, think "Network Installation" and you may at least eliminate some of the answers.

Even though the product documentation or other books refer to Windows NT Server Resource Kit utilities, you can bet that the exam doesn't cover them. Microsoft doesn't include questions regarding programs or utilities on the kits because not everyone has access to them. The same applies to enhancements via service packs that have occurred since the original exam.

An easy Sysdiff question may ask "Which utility could you use to create images of programs for installations on other computers?"

Winnt and Winnt32

Winnt and Winnt32 are separate and distinct commands that you use to set up NT in different situations. Know when to use one or the other.

You use the Winnt command if you're in Windows 95 or MS-DOS; you use Winnt32 if you're in Windows NT.

Repeat after me: WINNT for Win95 and DOS; WINNT32 for NT.

Never choose anything on the test that has to do with Setup.exe. Hundreds of programs use Setup.exe, but not Windows NT.

Creating a boot disk

You need to know how to create a *network client installation disk,* a boot disk that contains the drivers that your network card needs to gain access to a network share. Questions about creating a network client installation disk often reference Network Client Administrator, the utility that you use in Windows NT Server to make boot disks.

You need to know what network card is in your computer (choose Control Panel⇨Network⇨Adapters to view the configuration of the network card). If you don't have an operating system installed, use the disk that came with the network adapter card. You must use an old DOS floppy disk to boot the machine, and then drop in the network adapter configuration utility to view the current adapter settings. Network Client Administrator requires the brand of network adapter card when you create a boot disk. You also need to input network adapter settings when Windows NT asks you for them. If you already have access to an NT Server, use the Network Client Administrator program, shown in Figure 7-1, located in the Administrative Tools section.

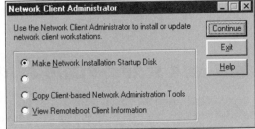

Figure 7-1:
Network
Client
Administrator.

The Network Client Administrator creates a boot disk that loads the driver for your network card, points to the network share, and begins the setup. It gives you only two choices, though: DOS and Windows 95 clients.

Installation Roles

I cover all of the server roles in-depth in Chapter 2. You need to make a couple decisions during installation involving domains.

Primary domain controller

The primary domain controller (PDC) is the first server you install in a domain. You can't have more than one PDC on the domain, but if for any reason the PDC cannot fulfill its duties, you can promote a BDC to PDC.

You also can demote the PDC. Be sure to promote your best BDC to PDC *before* the domain goes to chaos. If you promote a BDC without demoting the current PDC, the new PDC automatically ousts the old PDC from the domain.

If you install a server without making it a PDC, you cannot make it a PDC later without having to reinstall NT.

When you create a domain, designate the first server you install the PDC.

Backup domain controller

The BDCs of the domain keep everyone up-to-date on changes. Each BDC keeps a copy of the SAM and makes sure that it's up to date with the PDC. Unless your domain is gigantic (2,000 workstations), you need only one BDC. For every 2,000 additional workstations, add another BDC. Once you create a BDC, you can't just make it go away. You must reinstall NT Server.

You cannot just make BDCs go away. You must reinstall NT Server. Don't rule out the possibility of a question asking you to recommend the best number of BDCs for an organization that has *x* number of users.

Member servers and stand-alone servers

Member servers are servers that fulfill a certain purpose, such as file serving, remote access, and Internet access. Remember, you cannot have a member server before you designate at least two other servers as a PDC and a BDC. Thereafter, you can have as many member servers as you like. You can have hundreds. If you forget who's who in your domain, you can use Server Manager in the Administrative Tools to see each server and its role.

A member server serves a domain like a stand-alone server serves a workgroup.

If you install a server that is not part of your domain, it is called a stand-alone server (just another type of member server).

Member servers are always member servers. If you want to promote a member server to a PDC or BDC, you must reinstall NT.

Upgrading to Windows NT Server 4

Questions that focus on upgrading confuse the candidate with Winnt.exe and Winnt32.exe commands. If you perform an upgrade, use Winnt32.exe.

You install Windows NT Server 4 in the same directory as your existing version of Windows NT. If you want to make changes to your settings, install it in a separate directory.

Server and domain names

Domain names, like server names, should reflect the location or purpose of the domain. If you are a branch office of the corporation, the name of the domain should represent the physical location, such as the Seattle or Denmark domain. If you are a logical separation, you name the domain along the lines of Sales or Support. For the exam, when you install your server, you have to know the name of the domain you are joining. You aren't shown a list of available domains. You know something's wrong if you see this error message:

```
The domain controller for this domain could not be located.
```

You can get this message if you use the wrong domain name. You also may get this message if your network hardware and configuration is set up incorrectly. If this happens, you can install the computer in a workgroup and then install and configure the networking components. After you correctly configure the networking components you can go back and join the domain.

Don't worry much about domains for the Windows NT Server exam. As far as installation goes, the only additional piece of information you may need to know is that a server name cannot exceed 15 characters.

The Installation Process

The important installation steps to review are

- ✔ The various options available in different dialog boxes
- ✔ Decisions involving your selection of a file system
- ✔ Creation of an emergency repair disk
- ✔ Use of the RDISK utility
- ✔ Decisions about protocol selection
- ✔ Removing a file system
- ✔ Customizing the Boot.ini file

Don't worry about

- ✔ The differences between Custom, Typical, and Compact installations
- ✔ Removing NT Server (but don't skip removing NTFS — you may need to know that)

You can install NT Server in many ways, although they all end up in the same place. For this example, we begin an installation from within Windows NT Workstation, just by inserting the *Windows NT Server* CD-ROM.

When we use this method, even if we don't specify the switch to exclude creation of the boot floppies, the installation program doesn't create them. When we select Continue in the Installation/Upgrade dialog box, NT begins to copy the files. Feel free to take a break (or use the time to memorize those switches) — copying those files can take a long time.

Starting Setup

After NT copies the temporary files to your computer, you need to restart your computer to begin the installation process (unless you're using the three floppy disks to install NT Server, because taking that approach doesn't create a large temporary installation before you begin setup).

After you restart the computer, you see a new option on the boot menu: Installation/Upgrade. Select the Installation/Upgrade option. Setup then starts to inspect your computer's hardware. After Setup finishes its inspection, the first setup window appears. (We cover the Setup program in the next section.) No matter how you start Setup, you get the same opening screen.

Setup program

Although the Setup program presents you with numerous options, I cover only the options you're most likely to see on the exam. From this main setup screen, you have a few installation options:

- ✔ Set up a new installation of Windows NT
- ✔ Repair a damaged version of Windows NT
- ✔ Quit setup

The next screen lists the various devices in your system that Windows NT recognizes. Know the options on this screen for the exam. I thought I was good at installing Windows NT until an exam question concerning this area totally stumped me.

The screen following the list of recognized devices presents the license agreement and the next one after that lists previous Windows NT installations. The list of previous installations is an important screen, because you must make an important decision:

✔ Upgrade a current installation

✔ Install a fresh copy of Windows NT

The next major screen lists the partitions and space available for creating new partitions. You have many choices to make:

✔ Install NT on an unused partition

✔ Delete a partition

✔ Create a partition in the unused space

When you select the partition on which you want to install Windows NT, Setup asks you to make another decision — you may receive a question covering this: Do you want to leave the current file system intact or do you want to format the partition with a new file system?

Here's the key: You can choose to format the partition with the FAT file system now; you can always convert it to NTFS later. *After you choose the NTFS file system, you cannot convert your partition back to FAT without losing information.*

So when would you go with NTFS? You need to go with NTFS if you need new features that only the NTFS file system provides, such as compression on-the-fly, security permissions on files and folders, and support for those gigantic hard drives that are on the market today.

Want to review FAT and NTFS? Good idea. Go back to Chapter 5.

After Setup examines your hard disk, it copies the files from the temporary directory created at the beginning of setup to the new directory. Then you can restart your computer. Shortly thereafter, the graphical user interface portion of setup begins.

If you exit installation of Windows NT during the text-based setup and then restart the computer, the Installation/Upgrade menu may remain on the boot menu. To fix this, you may need to edit your Boot.ini file to remove the reference to this failed installation. If so, you also need to delete the temporary files left behind in a directory.

Choosing setup options

When you enter the setup portion of the installation, you see the graphical user interface — no more of those old DOS-looking screens. What is convenient about these screens is that you can use the Back button if you enter something incorrectly. Among the first options you see in the GUI-based setup are the Setup options.

Express versus custom: Paper or plastic?

Don't expect any questions on the exam about what you install during a Compact install or which dialog boxes appear in a Custom install.

The next major decision concerns the server type. Choose wisely, because you have to start all over if you choose wrongly. Also, be aware of the fact that some of the BackOffice products that require Windows NT Server may require that your server be a BDC or PDC. For example, Microsoft Exchange Mail Server requires a BDC or PDC because it works constantly with user accounts and authentication. Systems Management Server also requires that your computer be a BDC or PDC before installing.

Emergency repair disk (ERD)

The next option is whether you want to create an emergency repair disk (ERD). Windows NT repair disks are unique to the computer that you create them on. The exam also may hit you with a question about the purpose of the RDISK utility. You use RDISK to go back and create another ERD.

Protocols

A very possible exam question concerns which protocols to use on your network. If you don't use it, remove it!

If you choose to install the TCP/IP protocol, you must decide whether to enable Dynamic Host Configuration Protocol (DHCP).

- ✔ If you do not enable DHCP, you must correctly configure the required TCP/IP settings: the IP address, subnet mask, and default gateway.
- ✔ If you enable DHCP, a certain server on the network should assign you the necessary TCP/IP information.

Don't worry about WINS or DNS for now. If you prefer, you can just not even use TCP/IP, and use an easier protocol like NetBEUI. NetBEUI does not require as much configuring as TCP/IP.

Almost everything you learn for this test, you can apply directly to the Windows NT Workstation exam and the Windows NT Server in the Enterprise exam. That means less studying! It also means more money when you become a hot commodity as an MCSE. So don't give up, you can do it! The bad news is that the subtle differences between the two operating systems

can be confusing; differences such as the number of RAS connections and
those additional utilities that come with NT Server. These are hot topics
for exams. Microsoft wants to make sure that you understand the requirements and the differences, and when to implement them. Table 7-3 takes a
quick look at what the major differences are between NT Server and NT
Workstation:

Table 7-3	Major Differences between Server and Workstation	
Functionality	*Windows NT Server*	*Windows NT Workstation*
Number of CPUs supported	32	2
Number of RAS connections	256	1
Number of client connections	Unlimited	10
Fault Tolerance	Disk Striping with Parity, Mirroring	None

We guarantee that you will be much better off if you install NT Server many
times before the exam. Working with the program hands-on gives you
experience that makes the facts of installation second nature.

Removing Windows NT Server

Rollback.exe removes all of the NT information from your computer and
returns you to the end of the DOS-looking portion of setup. You do not have
to start over with a formatted hard disk.

Chances are you won't get a question on the exam about removing NT
Server. If you do, look for an answer that includes the Rollback.exe utility.

Removing NTFS

Questions on NTFS often focus on installing it and choosing between NTFS
or FAT. They also may focus on removing it altogether. And you can't exactly
remove NTFS. You must back up your data and format the partition using
the FAT file system, and then restore your data from the backup.

Changing the boot operating system

NT administrators customize the NT boot menu, as well as the Boot.ini file.
And Microsoft commonly includes exam questions on the Boot.ini file,

especially ones that ask what you can customize using Boot.ini — such as adding switches. You see more of the Boot.ini file when it comes to trouble-shooting — you can expect several questions on the Windows NT Server exam, as well as on the Windows NT Workstation exam.

Boot.ini is the file that decides what disk and what partition to install the operating systems on. NT has a boot menu to choose which operating system to boot up into. You can customize the startup menu by

✔ Changing the names of operating systems listed

✔ Changing the default operating system

✔ Adjusting the countdown before an operating system loads

Lab 7-1 reviews customizing the Windows NT boot menu and the Boot.ini file.

Lab 7-1   Customizing the Windows NT Boot Menu

If you want to customize the Windows NT boot menu, you have two choices: the easy way and the hard way. Here's the easy way

1. Choose Control Panel⇨System.

2. Click the Startup/Shutdown tab.

3. In the System Startup portion, use the drop-down menu to select the default operating system.

4. Adjust the amount of time you want Windows NT to sit there before it starts booting.

If you choose the hard method, follow in Windows Explorer:

1. Start Windows Explorer.

2. Find the Boot.ini file.

It's probably in the root directory of your system partition, probably C:/. The Boot.ini file is hidden (and read-only), so you may have to choose View⇨Options and then click the Show All Files radio button.

3. Open the Boot.ini file.

Yikes! You can manually adjust the options in the System applet in the Control Panel from this file, but it's more difficult.

4. To change the default operating system, find two lines in your Boot.ini file that resemble the following:

```
default=multi(0)disk(0)rdisk(0)partition(4)\WINNT
[operating systems]
```

1 What is the minimum amount of RAM for a RISC-based system?

A ○ 12MB

B ○ 16MB

C ○ 20MB

D ○ 24MB

2 (True/False). DOS can read an NTFS partition if it is installed on an NTFS partition.

3 How would you create the three boot floppies that came with NT Server if you have lost them?

A ○ Use the /b switch with SETUP to specify boot floppies only.

B ○ Use the /b switch with WINNT to specify boot floppies only.

C ○ Use the /ox switch with WINNT to only create the boot floppies.

D ○ Use the /f switch with WINNT for floppies only.

4 You want to install Windows NT Server on your Pentium Pro computer, which does not have a CD-ROM drive. The computer does not have an operating system installed yet; however, it does have a network adapter. The source files are located on a Windows NT 3.51 Server. What is the most efficient way to begin the installation?

A ○ Make a network client installation disk, attach to the network share, and issue the Winnt32 command.

B ○ Make a network client installation disk, attach to the network share, and issue the Winnt command.

C ○ Install Windows NT Server 3.51, attach to the network share, and issue the Winnt command.

D ○ Install Windows NT Server 3.51, attach to the network share, and issue the Winnt32 command.

5 Which of the following is possible with the Boot.ini file?

A ○ Specify the path for applications to search.

B ○ Add switches to be used during startup.

C ○ Specify minimum amount of memory for each operating system installation.

D ○ Add device drivers to be used during startup.

PY 123-124

6 Which tab would you click to modify the boot menu options?

A ○ Startup tab

B ○ Shutdown tab

C ○ Startup/Shutdown

D ○ System Startup tab

7 You used Server Manager and found out that you have too many backup domain controllers in your domain. What is the quickest way to demote this extra backup domain controller to a member server?

A ○ Select the backup domain controller that you want to demote in Server Manager and select Demote to Stand-Alone server in the File menu.

B ○ Select the backup domain controller that you want to demote in Server Manager and select Demote to Member Server in the File menu.

C ○ Reinstall the operating system and select stand-alone server.

D ○ Edit the Registry.

8 If you have 8,000 workstations in your domain, about how many backup domain controllers should you have?

A ○ One

B ○ Two

C ○ Three

D ○ Four

9 What is the correct way to upgrade a Windows 95 machine to Windows NT Server?

A ○ Install NT in the same directory as Windows 95.

B ○ Install NT in the same directory as Windows 95 and import the Registry settings.

C ○ Start the install using WINNT32 instead of WINNT, select a directory other than the Windows 95 directory, and reinstall all of the applications.

D ○ Start the install using WINNT, select a directory other than the Windows 95 directory, and reinstall all of the applications.

10 If you do not use DHCP, which three settings must you configure? (Choose all that apply.)

A ❏ WINS Server

B ❏ IP address

C ❏ Default gateway

D ❏ DNS server

E ❏ Subnet mask

Answers

1 B. 16MB. The minimum for x86-based systems is 12MB of RAM. *Review "Hardware Preparation"* (**hint:** *see Table 7-1).*

2 *False.* You can't install MS-DOS on an NTFS partition, period; therefore, DOS cannot read an NTFS partition under any circumstance. *Review "Booting multiple operating systems."*

3 C. Use the /ox switch with Winnt to create the boot floppies without having to do the entire installation. The /ox switch, for making boot floppies, and the /b switch, for skipping the creation of boot floppies during installation, are the most popular Winnt\Winnt32 switches. *Review "Winnt and Winnt32."*

4 B. The answer is definitely not Winnt32, because you don't have an operating system yet — the source files just happen to be located on an NT 3.51 server. *"Review "Winnt and Winnt32."*

5 B. Add switches to customize startup. You can add switches to show the drivers as they load, start the computer in VGA mode, and more. *Review "Changing the boot operating system."*

6 C. Startup/Shutdown. The tab to modify the boot menu options is the Startup/Shutdown tab in the System applet of the Control Panel. *Review "Changing the boot operating system."*

7 C. Reinstall the operating system and select stand-alone server. Unfortunately, this is the quickest way to demote a BDC or PDC to member server. *Review "Backup domain controller."*

8 D. 4. You should have at least one BDC for the first 2,000 computers. After that, you should have another BDC for every additional 2,000 computers. *Review "Backup domain controller."*

9 D. Start the install using Winnt, select a directory other than the Windows 95 directory, and reinstall all of the applications. There is no upgrade path for Windows 95 to Windows NT. *Review "Winnt and Winnt32."*

10 B, C, and E. IP address, default gateway, and subnet mask. *Review "Protocols."*

Chapter 8

Configure This! Making NT Server Work for You

Exam Objectives

▶ Using the Control Panel applications

▶ Understanding the NT system Registry

▶ Editing the Registry

▶ Backing up and restoring the Registry

*A*h, the Control Panel. The system administrator's second-best friend. In this chapter, we discuss some of the tools you can use to configure an NT 4.0 Server. First, I review the Control Panel, which allows you to tweak many aspects of the NT system in a matter of mouse clicks. Later in the chapter, we cover the system Registry and its components.

The primary goal here is to merely review the Control Panel and the Registry, to help you study for the exam, not to go over every gory detail.

Quick Assessment

Using the Control Panel Applications

1 Which Control Panel application lets you change the minimum and maximum size of the system's paging file?

(2) After installing a new Ethernet adapter in your NT server, use the _____ tab of the _____ application to install the proper driver to enable the adapter.

PG . 141

(3) Your server has been crashing unexpectedly, and you need to config-ure the system to write information to a debug file. You also want the system to automatically reboot the next time it crashes. You can accomplish both goals from the _____ tab of the_____ application.

PG 144-145

Understand-ing the NT System Registry

(4) Five_____ comprise the top level of the NT Registry hierarchy.

PG 148-149

Using the Control Panel Applications

5 You can use the_____ tab of the _____ application in the Control Panel to add IPX/SPX protocol support to your NT server.

6 Where can you check that the Netlogon service is running and, if necessary, restart it?

7 The _____ tab of the _____application lets you reduce the priority given to your server's foreground applications?

Backing Up and Restor-ing the Registry

8 (True/ False). Using the Emergency Repair Disk application via Windows Explorer is the *best* way to back up the NT Registry.

Editing the Registry

(9) Which Registry editor has both a Security menu and a Read Only mode: Regedt32.exe or Regedit.exe?

PG 149- 150

Answers

1 *System.* Review "Using the Control Panel Programs."

2 *Adapters; Network.* Review "Using the Control Panel Programs."

3 *Startup/Shutdown; System.* Review "Using the Control Panel Programs."

4 *Subtrees.* See "Structure of the Registry."

5 *Protocols; Network.* Review "Using the Control Panel Programs."

6 *Services.* Review "Using the Control Panel Programs."

7 *Performance; System.* Refer to "Using the Control Panel Programs."

8 *False.* Review "Backing up and restoring the Registry."

9 *Regedt32.exe.* Review "Editing the Registry."

Drivers

Drivers are software that act as an interface between your hardware and the NT operating system. As an NT system administrator, driver issues revolve around installing and configuring new peripheral hardware components, such as

- ✔ CD-ROM drives
- ✔ Tape devices
- ✔ Network adapter cards

The NT 4.0 Server exam does not question you about the workings of drivers, and the seemingly infinite number of hardware vendors out there makes it impractical (not to mention cruel) for the exam to ask you about the features of various drivers. What you do have to know, however, is *how and where* you install new drivers from within your NT system.

Installing drivers usually consists of

- ✔ Installing the hardware
- ✔ Telling NT to find the new hardware
- ✔ Providing NT with the new driver when it asks for it

The trick is in knowing where to begin, which is the Control Panel.

Using the Control Panel Programs

The Control Panel is a front-end to the NT Registry. The applications in the Control Panel read and change two of the five Registry subtrees:

- ✔ HKEY_LOCAL_MACHINE
- ✔ HKEY_CURRENT_USER

I cover the Registry in more detail in "The Windows NT Registry" later.

The NT 4.0 Server exam is about system administration issues, so the questions emphasize managing your network's resources via NT servers.

The Control Panel allows you to configure *the local NT server* only. Although it helps you fix *the local NT server's* problems, it isn't your primary network troubleshooting tool. Know the Control Panel, but don't agonize over it. What you really need to know boils down to this: Use the Control Panel to

✔ Improve system performance

✔ Change startup/shutdown settings

✔ Set key environmental variables

The applications in the Control Panel, shown in Figure 8-1, break down into two distinct categories:

✔ **Software:** Applications that you can use to alter software settings; in other words, applications that are *user-centric*.

✔ **Hardware:** Applications that you can use to alter hardware settings; or, applications that are *computer-centric*.

User-centric applications enable each user to customize several aspects of the server:

✔ Keyboard preferences

✔ System fonts

✔ Mouse settings

✔ Printers

These changes usually involve software settings and typically affect only the user who makes them.

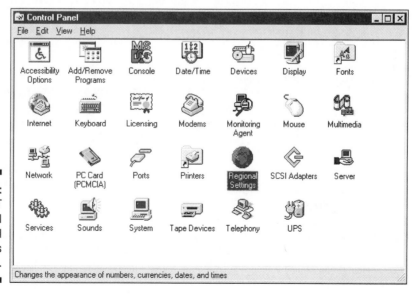

Figure 8-1:
The NT
Control
Panel
and its
applications.

Changes that you make by using the software settings applications mainly alter the HKEY_CURRENT_USER subtree, although as always, a few exceptions do apply. I suggest that you don't spend too much time memorizing everything these apps can do, because the exam has few (if any) questions about them.

Roughly half of the applications in the Control Panel allow you to configure software settings, such as default system fonts and keyboard preferences. The software settings applications are handy, but they are not the focus of the NT Server exam. I recommend that you spend a little more time on the other applications, which allow you to configure *hardware settings*.

The computer-centric applications enable you to configure system hardware:

- Modems
- Tape devices
- UPS devices

These types of changes usually affect the whole system. Changes that you make by using computer-centric applications typically are stored in the HKEY_LOCAL_MACHINE subtree. Spend more time learning these applications and how you can use them to make configuration changes. The exam may slip in some configuration questions, and assumes that you know what application in the Control Panel to use for making the changes.

Applications that affect hardware settings are typically restricted to administrative users, so that anyone who doesn't log in with local administrator privileges can't use these apps.

Accessibility

The Accessibility application is available only if you selected the Accessibility option during setup or added it. The Accessibility app provides features and options for users who have disabilities or special considerations. I wouldn't spend much time on this application.

Console

Console allows you to customize the properties of the *character-mode application environment* (a fancy way of saying the *command prompt window*). Console is a software settings application, so settings here alter:

```
HKEY_CURRENT_USER\Console
```

Dial-Up Monitor

Dial-Up Monitor lets you view the status of current dial-up network connections. If RAS (Remote Access Server) is installed on your server, Dial-Up Monitor is quite handy for troubleshooting problems. The Status tab shows you who is currently dialed in; the Summary tab gives you a bigger picture:

- ✔ Networks currently connected
- ✔ Users online
- ✔ Devices users are connected via

The Preferences tab lets you change some behavior, such as whether to make a noise when someone connects.

Display

If you like to customize your desktop's appearance, Display is your friend. It allows you to configure:

- ✔ Screen resolution
- ✔ Background color
- ✔ Screen saver properties

See Figure 8-2 for a peek at this application.

Settings in Display edit

```
HKEY_LOCAL_MACHINE\SYSTEM\CurrentControlSet\Services\<video
          driver>\Device0\
```

Even though some of the settings are software settings, it makes changes to the HKEY_LOCAL_MACHINE key. Actually, changes occur in the HKEY_CURRENT_USER Registry Subtree as well.

You may have noticed that you also can access this application by right-clicking any open space on your desktop and choosing Properties.

Fonts

Fonts doesn't really do anything, other than display the installed system fonts and install new ones — the exam has no questions about the Fonts app.

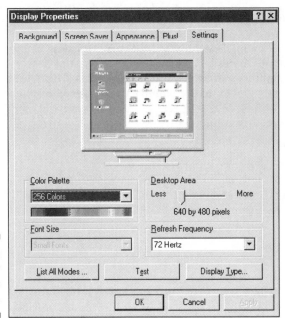

Keyboard

Keyboard enables you to modify such exciting settings as

- Key repeat rate
- Repeat delay
- Cursor blink rate
- Keyboard layout properties

Don't worry about the Keyboard application. Changes you make are stored in

```
HKEY_CURRENT_USER\ControlPanel\Keyboard
```

Mouse

The Mouse app is basically the same as the Keyboard application, but these settings affect the mouse. The changes are stored in

```
HKEY_CURRENT_USER\ControlPanel\Mouse
```

Printers

The Printers application, also available from the Start menu, under Settings, displays the currently installed printers and lets you view their print queues. You use this app to set the default printer. Printing is a big part of the exam, so get to know this application. Changes you make here are stored in

```
HKEY_CURRENT_USER\Printers
```

Don't be lulled into a false sense of security because you know the Printers app backward and forward. Printing involves more than what you can do via the Printers application. Chapter 12 discusses printing in detail.

Regional Settings

Regional Settings allows you to make changes according to your geographic (or other) preferences. This application allows you to alter the way the following values appear on-screen:

- ✔ Currency
- ✔ Dates
- ✔ Numbers
- ✔ Time

Changes made here are stored in

```
HKEY_CURRENT_USER\ControlPanel\International
```

Sounds

The Sounds application lets you link sounds to various NT system events. You can have auditory accompaniment to such events as

- ✔ Maximizing or minimizing a window
- ✔ Starting up an application
- ✔ Exiting NT

Fun for customizing your system, not relevant to the exam. Settings are stored in

```
HKEY_CURRENT_USER\ControlPanel\Sounds
```

Telephony

The Telephony application, shown in Figure 8-3, is one you should get to know. Telephony lets you configure your telephony settings, such as

✔ Your area code

✔ Whether you have to dial 9 to get outside the local switchboard

✔ The area of the country you're in

You can also install new telephony drivers here.

Add/Remove Programs

Add/Remove Programs Properties dialog box, shown in Figure 8-4, is a *very* handy application and you use it often. It enables you to perform the following tasks:

✔ Install new applications

✔ Add or remove NT components from the system

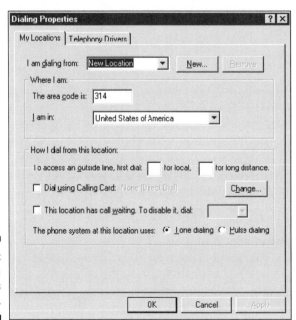

Figure 8-3:
The Dialing
Properties
dialog box.

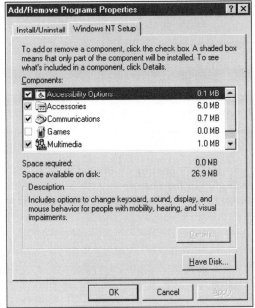

Figure 8-4:
Adding and
removing
NT
components.

The Install/Unistall tab enables you to add or delete applications, or remove or modify components of applications. The Windows NT Setup tab provides a mechanism to add or remove components of the NT operating system. I didn't have any questions about this application on my exam, but it certainly can play a workhorse role for the system administrator.

Date/Time

Date/Time directly affects the system clock. You use it to set your time zone. You can also view values in

```
HKEY_LOCAL_MACHINE\SYSTEM\Setup
```

Licensing

Licensing, shown in Figure 8-5, is an important application to know for the exam. Microsoft is keen on licensing these days, and they're going to ask questions about proper licensing and how to configure it. You can view the current licensing agreement here, and you may need it to make changes if you migrate from Per Server to Per Seat licensing mode.

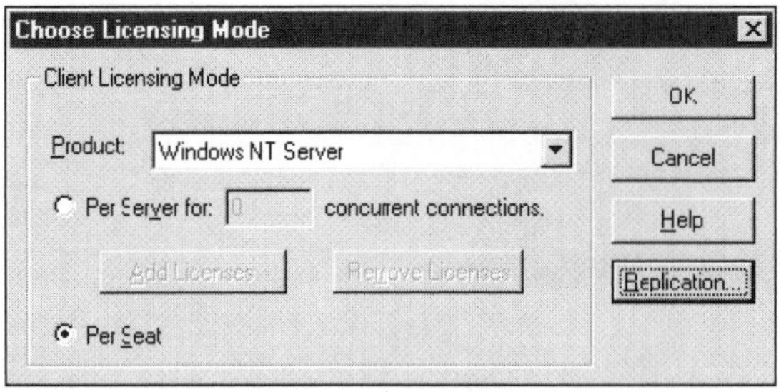

Choose Licensing Mode

Client Licensing Mode

Product: Windows NT Server ▼

○ Per Server for: ☐ concurrent connections.

Add Licenses   Remove Licenses

⦿ Per Seat

OK   Cancel   Help   Replication...

Figure 8-5:
The
Licensing
application.

The exam is Microsoft-centric, so questions focus on NT's ease of use. Most configuration questions highlight *the easiest* way to do something, so if you can do it via an application in the Control Panel, it's the easiest way.

Modems

The Modems application enables you to

 ✔ Install modems
 ✔ Configure modems
 ✔ Remove modems

The exam may well ask a question or two about doing this because RAS (Remote Access Server) is such an integral part of the NT server environment. A really nice feature of the Modem application is NT's capability to autodetect installed modems.

Multimedia

The Multimedia application allows you to

 ✔ Add multimedia devices
 ✔ Configure multimedia devices
 ✔ Remove multimedia devices

You can make changes to the CD music, audio, video, and MIDI settings. The exam doesn't care about this application, however, so don't lose any sleep over it. You can view settings in

```
HKEY_LOCAL_MACHINE\SYSTEM\CurrentControlSet\Services
```

Network

The Network application is another *major* tool in the Control Panel arsenal. The Network application lets you

- ✔ Change your machine name
- ✔ Join new workgroups
- ✔ Join new NT domains
- ✔ Add network services and adapters
- ✔ Configure network services and adapters
- ✔ Remove network services and adapters

The Identification tab lets you view or change the machine's current name, and the NT domain or workgroup to which your server belongs. You also can find these settings in

```
HKEY_LOCAL_MACHINE\SOFTWARE\Microsoft\Windows
        NT\CurrentVersion\WinLogon
```

The Services tab adds, removes, or configures network services, such as

- ✔ TCP/IP protocol
- ✔ Client Services for NetWare
- ✔ Remote Access Service

You can also use the Services tab to make changes to these services' properties, such as your server's IP address and subnet mask, and WINS and DNS entries.

The Adapters tab lets you

- ✔ Add network adapters
- ✔ Remove network adapters
- ✔ Configure network adapters

Changes you make via the Network app are stored in

```
HKEY_LOCAL_MACHINE\SYSTEM\CurrentControlSet\Services
```

Most configuration changes you make via the Network application require access to the NT server source files, and they also usually require a system restart for the changes to take effect.

The exam has a number of questions about NT networking, so bear down on Chapters 9 and 10, which covers Network application.

PC card (PCMCIA)

The PCMCIA application is applicable only installed on the system. If you do, you can use it to install and configure device drivers for PCMCIA cards. My exam didn't have any questions about this app.

Ports

The Ports application gives you a list of the available serial ports on the system not currently used by existing devices. Changes via the Ports application affect the following Registry key:

```
HKEY_LOCAL_MACHINE\SYSTEM\CurrentControlSet\Services\Serial
```

If you click the Settings button for a given port, you get information about various features of that port, including:

- ✔ Baud rate
- ✔ Data bits
- ✔ Stop bits
- ✔ Parity
- ✔ Flow control

SCSI adapters

The name suggests this application only deals with SCSI devices. In fact, you use this app to

- ✔ Install and configure new SCSI adapters
- ✔ Install or remove new IDE CD-ROM devices and drivers

SCSI and IDE are totally different animals. The name should at least imply the dual role of this application, but it doesn't.

This app has two tabs (as shown in Figure 8-6):

- ✔ Devices
- ✔ Drivers

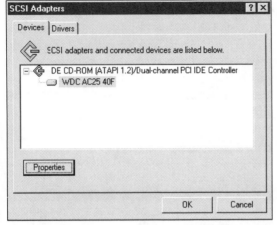

Figure 8-6:
SCSI and
IDE,
together
at last?

The Devices tab lets you view the devices and the Drivers tab lets you add or remove drivers. You also can click the Properties button if you want to check out SCSI IDs and firmware levels.

Server

The Server application, shown in Figure 8-7, may look familiar to you if you've used Server Manager. The Server app shows you the current connections to your server and lets you administer them. You can view Usage Summary for your server, or you can view the five following configuration windows individually by clicking the appropriate buttons:

- ✔ **Users:** Gives you info about users currently logged in to your system.
- ✔ **Shares:** Shows you the status of current shared resources on your server.
- ✔ **In Use:** Displays any of your server's resources that are currently in use.
- ✔ **Replication:** Allows you to configure the Directory Replicator service.
- ✔ **Alerts:** Lets you enter a list of users or workstations that can receive alert messages when important server events occur.

Services

Services, shown in Figure 8-8, is perhaps one of the most critical applications in the Control Panel. Services allows you to stop and start key NT services, such as the Server service. The exam does address the Service application, believe me. You need to know that you can use the Services app to stop, start, and pause key services, as well as change the startup properties of services (that is, manual, automatic, and disabled).

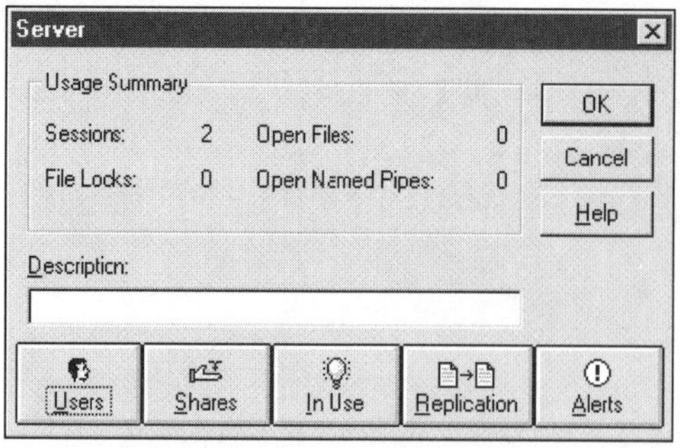

Figure 8-7:
The Server
application.

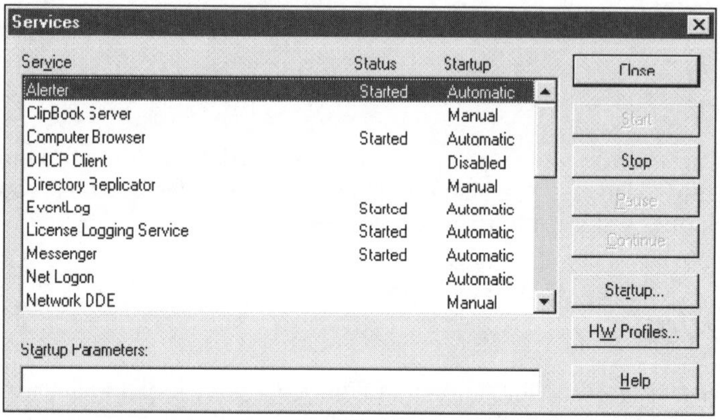

Figure 8-8:
Configuring
services.

Services are background processes that run all the time, regardless of whether anyone is logged in. For the UNIX-literate out there, services are roughly equivalent to a *daemon* process. Services rarely interact with the user interface, which means that you usually aren't aware of them. Changes you make here are stored in

```
HKEY_LOCAL_MACHINE\SYSTEM\CurrentControlSet\Control\Services.
```

System

The System application in the Control Panel is perhaps the most relevant to the NT Server exam. This little gem is the key to

✔ Improving system performance

✔ Changing startup/shutdown settings

✔ Setting key environmental variables

The System app alters aspects of system performance and changes startup/shutdown options. It has six tabs:

- ✔ **Startup/Shutdown:** This tab, shown in Figure 8-9, sets the default menu choice and the default countdown for the boot loader portion of startup. Each time the system starts, the Boot.ini file builds the boot loader menu, which asks you to select the operating system to load — typically either Windows NT Server 4.0 or Windows NT Server 4.0 (VGA Mode). The changes you make are stored in the Boot.ini file. The tab includes a Recovery area, which lets you specify what can happen in the event of a system crash. You can specify a system log event, send an alert, write debugging information to a file, and automatically reboot.

- ✔ **Performance:** The second most important tab of the System application, Performance, lets you make two important changes to your system: change the paging file size and location and set the priority for foreground applications versus other system activities. Chapter 19 covers performance tuning in greater detail, but, *when* (not *if*) the exam asks where to increase the size of the paging file, the answer is in the Performance tab of the System app in the Control Panel.

- ✔ **General:** This tab provides you with information about your system, such as operating system and version number, the product's registered name, amount of RAM installed, and processor type.

Figure 8-9:
The
Startup/
Shutdown
tab.

✔ **Hardware Profiles:** Hardware profiles allow the user to store information about devices and configurations. A good example of when hardware profiles come into play is laptop computers. Laptop users may set-up two different hardware profiles, one for office use when they can connect to a LAN, and one for travel use, when they are running stand-alone. You can choose a different hardware profile at boot time. Granted, this may not be a likely scenario for an NT server, but you may need to know how and where to set hardware profiles for your users' workstations. The exam is not likely to talk about hardware profiles, but be aware of it.

✔ **User Profiles:** This tab can show you a list of all user profiles stored in the server or just the user profile you're currently logged in with, depending on whether you are logged in with administrator privileges. You can choose which copy of your profile you want to use at login time: the locally stored copy or a roaming copy copied from a domain controller. You also can copy profiles from one place to another. The exam focuses on centrally storing profiles and user policy for all domain users. See Chapters 14 and 15 for more on user profiles.

✔ **Environment:** Environment variables allow NT to run successfully and allow applications to successfully interact with the NT operating system. *Environment variables* are strings that contain drive letters, paths, and files.

The two types of environment variables are *system* and *user:*

- System environment variables typically are defined by NT at the initial NT system install, but you can make changes later.

- User environment variables are different for each individual user of the system, and typically contain Path statements for specific applications.

Tape Devices

The Tape Devices application is nearly identical in function to the SCSI Adapters application, except that it deals with, you guessed it, tape drives. This app has an added bonus, a Detect button, which you can click to have NT detect your newly installed tape drive.

UPS

A UPS, or *uninterruptible power supply,* can keep your system up if the main power goes out for a few minutes.

The UPS application makes changes to UPS settings. The UPS service communicates with the UPS to keep your system running until

✔ The power comes back on

✔ The UPS runs out of juice

✔ An administrator shuts the system down gracefully

The exam does have a few questions about UPSs. If you don't have one to play with, I suggest you review UPSs and Windows NT.

The settings in the UPS application are specific to the brand of UPS you use. Refer to the documentation for UPS before you configure it for NT. You can set the following options as shown in Figure 8-10:

✔ Send an alert when a low power threshold occurs

✔ Send an alert when the power supply fails

✔ Execute a local command on the server just before it shuts down

✔ Change the interval between the power failure and when the first warning message is sent to users

✔ Change the amount of time between warning messages sent to users

✔ Configure the expected battery life

✔ Specify the amount of time needed to recharge the batteries (in re-charge minutes per battery run time minutes)

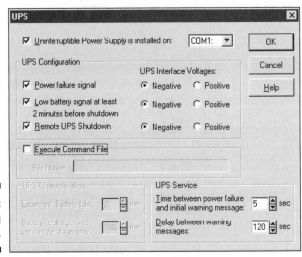

Figure 8-10:
Configuring
the UPS.

Changes made here are stored in

```
HKEY_LOCAL_MACHINE\SYSTEM\CurrentControlSet\Services\UPS
```

The Windows NT Registry

The system's Registry is the heart and soul of Windows NT — it's a centrally located database that contains every bit of system configuration information, and every NT system has one. The NT Registry helps you, the administrator, support your systems because the configuration information you need is in one location — safe from unwanted meddling by non-administrative users. One of the beautiful aspects of NT is how you can support your systems remotely, and this is true of the Registry as well.

Get to know the Registry keys (HKEY_LOCAL_USER, HKEY_LOCAL_MACHINE, and so on) and what they affect. The exam doesn't expect you to know every nook and cranny of the Registry, but you need to know how to navigate, understand the Registry's high-level organization, and know why it's organized that way.

The Registry is a new innovation from Microsoft, but is roughly comparable in function to the old WIN.INI and CONFIG.SYS files used in Windows 3.*x* and MS-DOS. The NT Server exam assumes that you know your way around the Registry, so I *highly recommend* opening it up and wandering around it a bit.

Structure of the Registry

The best thing Microsoft did when they dreamed up the Registry concept was organize it in a folders/files format. It has a hierarchical structure that makes finding what you need simple — once you understand its organization. The first step in understanding the Registry's structure is to look at the components that comprise the Registry, in order of hierarchy:

- ✔ **Subtree:** The highest level of the Registry, subtrees organize configuration data by how they affect the system. Here are the five subtrees:

  - **HKEY_LOCAL_MACHINE:** This key contains all the configuration data about the local system, including hardware data and operating system info, such as the bus type, system memory, and device drivers. Some of the data necessary for booting the system comes from this subtree. This data is not user dependent.

  - **HKEY_CLASSES_ROOT:** This subtree contains the associations that link applications and file types, using filename extensions like DOC for Word, XLS for Excel, and so on.

- **HKEY_CURRENT_CONFIG:** This subtree contains the info affected by changes you make on the Hardware Profiles tab (of the System application on the Control Panel section). You can find the currently booted hardware profile's information here, too.

- **HKEY_CURRENT_USER:** All the configuration information for the user currently logged in. Accordingly, this subtree is dynamic and rebuilds with each login. Every user who logs in to the system has all relevant data stored in *winnt_root*\profiles*username* so that this subtree can rebuild for them whenever they log in.

- **HKEY_USERS:** The default user profile and the *SID* (security ID) of the currently logged-in user.

✔ **Hive:** A grouping of keys and subkeys. Hives are permanent components of the Registry and are not built dynamically at boot time. Hive data has corresponding files in the %SystemRoot%\Config folder.

✔ **Keys and subkeys:** Keys and subkeys are kind of like folders and subfolders. Each hive can contain both keys and subkeys.

✔ **Data types:** The Registry has several data types and each one specifies the kind of configuration data the value contains.

- **REG_DWORD:** One value present, up to 8 hexadecimal digits in length.

- **REG_BINARY:** One value present, the hexadecimal string converted, in pairs, to a byte value; for example, 7f d2 = 128, 210.

- **REG_SZ:** One value present, interpreted as a string to be stored.

- **REG_EXPAND_SZ:** One value present. Similar to REG_SZ, except that the string can contain a variable that represents something else; for example, *%SystemRoot%*\drivers, where *%SystemRoot%* represents the path, such as c:\winnt\system32.

- **REG_MULTI_SZ:** Multiple values can be present.

✔ **Values:** Values are like files. You can find values inside keys and subkeys. They're sometimes hard to interpret at first because they actually have three parts: the *name,* the *data type,* and the *actual value.* For example:

```
RegistrySizeLimit : REG_DWORD : 0x800000
```

RegistrySizeLimit is the name, REG_DWORD is the data type, and 0 x 800000 is the actual value.

Editing the Registry

You can take care of most necessary configuration changes by using the Control Panel applications. If you do have to roll up your sleeves and edit the Registry manually, here's how you do it.

The *Windows NT Registry Editor,* Regedt32.exe, is the application that lets you see and modify the NT Registry. Making mistakes in editing the Registry can mean having to reload NT and losing everything, so Microsoft decided to not provide a Regedt32 icon. The only way to start Regedt32.exe is to run it directly from the Start menu (choose Run and type Regedt32) or the command line (for the command line commando in you, the EXE lives in the *winnt_root*\System32\ folder). Of course, you can always just create your own shortcut.

Now for a bit of confusion. For those of you who have worked with the Windows 95 Registry (yes, it has one too), the NT Registry looks suspiciously like the Regedit.exe tool. In fact, they are almost identical if you take away Regedit.exe's 16-bit nature and its lack of

- ✔ A security menu
- ✔ Read-only mode

NT installs both of these Registry editors during setup. Why, I'm not sure.

Under NT, you can use either Registry editor, but you SHOULD use Regedt32 to edit the Registry. Remember that. Microsoft *recommends* that you use Regedt32.exe. The exam asks a few questions about editing the NT Registry, and at least one tricky question asks you to identify the proper tool to use.

By default, only administrators have rights to make changes in the Registry. Users have Read access only. As administrator, however, you can alter the security settings of the Registry via the Security menu of Regedt32.exe to allow other non-administrators to make changes.

When you bring up Regedt32.exe, click Read Only Mode in the Options menu to avoid making mistakes that can ruin your day.

Searching the Registry

The Registry Editor includes some excellent tools. Check under the Registry and View menus for these new friends:

- ✔ **Find Key:** Lets you search for a key in the current subtree only.
- ✔ **Save Key:** To test a new configuration, save a key and all subkeys in binary form. To restore those keys, use the Restore Key command.
- ✔ **Restore Key:** Restore a section of keys from a file.
- ✔ **Save Subtree As:** Save a section of Registry to a text file so you can search the section for a specific value.
- ✔ **Select Computer:** Lets you access the Registry of a remote machine.

Backing up and restoring the Registry

The exam almost certainly will test you on backing up and restoring the Registry. The Registry is too vital to NT to ignore. You must know how to ensure that the Registry is safely backed up. You can use several methods to perform a backup, some not as complete as others.

- ✔ **Use the Save Registry option in the Backup utility:** You can find the Backup utility in Administrative Tools. *This method works only if you have a tape device.*

- ✔ **Use the Save Key option of the Registry Editor:** Not the preferred method, because restoring a saved key while running NT is not a guaranteed proposition and may fail.

- ✔ **Use an Emergency Repair Disk:** You can use an Emergency Repair Disk to back up the important Registry files necessary to boot the system. Using this method does not back up Security, Default, or SAM files unless you run rdisk from the command line and include the /s option.

✓ **1** Which of these Control Panel applications makes changes to NT hardware settings? (Choose all that apply.)

A ❑ System
B ❑ Keyboard
C ❑ Ports
D ❑ Network

✓ **2** REG_DWORD is an example of which type of Registry component?

A ○ Subtree
B ○ Hive
C ○ Value
D ○ Data Type
E ○ Key

3 You have purchased and installed a UPS for your Windows NT server. Using the UPS application in the Control Panel, which of the following tasks can you configure? (Choose all that apply.)

A ❑ Send an alert to users when the power fails.
B ❑ Change the text of the alert that is sent.
C ❑ Execute a local command on the server before shutdown.
D ❑ Change the interval between warning messages sent.
E ❑ Reboot the server.

4 Which subtree of the NT Registry contains data about the local system's hardware and operating system?

A ○ HKEY_CURRENT_CONFIG
B ○ HKEY_CURRENT_USER
C ○ HKEY_LOCAL_MACHINE
D ○ HKEY_USERS
E ○ HKEY_CLASSES_ROOT

5 You need to decrease the time it takes to remotely reboot your server. From what application can you reduce the default wait time during the boot menu portion of startup?

A ○ System
B ○ Network
C ○ Performance
D ○ Startup

6 The configurable software component that acts as an interface between hardware and the NT operating system is typically called a _____.

A ○ Connector

B ○ Driver

C ○ Adapter

D ○ Stabilizer

✓ **7** Complete the hierarchy of the NT Registry, listing from highest level to lowest: Subtree, Hive, _____, _____, and _____.

A ○ Key, Value, Data Type

B ○ Key, Data Type, Subkey

C ○ Keys and Subkeys, Data Type, Value

D ○ Data Type, Value, Key

✓ **8** One of your mobile users is complaining that when she travels, she gets error messages about services failing to start at bootup that she doesn't get when she is in the office connected to the LAN. What Control Panel application can you use to configure a new hardware profile for her to prevent these startup errors?

Pg 146

A ○ The Hardware Profiles tab of the System app

B ○ The Protocols tab of the Network app

C ○ The User Profiles tab of the System app

D ○ The Performance tab of the System app

9 You have just added an IDE CD-ROM drive to your system. What Control Panel application lets you add the necessary driver to support this device?

A ○ SCSI Adapters

B ○ System

C ○ Server

D ○ Tape Devices

10 Your server has been crashing unexpectedly lately, and you need to configure the system to write information to a debug file and also to automatically reboot the next time it happens. You can accomplish this by using the _____ tab of the_____ application.

Pg 145

A ○ Adapters tab of the Network application

B ○ Hardware tab of the System application

C ○ Startup/Shutdown tab of the System application

D ○ Recovery tab of the Server application

Answers

1   *A, C, D.* System, Ports, and Network all makes changes to hardware settings under NT. The Keyboard application is user-centric, and makes changes to software settings. *See "Using the Control Panel Programs."*

2   *D.* REG_DWORD is a data type. Data types specify what kind of data the value in a key can be. Other data types include REG_MULTI_SZ, REG_BINARY, and REG_SZ. *See "Structure of the Registry."*

3   *A, C, D.* Only these options are valid. When configuring a UPS via Control Panel, you cannot request a system reboot, and cannot customize the alert message that goes to users when the power fails. *See "UPS."*

4   *C.* The HKEY_LOCAL_MACHINE subtree contains configuration data about the system's hardware. *See the introduction of the "Using the Control Panel Programs" section.*

5   *A.* Only the System application lets you do this. In the Startup/Shutdown tab of the System app, you can change the default time from 0 to 99 seconds. The Performance app does not offer this feature, and the other two choices are not Control Panel applications. *Review the "System" section.*

6   *B.* Drivers act as an interface between hardware and the NT operating system. Users can sometimes configure drivers. *Review the "SCSI Adapters" section.*

7   *C.* Keys and subkeys are next in the Registry hierarchy, followed by data types, and then actual values. *Review "Structure of the Registry."*

8   *A. See the "System" section.*

9   *A.* Only choice A, the SCSI Adapters application, is correct. Though the name is confusing, this application allows you to add and configure both SCSI and IDE devices. *Review "SCSI adapters."*

10   *C.* The Startup/Shutdown tab of the System application allows you to configure some basic recovery options when the system crashes, such as writing a memory DMP file, automatically rebooting, and sending an administrative alert. *See "System."*

Chapter 9

Network Protocols: Who You Gonna Call?

Exam Objectives

▶ Choosing a protocol

▶ Identifying the most popular protocols available for Windows NT

▶ Examining IPC mechanisms

▶ Installing and configuring protocols and protocol bindings

*T*he NT Server certification exam usually gives you several questions that rely heavily on you knowing how to select and configure transport protocols for a Windows NT Server. To that end, this chapter gives you an overview of Windows NT network architecture and provides explicit instructions for configuring the transport protocols.

Quick Assessment

Examining IPC mechanisms

✓**1** Name four interprocess communication mechanisms that allow access to resources over the network: _____, _____, _____, and _____.

2 You normally should configure NWLink to use _____ Frame Type Detection.

Choosing a protocol

3 A set of rules used to regulate communications between computers is called a _____.

4 NetBEUI, TCP/IP, and NWLink are known as _____ protocols.

5 _____ is a nonroutable protocol.

Installing and configuring protocols and protocol bindings

✓**6** A module of software used to integrate a network adapter into a network configuration is called a _____.

7 _____ allows multiple protocols to be bound to a single network adapter card.

✓**8** The Workstation Service is an example of a _____ driver.

9 How many parameters can you change under the NetBEUI protocol's Property dialog box?

Answers

1 *NetBIOS, Windows Sockets, RPC,* and *NetDDE.* Review "Interprocess Communication (IPC) Mechanisms."

2 *Auto.*

3 *Protocol.* See "Network architecture."

4 *Transport.* See "NetBIOS."

5 *NetBEUI.* See "Transport protocols."

6 *Driver.* Review "Drivers."

7 *NDIS.* See "Network Device Interface Specification (NDIS)."

8 *File system.* Review "File system drivers."

9 *Zero.* Review "NetBEUI."

Protocol Overview

The Microsoft NT Server exam covers protocols and protocol bindings in depth. If you are comfortable with the network-related concept of a protocol, skip ahead to the sections on the various protocols (but don't skip them — the exam has questions on the various protocols). If you need a refresher course in protocols, read this section for a quick review.

When computers exchange data, they must abide by rules, or *protocols*. These protocols govern network communications, including

- ✔ The format of information
- ✔ What the information means
- ✔ When the computers can exchange the information

They also apply to other aspects of communications, including establishing and concluding communications and recovering when communications fail.

In the most general sense, protocols are sets of rules, which you can implement in hardware or software. Windows NT Server is a software product, so the protocols you configure in Windows NT are software modules. In the context of Windows NT, we can use the word *protocol* to refer to the rules themselves or to the software modules that implement the rules.

Here are the key concepts you need to follow protocol discussion:

- ✔ **Protocol stack:** A formal separation of various computer communications processes that enables developers to introduce new and different technologies without upsetting an entire network.
- ✔ **Interface:** The point where one protocol interacts with another protocol.
- ✔ **Drivers:** Programs that operate specific devices based on commands that they give through device-specific interfaces.
- ✔ **Bindings:** The explicit specification of the connections you can make between drivers' communications adapters and protocols.
- ✔ **Reference models:** Models for developers to model their products to be compatible with other developers' products.

Although questions about the layers of the Open Systems Interconnect (OSI) model are unlikely, it is useful to describe Microsoft's implementation of networking on Windows NT.

Interprocess Communication (IPC) Mechanisms

On the Windows NT Server certification exam, you need to know about several of the more important interprocess communication mechanisms, particularly these:

- **NetBIOS:** At the most basic level, NetBIOS is a naming scheme that enables us to identify domains, computers, and resources. In Windows NT, the file and printer services depend on the NetBIOS interface for file- and printer-sharing. You also can use NetBIOS to support RPC. NetBIOS can work with the following transport protocols:
  - NWLink
  - NetBEUI
  - TCP/IP

- **Windows Sockets (WinSock):** A programming interface that utilizes transport protocols such as TCP/IP and IPX to form a bidirectional guaranteed channel for communication between a client and a server.

- **RPC:** Remote Procedure Calls let programs on one computer call procedures (programs) on another computer.

- **NetDDE:** Network Dynamic Data Exchange allows applications to share information. An example of a NetDDE utility is Chat.

- **Named pipes:** A *named pipe* is a two-way communications channel that provides guaranteed messaging between a client and a server.

- **Mailslots:** A faster, primitive form of IPC. NetBIOS datagrams transmit information from the client task to the server. Unlike named pipes, mailslots offer only one-way communications.

Windows NT offers programmers and systems integrators hundreds of programming interfaces. Within the context of computer networks, dozens of programming interfaces provide applications with access to networking resources available to Windows NT. In fact, each installed protocol, service, or driver provides a programming interface that allows it to provide services to protocols above it in the protocol stack.

When reviewing the programming interfaces, focus on NetBIOS, RPC, Windows Sockets, and NetDDE. A possible Remote Access Service (RAS) question attempts to trick you by asking which of these interfaces are available if you establish a network connection remotely. *All* of them are available via a remote connection.

File system drivers

File system drivers allow programs to access data on different types of
storage devices without knowing details about that device. You can use the
same COPY or XCOPY command to move files from any of the following:

- ✔ Hard disks
- ✔ Floppy disks
- ✔ CD-ROMs
- ✔ Zip drives

Each device has its own file system driver to integrate it into the operating
system. In addition, several different file system drivers are designed just for
hard files, including FAT, HPFS, and NTFS.

In a networking environment, two major networking components — the
Workstation Service (more commonly known as Redirector) and the Server
Service (both covered in the following sections) — are file system drivers.
When a file is requested, as in a COPY or XCOPY command, these file system
drivers can move files from one computer to another.

Workstation Service (Redirector)

In older software products (Microsoft LAN Manager and IBM LAN Server),
the Workstation Service was known as "the Redirector." The Redirector
intercepts calls to file and print functions and determines whether the calls
are for a local network resource. If a call is for a local resource, the
Redirector passes the request to the driver that services the local resource.
If the request is for a network resource, the Redirector operates the NetBIOS
programming interface to pass the request to the remote resource.

The exam also refers to the Redirector as the Workstation Service, so be
sure you know that they're the same!

Server Service (Server)

The Server Service helps the Workstation Service (the Redirector). It
receives requests for access to local resources from remote Workstation
Services. The Server Service's coordinates access from remote Workstation
Services. This coordination includes file-locking so that if multiple workstations access the same resource, they don't undermine each other.

Also, the Server Service manages the security associated with a local
resource (if it is located on an NTFS partition). Whenever a user requests a
file, the Server Service checks the userid against the Access Control List
(ACL) for the requested file to determine what type of access the user has to

the file such as Read or Full Control. In the event that the user has been assigned the No Access NTFS Permission, the request for the file fails, manifesting as an "access denied" message.

Transport Driver Interface (TDI)

The Server Service and the Workstation Service (Redirector) use the NetBIOS interface to communicate with a variety of protocols, including:

- ✔ NWLink
- ✔ NetBEUI
- ✔ TCP/IP

The homogenization that allows all of these transport protocols to function interchangeably is *Transport Driver Interface* (TDI). The TDI is important because it allows the selected protocol for network communication to change without impacting services like Server and Workstation.

Transport protocols

Five transport protocols ship with Windows NT Server. The exam expects you to know them all.

TCP/IP

TCP/IP is the language of the Internet. Few, if any, computers or operating systems cannot communicate using TCP/IP. TCP/IP is routable and works well over *WANs (wide area networks)*.

On the downside, TCP/IP is relatively complex to administer, especially if you don't deploy Domain Name Services (DNS) or Dynamic Host Configuration Protocol (DHCP). These services automate the process of distributing IP addresses and provide the capability to resolve fully qualified domain names (FQDNs). These are machines that can be identifed by *computer_name.domain_name* (for example, kyle.microsoft.com). Also, TCP/IP employs a 32-bit addressing scheme that limits the number of addressable nodes (*hosts* in TCP/IP lingo) to a mere 2 billion.

NetBEUI

NetBEUI was once the default protocol for Microsoft networking products. NetBEUI is small and very fast, and easy to administer. The evolution of networks from routers to switches has made NetBEUI more applicable technically, but many network designers no longer consider it viable.

The main problem associated with NetBEUI is that it isn't *routable*. NetBEUI was designed for small networks (2 to 200 computers). Consequently, the ability to route packets to remote networks was omitted. Other protocols, such as TCP/IP and IPX, are designed to work with thousands of computers across multiple networks. Also, the features that make NetBEUI easy to administer require bandwith. NetBEUI is renowned for the problems that its broadcasts cause. Generally, NetBEUI is appropriate only for small, isolated LANs (local area networks) and LANS connected via bridges instead of routers.

NWLink

Before the Internet made TCP/IP the protocol suite of choice, Novell installed millions of NetWare servers using IPX protocol. Many network designers used NetWare servers as routers as well as servers. Networks that used NetWare servers as routers were virtually closed to Microsoft servers because NetBEUI is not routable.

Microsoft responded by developing NWLink, which is similar to Novell's IPX. Like Novell's IPX, NWLink supports NetBIOS applications.

If you want to place Windows NT Server on a Novell-centric network, NWLink is a good choice. However, NWLink doesn't have TCP/IP's broad interoperability. Also, NWLink (like IPX) is particularly slow over WANs. NWLink is significantly slower on WANs than TCP/IP and NetBEUI are.

NWLink does not allow NetWare clients to access Windows NT Server for file and print services. You must install FPNW on the NT Server before that can happen.

AppleTalk

AppleTalk, installed as part of Windows NT Server's Services for Macintosh, allows Macs to access file and printer resources on an NT Server.

Some people argue that AppleTalk isn't really a transport because it never shows up in the list of protocols under the Windows NT network configuration program, but the fact is that Microsoft documentation does refer to it as a transport protocol. And who writes these exams? You got it: Microsoft.

DLC

DLC (Data Link Control) is a more primitive protocol than TCP/IP, NWLink, or NetBEUI, and cannot support the Server and Workstation Services on its own. The primary use for DLC is to support IBM's SNA communications and HP's network printer products.

Network Device Interface Specification (NDIS)

Network Device Interface Specification (NDIS) 4.0 is the network driver interface for Windows NT Server. NDIS provides a means of managing multiple protocols across a broad array of network adapters from many vendors.

NDIS specifies the interface that protocols use to communicate with network adapter device drivers. In the Windows NT network architecture, NDIS allows adapters to bind to transport protocols without having to contain specific blocks of code for every protocol possible to implement. Rather, the protocols are designed as NDIS-compliant so that they can work with any other network adapter card driver also written to NDIS specifications. Some of the benefits NDIS provides include:

- Ability to operate several protocols through a single network adapter
- Simplification of the installation of network adapter drivers
- Flexibility in configuring protocols with network adapters

NDIS allows binding of multiple protocols to a single network adapter card.

Network adapter card drivers

Network adapter card drivers are software, generally written by a network adapter manufacturer, that ships with network adapter cards. These drivers are written as NDIS 4.0 compliant for Windows NT, so that they can interoprate with any other protocol implemented on the server.

Because of the Windows NT Hardware Abstraction Layer (HAL), drivers written for DOS or Windows 3.1 do not work under NT.

Installing and Configuring Network Protocols

To start configuring protocols on your Windows NT Server, choose Start⇨Settings⇨Control Panel and then double-click the Network icon.

Review the Network Configuration dialog box and all of its settings.

Figure 9-1 shows the Protocol tab of the Network Configuration dialog box. The word *protocol* can get a little confusing sometimes. Some *protocols*, such as DHCP, are installed and configured as *services*. You can refer to the protocols listed in Figure 9-1, using Microsoft terminology, as *transport protocols*.

Lab 9-1 steps you through adding a protocol.

Lab 9-1	**Installing a Protocol**

1. **Click the Add button.**

   A list of protocols appears.

2. **Choose the desired protocol and then press OK.**

3. **Insert your Windows NT CD-ROM or point the install program to the path where the protocol is stored.**

4. **Click Close to finish the installation.**

5. **Click Yes to restart your server.**

TCP/IP

If you select the line "TCP/IP Protocol" from the list of transport protocols on the Protocols tab, and then click the Properties button, the TCP/IP Properties dialog box opens. The following sections discuss its five tabs.

IP Address

The IP Address tab (see Figure 9-2) enables you to manually assign an IP address to a network card. If your Windows NT Server has more than one adapter, select the correct adapter before making any changes on this tab.

If the adapter is correct, you can set the IP address of this server. Most servers have explicit (static) addresses and don't use DHCP.

Unless you use DHCP to obtain an IP address, you must fill out the IP Address field and the Subnet Mask field.

If your Windows NT Server has more than one network adapter and is set up for routing, the Default Gateway field isn't relevant and you can leave it blank. Otherwise, set the Default Gateway field to the address of a router located on the same segment as your Windows NT Server.

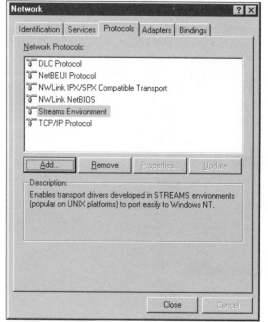

Figure 9-1:
The
Protocols
tab in the
Network
Configuration
dialog box.

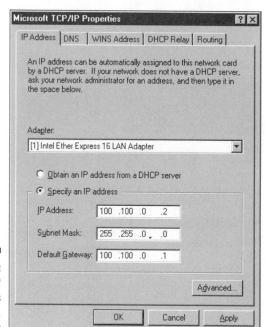

Figure 9-2:
The TCP/IP
Properties
dialog box.

DNS

The DNS tab (see Figure 9-3) allows you to specify the TCP/IP host name of your Windows NT Server. It also allows you to specify the IP address of the domain name server. A *domain name server* allows users to refer to a specific host with a symbolic name (such as www.microsoft.com or www.dukepress.com) instead of the numeric IP address. The address of the domain name server tells applications where to send a symbolic name to have it resolved to a numeric IP address.

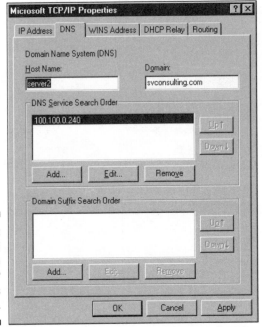

Figure 9-3:
The DNS
tab of the
TCP/IP
Properties
dialog box.

WINS Address

Windows Internet Name Servers (WINS) is a facility for resolving NetBIOS names to IP addresses. If you're using NetBIOS over TCP/IP in a network that contains routers, you may need to specify the IP address of the WINS server; you don't have to do this if your NT Server is running the WINS service tab.

Routing

If your Windows NT Server has multiple network adapters, you can use it as an IP router. To do so:

1. Click the Routing tab of the Microsoft TCP/IP Properties dialog box.

2. Check the Enable IP Forwarding check box to configure your Windows NT Server as an IP router.

DHCP Relay

If your Windows NT Server is a router, and your organization uses a DHCP server to manage client workstations, configure your server to relay DHCP requests and responses. To do that, you use the DHCP Relay tab (see Figure 9-4).

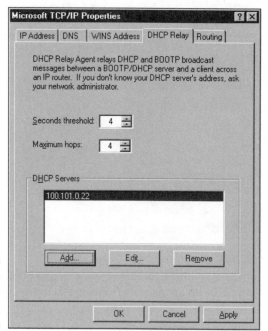

Figure 9-4:
The DHCP
Relay tab.

NWLink IPX/SPX

If you select the line "NWLink IPX/SPX Compatible Transport" from the list of transport protocols and then click the Properties button, you get the NWLink IPX/SPX Properties dialog box, shown in Figure 9-5.

Generally, you don't want to change anything in the NWLink configuration. The default network address is 0, which allows the protocol to accept frames with any network address. If you place a value in the Internal Network Number field, it must match the same value as the other NetWare servers on your network.

In today's networking environment, you want to enable the Automatic Frame Type Detection setting. However, you may run into an old network adapter that doesn't detect frame types properly. If you do, you can use this dialog box to add one or more frame types manually.

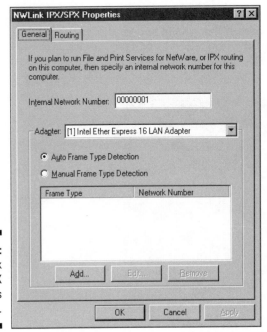

Figure 9-5:
The NWLink
IPX/SPX
Properties
dialog box.

If you have multiple network adapters, you may want to use your Windows
NT Server as an IPX router. To do so, use the Routing tab in the NWLink
IPX/SPX Properties dialog box.

Checking the Enable Rip Routing check box configures your Windows NT
Server as an IPX router.

NetBEUI

NetBEUI doesn't have configurable parameters, so after you add it to your
protocol list, that's it — no configuring necessary.

AppleTalk

You cannot add AppleTalk to the protocols. You install the AppleTalk
protocol automatically when you install Services for Macintosh from the
Services tab of the Network dialog box.

Prep Test

1 Protocol stacks evolved because?

A ○ Networking and communications technology has been very stable.

B ○ They ensure the highest performance.

C ○ They allow network developers to introduce new technologies without disrupting the entire network.

D ○ Communications functions are constantly being embedded in hardware.

2 Which of the following are routable protocols? (Select all that apply.)

A ❑ AppleTalk

B ❑ NetBEUI

C ❑ TCP/IP

D ❑ IPX

3 How do you add the AppleTalk protocol?

A ○ You add it via the Protocol tab in the Network dialog box.

B ○ You add it via the Services tab in the Network dialog box.

C ○ You add it to the protocol list automatically if you add Services for Macintosh via the Services tab in the Network dialog box.

D ○ You add it automatically if you add Services for Macintosh via the Services tab in the Network dialog box, but it doesn't show up in the protocol list.

✓**4** How do you configure your Windows NT Server to act as a TCP/IP router?

A ○ Check the Enable IP Forwarding check box on the Routing tab of the Microsoft TCP/IP Properties dialog box.

B ○ Check the Enable IP Routing check box on the Routing tab of the Microsoft TCP/IP Properties dialog box.

C ○ Install more than one network adapter with TCP/IP and you get routing automatically.

D ○ Windows NT Server can route IPX but cannot route TCP/IP.

✓**5** Which transport protocols ship with Windows NT Server? (Select all that apply.)

A ❑ DLC

B ❑ NWLink

C ❑ NetBEUI

D ❑ DHCP

6 You want to add the NetBEUI protocol to your Windows NT server. Which of the following are valid ways to accomplish this task? (Select all that apply.)

A ❑ Do nothing. NetBEUI is installed automatically during Windows NT setup, so you don't need to add it later.

B ❑ Choose Start➪Settings➪Control Panel and then double-click the Network icon. Then select the Protocol tab, click the Add button, and select NetBEUI from the list.

C ❑ Double-click the My Computer icon, then the Control Panel, then the Network icon. Click the Protocol tab and then click the Add button, and finally, select NetBEUI from the list.

D ❑ Insert the Windows NT Server CD, choose Windows NT Setup, and perform Network Setup.

7 You are setting up a 15-workstation Ethernet LAN at a small insurance agency. Which transport protocol is most appropriate?

A ○ DLC

B ○ TCP/IP

C ○ NetBEUI

D ○ NWLink

8 You must set up a 10-workstation Token Ring LAN to communicate with a remote Windows NT Server over a routed network. Which transport protocol is most appropriate?

A ○ DLC

B ○ TCP/IP

C ○ NetBEUI

D ○ NWLink

9 You want to change your TCP/IP host name. Which of the following are appropriate ways to do it?

A ❑ Use the IPCONFIG.EXE program.

B ❑ You can't change the host name after installing TCP/IP.

C ❑ Use the Host Name field under the DNS tab of the Microsoft TCP/IP Properties dialog box.

D ❑ Contact your Domain Name Server administrator.

Answers

1 C. The idea behind a protocol stack is that by formally separating the different processes of communications, you can introduce different technologies without disrupting the whole network. *Review "Protocol Overview" for more information.*

2 A, C, D. All but NetBEUI. *Refer to "Transport protocols."*

3 D. You cannot add AppleTalk to the list of protocols as you can NetBEUI, TCP/IP, and NWLink. *Review "AppleTalk."*

4 A. Enabling IP routing allows your NT Server to send packets from your local network to a remote network. *Review "TCP/IP."*

5 A, B, C. DHCP is not a transport protocol; you implement it as a service under Windows NT. *See "Installing and Configuring Network Protocols."*

6 B, C. There are a couple of ways to install network protocols. *See "Installing and Configuring Network Protocols."*

7 C. With only 15 Ethernet-attached workstations, the small insurance agency doesn't need routers, so NetBEUI's nonroutable nature is not an issue. NetBEUI, with its superior speed and simplicity of administration, is ideal in this situation. *Review "NetBEUI" under "Transport protocols."*

8 B. Even though the number of workstations is small, the fact that the clients must communicate with the server over a routed network eliminates the use of NetBEUI as the transport protocol. TCP/IP and NWLink could both work here, but TCP/IP is a better choice because it has broader interoperability and is faster over a WAN. *Review "Transport protocols."*

9 C, D. See the DNS tab under Microsoft TCP/IP Properties configuration dialog box. The reason you also should contact your DNS administrator is to have the administrator associate this host name with its IP address in the DNS Server so that other computers can refer to your server by its host name instead of its IP address. Your DNS Server may or may not be the same computer as your Windows NT Server. *Review "TCP/IP."*

Part IV
Configuration

The 5th Wave   By Rich Tennant

"GET READY, I THINK THEY'RE STARTING TO DRIFT."

In this part . . .

1 help you study how to configure protocols, services, and adapters — and even printers. I also cover support for clients, as well as configuring NT Server with various clients: Workstation, Windows 95, and more. Knowing how a Windows NT client interacts with a Windows NT Server can help you pass the Server exam and is key to your success as an MCSE *after* you pass the exam. Read on!

Chapter 10

Networking Services

● ●

Exam Objectives

▶ Describing what makes a Windows NT Server a server

▶ Examining how services are implemented within Windows NT networking architecture

▶ Identifying the most common services available for Windows NT

▶ Describing how Windows NT security architecture relates to the services Windows NT Server provides

▶ Troubleshooting information on Windows NT networking

● ●

*T*he essence of a Windows NT Server is its facility for information-sharing. Several programs allow Windows NT Server to share different kinds of information. These programs are called *networking services* (or more commonly, just *services*) in the Windows NT networking architecture — and the Server exam tests you heavily on these services.

In this chapter, I examine the nature of these services. I tell you how these services distinguish Windows NT Server from Windows NT Workstation. And I give you a few pointers on how to handle networking services that don't perform as expected.

Quick Assessment

Services
Available
for Windows
NT

√1 Name five services required on a Windows NT Server in order to share files and printers: _____, _____, _____, _____, and _____.

2 A domain master browser can exist only on a _____ type of server.

3 If you're looking for a computer to designate as a master browser, your best choice is a machine that has the _____ operating system installed on it.

Trouble-
shooting
Windows NT
Networking

4 You can use the _____ utility to check available IRQs, I/O port addresses, and base memory addresses.

Services
Within
Windows NT
Networking
Architecture

5 (True/False). Workgroup administration is centralized.

6 You store the domain database on what types of Windows NT Servers?

7 Another name for a workgroup network is a _____ network.

√8 A user's access token is created during the _____ process.

Windows NT
Security
Architecture

√9 Name three types of objects that you can secure under Windows NT Server: _____, _____, and _____.

Answers

1 *Computer Browser services, NetBIOS Interface services, RPC Configuration services, Server services,* and *Workstation services.* See "Networking Architecture Overview."

2 *primary domain controller.* See "Directory Services."

3 *Windows NT Server 4.0.* See "Directory Services."

4 *WinNT Diagnostic utility.* See "Network interface card installation."

5 *False.* See "Workgroups."

6 *Primary domain controllers and backup domain controllers.* See "Domain."

7 *Peer-to-peer.* See "Workgroups."

8 *logon.* See "Logon."

9 *Devices, directories, files, network shares, ports, printers, processes, symbolic links, threads,* and *windows.* See "Security."

Windows NT Workstation 4.0

Windows NT Workstation has a rather steep hardware requirement compared to DOS and Windows 95, but offers a higher level of stability and security than the others.

Hardware requirements: Windows NT Workstation 4.0 requires at least a 486SX processor, with a minimum of 12MB of RAM. The recommended minimum platform, however, is a Pentium processor and at least 16MB to 24MB of RAM. Windows NT supports neither Plug and Play nor the APM (advanced power management) features available in Windows 95.

Compatibility: Owing to its stringent security model, Windows NT Workstation 4.0 does not support any application that directly manipulates the computer's hardware. Windows NT's layered security model, with its multiple transition and interface layers (TDI, NDIS, and so on), prohibits applications from touching the devices directly. Unfortunately, this security model causes problems with many DOS applications, as well as more than a few Windows 95 applications.

Security and stability: If you're aware of the compatibility problems inherent in NT, you probably wonder why anyone would use NT Workstation. Two words: *security* and *stability*. Windows NT Workstation 4.0 operates applications in protected memory areas with a highly refined object-based security model. By limiting the likelihood of any single application failure to cause a machine failure, the stability of the Windows NT platform far exceeds that of both the Windows 95 and DOS platforms.

Networking: Windows NT Workstation ships with support for the NetBEUI, IPX, DLC, and TCP/IP protocols.

Windows for Workgroups and DOS

Windows for Workgroups and DOS are hot topics on the Windows 3.51 exams, but the Windows NT 4.0 exams hardly even mention them. All you need to know about Windows for Workgroups and MS-DOS is that they are the only operating systems that you can run on systems that use a 386SX or slower processor, less than 4MB of RAM, or less than 35MB of free hard disk space.

Windows for Workgroups 3.11 and MS-DOS do not support long filenames. They also do not support NTFS; they support FAT only. Windows for Workgroups environments do, however, offer limited 32-bit application support via the Win32 driver.

To connect to Windows NT systems, your best bet is to use the Microsoft Networking Client that ships on the *Windows NT 4.0 Server* CD. The Microsoft Networking Client supports NetBEUI, IPX, and TCP/IP (including DHCP) configurations.

Installing the software

All of the client software that you might need is available on the *Windows NT 4.0 Server* CD-ROM in the \Clients directory. If you purchase this CD-ROM, know this: Although the copy of *Windows NT Server 4.0* does include the necessary client software, it does not include — I repeat, does *not* include — the required associated software licenses for Windows 95, Windows for Workgroups, and Windows NT Workstation. If you install any of these clients, you need separate software licenses from Microsoft for each client that you install. That's in addition to the client access license required for each Windows NT Server you install on your network.

Checking Out the Environment

Microsoft provides three key services for managing the environment.

Dynamic Host Configuration Protocol (DHCP)

The Dynamic Host Configuration Protocol (DHCP) is an extension of the BootStrap protocol (BOOTP) commonly used in the UNIX and diskless workstation environment. DHCP centrally manages the allocation and configuration of TCP/IP clients, effectively overcoming the most difficult aspect of an IP based-network, managing the pool of IP addresses. Figure 11-1 shows the DHCP Manager.

Although I cover DHCP in much more detail in Chapter 9, the few points most likely to appear on your exam bear repeating:

✔ You can assign a number of options with DHCP besides the IP address. A partial list of these include:

- IP lease expiration date

- The network gateway or router

- IP subnet mask

- WINS and DNS servers

- NetBIOS/WINS node-type

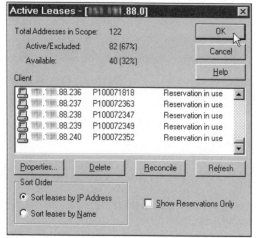

Figure 11-1:
The DHCP
Manager.

✔ The negotiation of IP addresses via DHCP uses the DORA process:

1. **Discover:** Client broadcasts request for an IP address.

2. **Offer:** Server broadcasts IP information for the client.

3. **Request:** Client selects IP configuration and broadcasts selection.

4. **Acknowledge:** Server acknowledges the request address if address is still available.

✔ DHCP messages are broadcast-based; therefore, they are limited only to the subnet, unless you enable BOOTP_RELAY on the TCP/IP routers or install the DHCP Relay Agent service on at least one computer on the machine's subnet.

✔ DHCP clients attempt to renew their leases from the DHCP server at boot time, at 50 percent of the lease time, at 87.5 percent of the lease time, and at 100 percent of the lease time.

✔ DHCP servers require static IP addresses. Obvious, but worth noting.

Windows Internet Name Service (WINS)

The Windows Internet Naming Service (WINS) is the server that resolves NetBIOS names for machines on a Windows NT network.

- NetBIOS names are 16 bytes long. The 16th byte identifies the *type* of name and is usually referred to by its hexadecimal equivalent. The most common entries are as follows:

  - **<00>** Workstation Service Name or the NetBIOS computer name

  - **<03>** Messenger Service Name or the NetBIOS user name

  - **<1B>** Domain master browser name (only found on the PDC)

  - **<1C>** Domain group name (contains up to 25 domain controllers)

  - **<1D>** Master Browser group name

- The four actions that WINS performs on your network are defined as the *4 Rs,* as follows:

  - **Register:** WINS clients register their NetBIOS names and IP addresses with the server.

  - **Renew:** WINS clients renew their NetBIOS names and IP addresses with the server on a predetermined interval defined by the *renewal interval,* which you set on the WINS server.

  - **Release:** When you shut a WINS client down properly, it notifies the WINS server via a *name release* message to the server.

  - **Resolve:** WINS-enabled machines use the WINS server to resolve NetBIOS names to IP addresses for other WINS-enabled resources.

- There are four types of NetBIOS node-types for WINS-enabled clients. The node-types define how name resolution functions on the client computers:

  - **B-node** *(Broadcast):* NetBIOS name resolution takes place via an IP broadcast only. B-node clients do not use WINS servers for name resolution.

  - **P-node** *(Point to Point):* P-node clients use the specified WINS server for name resolution. These clients do not use broadcasts for any name resolution.

  - **M-node** *(Mixed):* Combination of the B-node and P-node methods. M-node clients first *broadcast* and then perform *a WINS lookup* to resolve NetBIOS names.

  - **H-node** *(Hybrid):* Combination of the B-node and P-node methods. H-node clients first perform a *WINS lookup* then do a network *broadcast* to resolve NetBIOS names. H-node is the default mode for WINS-enabled clients.

- The following steps outline the name resolution process for H-node–enabled WINS clients:

  1. Check to see if the request is for the local computer.

  2. Client needs to resolve \\Server.

3. Check the NetBIOS Name Cache. Check all entries that have been accessed within the last 10 minutes and all entries that have been loaded in the LMHOSTS file with the #pre tag.

4. Query the WINS server. If the client doesn't find the name on the primary WINS server, it then queries the secondary WINS server (assuming one is specified).

5. Broadcast. An IP broadcast then attempts to resolve the name. If a WINS Proxy is configured on the network, the proxy receives this broadcast request and attempts to query the WINS server again.

6. Check the LMHOSTS file on the local computer (if configured to use LMHOSTS for name resolution).

7. Check the HOSTS file on the local computer (if configured to use DNS for name resolution).

8. Query the DNS server (if configured to use DNS for name resolution).

Domain Name Service (DNS)

Although Microsoft's DNS service isn't a major exam topic, you want to know the difference between WINS and DNS. DNS resolves host names to IP addresses, whereas WINS resolves NetBIOS names to IP addresses. I discuss each of these in more detail in Chapter 9.

Services for Macintosh Clients

Setting up and administering a Windows NT environment that uses Macintosh clients is no mean task. Before you can configure and support the environment properly, you need to understand several concepts that are foreign to most NT administrators. Just some of the concepts you need to be familiar with are AppleTalk, LocalTalk, seed routers, AppleTalk zones, network numbers, and LLAP.

Fortunately, for the exam, you need to understand only these three points:

✔ You must install Services for Macintosh (SFM) on your server before you can have Macintosh clients connect to a Windows NT network. SFM supports AppleTalk on your NT Server and does not offer NBT support to the Macintosh clients.

✔ After you install SFM, Macintosh clients can access PostScript (and some non-PostScript) printer queues on the NT network, and NT clients can print to Macintosh printers via print spools configured on the NT Server.

✔ Also before you can provide file services to Macintosh clients, you must configure your file system for NTFS — NTFS is necessary to support the extended Macintosh file system attributes, such as resource data forks.

You manage Windows NT SFM via the Windows File Manager and NT Print Manager programs.

Staying Legal: The MS License Manager

The Server exam does not test you concerning operation of the Microsoft License Manager utility, shown in Figure 11-2. You do need to know and understand the Microsoft Windows NT and BackOffice licensing model, however — the exam presents a scenario and asks you to recommend the correct model under the given circumstances.

Every client that needs to connect to a Windows NT Server or Microsoft BackOffice application needs a *client access license,* or CAL. Microsoft offers two licensing modes for assigning CALs to Windows NT Server and the various BackOffice components:

✔ **Per server licensing:** The licenses exist on the server and are assigned to client connections on a temporary basis. If a server has 100 licenses, it can accept 100 connections from clients, regardless of whether they're already connected to another Windows NT Server.

✔ **Per seat licensing:** The licenses exist on the clients, and therefore can serve to connect to any one of a number of Windows NT Server or BackOffice products.

Which licensing options you should use depends on the number of clients and the number and allocation of the NT Servers. Here's a general guideline to follow: If the number of licenses required across all of your servers exceeds the number of client computers in your installation, your best bet is a per seat license.

It is often recommended to have an environment that uses both licensing models. Consider an environment that has three file servers and five print servers for 50 users. Each user must access data on each of the three file servers. Equal numbers of users are assigned to the print servers. If you want to use per server licensing, you need 50 CALs for each server (150) plus 10 CALs for each print server (another 50). If you use per server licensing, you need to purchase 200 CALs. If you use the per seat licensing option, however, you need to purchase only 50 CALs.

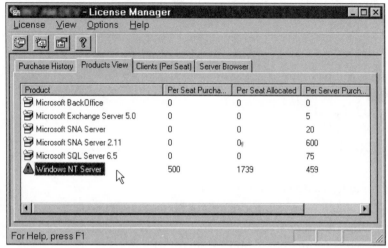

Figure 11-2:
License
Manager.

You are legally permitted a one-time change from per server to per seat licensing, so if you don't know which to choose, go with per server licensing. You are not permitted, however, to change from per seat to per server licensing.

Prep Test

1 What file will be referenced when a NetBIOS name needs to be resolved to an IP address?

   A ○ HOSTS.TXT

   B ○ LMHOSTS.TXT

   C ○ HOSTS

   D ○ LMHOSTS

2 How many bytes does a NetBIOS name contain?

   A ○ 14 bytes for the name and 1 byte for the service type

   B ○ 5 bytes for the name and 1 byte for the service type

   C ○ 16 bytes for the name and 1 byte for the service type

   D ○ 17 bytes for the name and 1 byte for the service type

3 Which of the following utilities do you use if you need to connect your Windows for Workgroups computer to a Windows NT network?

   A ○ Microsoft NetBEUI DHCP Client

   B ○ Microsoft IPX/SPX Client

   C ○ Microsoft Networking Client

   D ○ Microsoft DHCP Relay Client

4 The Microsoft license legally permits you to migrate from per seat to per server licensing how many times?

   A ○ Once

   B ○ Twice

   C ○ Thrice

   D ○ None

5 If a DHCP-enabled client cannot connect to a DHCP server on your subnet via a broadcast, what happens?

   A ○ The client contacts the server via the DHCP/IP protocol.

   B ○ The client contacts the server via the BOOTP protocol.

   C ○ A DHCP Relay Agent forwards the request.

   D ○ The DHCP/IP Relay protocol forwards the request.

PG
200 - 201

6 Which NetBIOS node-type first sends a broadcast and then performs a WINS lookup to resolve NetBIOS names?

A ○ P-node
B ○ H-node   *PG 202*
C ○ M-node
D ○ B-node

7 Which operating system do I choose if I require my older accounting and receiving programs to work flawlessly, but also require support for newer 32-bit applications?

A ○ Windows 3.1
B ○ Windows 3.11 (with network support)
C ○ Windows 95
D ○ Windows NT

8 What must you install (on what machines) before Macintosh clients can connect to a Windows NT network?

A ○ You must install Client for Microsoft Networks on each Macintosh client.
B ○ You must install Services for Macintosh on the Windows NT Server.
C ○ You must install Gateway Services for Macintosh Networks on the Windows NT Server.
D ○ You must install Client for Microsoft Networks on each Macintosh client and Gateway Services for Macintosh Networks on the Windows NT Server.

9 DORA is a quick and easy way to remember which process?

A ○ The WINS registration process
B ○ The DHCP IP negotiation process   *PG 201*
C ○ The Windows 95 installation process
D ○ The NetBIOS name resolution process

Clients

Answers

1 *D.* The LMHOSTS file is the static text file for resolving NetBIOS names to IP addresses on your local workstation. You should save the LMHOSTS file without an extension. *Refer to "Checking Out the Environment."*

2 *B.* NetBIOS names have a total of 15 bytes, plus 1 byte for the service type. *Refer to "Checking Out the Environment."*

3 *C.* To connect your Windows for Workgroups PC to a Windows NT network, you must use the Microsoft Networking Client, which also supports DHCP for automatic configuration of DHCP on the client. *Refer to "Choosing the Right OS."*

4 *D.* The license permits a one-time migration from per server to per seat licensing, but does not permit ever changing from per seat to per server licensing. *Refer to "Staying Legal: The MS License Manager."*

5 *C.* You must enable BOOTP_RELAY on the routers or install a DHCP Relay Agent on the subnet if you want to forward the DHCP broadcast requests off the subnet. *Refer to "Checking Out the Environment."*

6 *C.* M-node (which combines the B-node and P-node methods) clients first broadcast; then they perform a WINS lookup to resolve NetBIOS names. *Refer to "Checking Out the Environment."*

7 *C.* Windows 95 is more compatible with existing applications, but also includes support for newer 32-bit applications. *Refer to "Choosing the Right OS."*

8 *B.* Services for Macintosh enables AppleTalk support on the NT Server. You don't install any client software on the Macintosh clients. *Refer to "Services for Macintosh Clients."*

9 *B.* DORA stands for Discover, Offer, Request, and Acknowledge — that's the DHCP IP negotiation process. *Refer to "Checking Out the Environment."*

Chapter 12

Printing

· ·

Exam Objectives

▶ Understanding printing

▶ Reviewing NT Server print components

▶ Understanding network printing

▶ Creating and configuring NT Server printers

· ·

You can expect to see a handful of questions on your Server exam relating to printing to and from an NT print server. The exam can draw questions from a surprising amount of information for a topic as straightforward as printing. You need to know about spooler settings, network printing, printer pools, scheduling, and troubleshooting.

In this chapter, I introduce the basic concepts of the NT print model. Windows NT Server is designed to be a powerful, flexible, resource-sharing tool. I explore the ease with which you can create a new printer, the flexibility of the network administration functions, and the advantages offered by the advanced configuration options. This chapter also looks at NT Server's capability to accept print requests from any client platform that you may have in your organization, including NetWare, UNIX, and Macintosh clients.

Quick Assessment

Configuring Printers

1   What tool do you use to add a new printer in NT?

2   What are the six tabs available under the Properties option for an NT printer?

3   Associating multiple print devices with a single printer is known as a _____ _____.

Connectivity to Different Client Types

4   (True/ False). You must always install a print driver on Windows NT Workstation clients when printing to a Windows NT Print Server.

5   You must install the _____ network protocol before you can use a Hewlett-Packard Network Interface Print Device.

6   To print to a UNIX printer from NT, you can use the _____ utility, which is installed when you add the Microsoft TCP/IP Printing service.

Trouble-shooting

7   If your print device stops producing output, what is the first thing you should try?

Managing Resources, User/Group Rights

8   Which tab under Printer Properties would you use to limit the times when a printer can produce output?

9   (True/ False). By default, a user cannot delete a print job after submitting it to the printer.

Answers

1   *The Add Printer wizard.* Review "Creating a local printer."

2   *General, Ports, Scheduling, Sharing, Security, and Device Settings.* Review "Configuring a local printer: Plug 'n Pray."

3   *Printer pool.* Review "Diving into printer pools."

4   *False.* Review "NT print clients."

5   *Data Link Control (DLC).* Review "Network print devices."

6   *LPR.* Review "Using LPR."

7   *Stop and restart the Spooler service.* Review "Troubleshooting Print Problems."

8   *Scheduling.* Review "Scheduling."

9   *False.* Review "Security."

Don't Be Fooled by Spools and Pools

Microsoft has specific definitions for their technologies that you need to know for the exams. Don't fall into the trap of thinking that your technical vocabulary will match the definitions used on the tests. Review the definitions in Table 12-1, and pay close attention to the relationships between a printer, a print device, and a printing pool.

The following list gives you some points to focus on as you review for the Server exam:

- ✔ The five primary areas where you want to focus your studying efforts for the Server exam:

  - Spooler settings

  - Network printing

  - Printer pools

  - Scheduling

  - Troubleshooting

- ✔ The Server exam expects you to know which client platforms can direct print jobs to NT. Review "NT Print Clients."

- ✔ Information on connecting to resources on a non-NT platform applies to printing in the same way that it applies to file-sharing. Although this chapter doesn't explore connecting to resources such as NetWare printers and Macintosh printers, you should be aware that the process is the same for connecting to NetWare and Macintosh file resources.

Table 12-1	Official Definitions
Word	*Definition*
Printer	In Microsoft's dictionary, a *printer* is actually the software interface between a print device and the operating system. You define and manage your printers in the Printers folder.
Print device	The machine that produces your final document.
Printing pool	Multiple physical print devices associated with a single *printer*.
Print server	Network servers that define shared printers and receive documents for processing and management.
Print driver	Software that allows the operating system to communicate with a print device.

Word	Definition
Print processor	Software component that prepares a print job for printing depending on its content.
Local printer	A printer connected to and controlled by an attached computer. Only local users of the attached computer can print to the local printer. Note, however, that the local printer could print to the same *print device,* which you can define as a network printer.
Network printer	A printer that both local and network users can use.

Printing devices

Before you take the exam, understand the difference between a *printer* (NT's software interface between the operating system and the print device) and a *printing device* (the physical printer where the final hard-copy document is produced). Also, get familiar with the three types of print devices:

- ✔ Local print devices
- ✔ Remote print devices
- ✔ Network interface print devices

Printing software

In the good ol' days of DOS, every program that a user might need to print from had to have a programmatic software interface to handle the conversion of print requests into commands that a specific print device could understand. Then along came Windows, with the Graphical Device Interface (GDI), which allowed all programs to speak to all print devices in the same language, through a translator known as a *device driver*. This device driver is the software component you are configuring when you manage printers through NT's Printers folder. The "NT Print Architecture" section later in this chapter looks at this process in more detail.

Network printing

Resource-sharing, one of the greatest benefits of networking, is an important area on your Server exam. Purchasing a print device for every single desktop in a large multiuser environment is never cost-feasible. By the same token, having every user in a large environment printing to the same print device is also inefficient — not to mention somewhat insane. Network printing offers the tweener solution.

An application doesn't care whether a print device is attached to a local port or to another computer over the network. The network software handles redirection of print requests to the proper systems for print processing.

NT print clients

NT Server supports print services for a wide variety of network client platforms — all of which are fair game on the Microsoft exam. Be ready for questions that require you to know the following:

- Which clients can print to an NT print server without requiring client-side driver installations?
- Which platforms can print to NT?
- What additional software do you need to allow different platforms the capability to print to an NT print server?

Can you name the client platforms that can print to NT Server? If not, review the following list and then read the sections dealing with each for specific information.

- Windows NT clients
- Windows 95 clients
- Windows 3.x/Windows for Workgroups clients
- DOS clients
- TCP/IP (UNIX) clients
- NetWare clients
- Macintosh clients

Windows NT/Windows 95 clients

NT Print Servers can provide print drivers to NT and 95 clients automatically. When an NT 4.0 client sends a print job to an NT print server, the client can automatically download and use driver software from the server. To allow similar operation of NT 3.x clients and Windows 95 clients, you can install the device drivers for the different operating systems on the print server, and thus avoid having to install driver software on each client system. Just . . . under the Alternate Drivers box of the Printer Properties Sharing tab (see Figure 12-1).

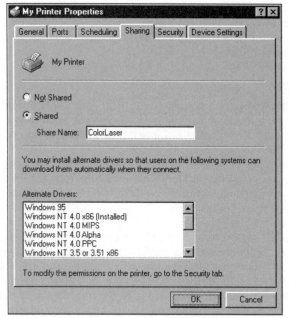

Figure 12-1:
The Printer
Properties
Sharing tab.

Windows 3.x/WFW/DOS clients

Using a Microsoft Networking Client Redirector allows DOS or Windows applications to send print jobs to an NT print share. DOS applications require their own internal print drivers, while Windows applications all use a single print driver that you must install on each client machine.

TCP/IP clients

TCP/IP-based printing clients, particularly UNIX clients, can print to NT print servers that are running the Microsoft TCP/IP Printing Service (LPD). Clients can use the LPR command to submit print jobs and the LPQ command to view the TCP/IP printer queue.

NetWare clients

A NetWare client can utilize NT print servers in two ways, and both are fair game on the Server test. In the first scenario, you need to have File and Print Services for NetWare (FPNW) installed on your NT Server. FPNW is a Windows NT network service that lets a computer running NT Server act as a NetWare 3.12-compatible file and print server. Using FPNW, NetWare clients can transparently access print services on a Windows NT Server without requiring additional client-side software.

The other option with NetWare clients is to install a client-side Microsoft Networking Client Redirector for NetWare clients. The downside of the second method is that you have to add and configure software on every NetWare client workstation.

Macintosh clients

Did you know that Macintosh clients could print to NT without additional client software? To allow Macintosh clients to submit print jobs to your NT Server, simply install and configure the Services for Macintosh on your NT Server.

Faced with an exam question on Macintosh printing, look for an answer that has "Services for Macintosh" in it. You may at least be able to eliminate some of the wrong answers that way.

The exam has questions about printing from non-NT clients. If you see a phrase similar to, "*without requiring configuration on the client workstation*," you can throw out answers that have the word "redirector" in them. Instead, look for answers that include the word "services." A *redirector* is client-side software that allows a non-Microsoft client access to Microsoft network services. A *service*, in this situation, is a server-side solution that can mimic the print server component of a client's native environment.

NT Print Architecture

This section presents a general overview of the NT printing process and then breaks down the functions of the individual components. For the test, you only need a general idea of how the printing process works; you are not expected to know the specific steps. Other areas you want to focus on for this section include

- ✔ The Registry location for your print spoolers
- ✔ Print monitors included with NT
- ✔ Printing to the HP Network Interface Printing Device

Printing process overview

The NT printing process begins when a client attempts to connect with a printer and ends when a print device receives processed data and produces a printed document. I review the whole printing process here, but remember that on the test, the most important step of this process to focus on is Step 1, the initial client connection. I include the additional steps for reference purposes, but you don't need to memorize them for the test.

1. Whenever you add a new network printer to a client machine and whenever a client machine tries to send a print job to a print server, if the client is running NT or Windows 95, the client first checks the version of the print driver on the server. If the server has a more recent driver, the client downloads the driver from the NT server into memory. If the version is the same or earlier, the client uses its local print driver. This version-checking and automatic downloading can occur only when NT clients or Windows 95 clients attach to an NT server.

2. The print job is sent to the client's local spooler via an RPC (remote procedure call), which then forwards the job to the server spooler. This step does not occur if the client and server are the same computer.

3. The server-side spooler passes the document to the router, which then determines the data type and passes the information to the appropriate print processor on the local print provider.

4. The print processor analyzes the type of data and determines whether further processing is required before returning the document to the local print provider.

5. If a separator page is to be used, this is the point in the process where the system creates and attaches the page to the beginning of the print job.

6. The print job is passed to the print monitor, which determines when the job should print and which port it should print through.

7. The print device receives processed data and produces a printed document.

That GD Interface!

The Graphics Device Interface (GDI) provides a single system-level interface for presenting graphical information to the user. This concept applies to printing to a printer as well as displaying images on a monitor. The GDI allows an application developer to create device-independent software, meaning that by writing to the GDI, the application appears and functions the same, regardless of the hardware used on the client platform. After a print request passes to the GDI, the GDI creates generic printer Device Driver Interface (DDI) calls to render the print job for interpretation by a print driver.

Print driver

A *print driver* is a software component that accepts the generic DDI calls that the GDI provides and translates them into device-specific commands. Every model of printer has its own custom print driver. The print driver provides model-specific characteristics of a printer, such as available resolutions, color translation, duplexing, and available paper sizes.

Print router

Know only that the printer router determines the format of data contained in a print job and passes the data to the appropriate print provider.

Print spooler

The spooler is responsible for routing print jobs to the appropriate printer. The print spooler is sometimes referred to as the *print provider*. When an application produces a print request, that request goes to the spooler.

If you want to change the default spool file folder, you must do so in the Registry. The locations of the spool folders are under the Registry key:

```
HKEY_LOCAL_MACHINE\SYSTEM\CurrentControlSet\Control\Print\Printers
```

You need to know for the exam that the Registry is where you can change the spool file folder location; however, you do not have to know the specific key where you make the change.

Print processor

A *print processor* translates print commands from an application into requests that a printing device can understand, often called *rendering a print job*. After a print processor renders a print job, the job is returned to the spooler.

Print monitor

The exam may ask about the print monitors that are included with NT. Table 12-2 lists these print monitors. The primary function of a print monitor is to transmit a print job to a printing device. In addition, a print monitor can

- ✔ Control the data stream to a printer port
- ✔ Acquire or release access to a printer port
- ✔ Report operational conditions of a print device (Paper Jam, Ready, Low Toner, you know the drill)
- ✔ Handle End-Of-Job notification so the spooler knows when to delete print jobs

Table 12-2	Print Monitors Supplied by NT
Monitor	*Description*
Localmon.dll	Processes output for LPT*x*, COM*x*, FILE:, remote shares, and named pipes.
Hpmon.dll	Sends output to the HP Network Interface Printing Device.
Sfmmon.dll	Transmits Macintosh print requests via AppleTalk protocol to network print devices. Both NT Workstation and NT Server can submit print requests to a Macintosh printer, but only Server receives print jobs from Macintosh clients.
Decpsmon.dll	Sends print jobs to Digital PrintServer printing devices.
Lexmon.dll	Sends output to Lexmark Mark Vision printers.
Pjlmon.dll	Communicates with printers that use the Print Job Language (PJL) communications standard.
Lprmon.dll	Sends print jobs to LPR printers. LPR is one of the printer components in the TCP/IP protocol suite. LPR allows a client application to send a print job to a spooler service on another computer via TCP/IP, which enables communication to and from systems running the TCP/IP protocol, such as UNIX.

Network print devices

A *network print device* is a print device connected directly to your network through the use of a special adapter, without requiring a connection to a physical port on a computer. You can think of a network print device as a Network Interface Card (NIC) for your printer. A network print device prevents you from needing a separate computer simply to provide a physical parallel port for each of your print devices. The print device may still be managed through an NT printer defined on an NT print server, which would definitely allow greater flexibility in the management functions; however, network print devices often are capable of performing their own rudimentary management functions independent of an NT print server.

A question about the HP Network Interface Print Device is likely. Now, not many people have experience with this technology, so here's a quick rundown of what you may need to know:

✔ An HP Network Interface Print Device requires the installation of the DLC network protocol. After you install the DLC protocol, the HP Network Interface Device appears as an option on the Ports tab for your printers.

✔ If you can't connect to an HP Network Interface Print Device, another user may already be attached using Continuous Connection Mode.

Local Printers

A *local printer* is any print device attached to a physical port and controlled by the attached computer. You can share a local printer, allowing other users across the network the option of printing to the print device associated with the printer, or you can configure it as not shared, meaning that no one on the network can view, access, or print to the printer. If you don't set a printer up as shared, only local users of the attached computer can print to the printer. Note, however, that a local, unshared printer could print to the same *print device* that could be defined on the same system as a shared printer. This is because you can define multiple NT printers with different properties and send them to a single physical device.

Creating a local printer

Are you familiar with the process for adding new printers in NT? You want to have at least a basic familiarity with the process for the server exam. You can create new printers, both local and remote, via the Add Printer wizard. Windows NT uses the Printers folder as the central management utility, providing an adding, sharing, deletion, and management interface for the NT printing environment. You can access the Printers folder in three ways:

- ✔ Choose Start➪Settings➪Printers
- ✔ Choose Start➪Settings➪Control Panel➪Printers
- ✔ Choose My Computer➪Printers

Lab 12-1 guides you through the process.

Lab 12-1   Adding an NT Printer

1. **Log on as an account with administrative authority.**

2. **Open the Printers folder.**

   Use one of the methods for opening the Printers folder covered in the section "Creating a Local Printer" later in this chapter.

3. **Double-click the Add Printer icon to start the Add Printer wizard.**

4. **Choose My Computer and click Next.**

   You should now see a list of available ports.

5. **Select the port that the local printer is attached to (usually LPT1).**

6. Select the manufacturer of your printer from the box on the left, the "Manufacturers" box, and then select the model of your printer from the resulting choices in the box on the right, the "Printers" box.

7. Choose a name for your printer and indicate whether this printer should be the default on this system.

8. Decide whether to share the printer. If you select Shared, you need to enter a Share Name, by which the computer can be referenced on the network.

9. If you share the printer, you can, at your option, install additional drivers for other client platforms that may need to print to the printer.

10. The Add Printer wizard asks you whether you want to print a test page.

11. At this point, you need to point the system to the location of the operating system installation media. Follow the instructions in the dialog boxes to complete this step.

   A new icon (labeled with a name that corresponds to the name you assigned your new printer) appears in the Printer window. Double clicking the new icon will open the properties window for the new printer, allowing you to configure the newly installed printer.

12. Explore the properties window for an idea of the configurable options on an NT printer.

   Do you recognize some of the same options from the Add Printer wizard screens?

Your best tool is experience. If you haven't worked with NT's Printers folder, take some time to explore it. You don't need to know every detail of every screen, but it's a good idea to get familiar with some of the main tabs.

Using LPR

The exam may ask about installing and using the Line Print Utility (LPR). To use the LPR protocol to connect to a network print device over TCP/IP, you must first install Microsoft TCP/IP Printing through the Networking control panel. After you install the Microsoft TCP/IP Printing Service, you need to go to the Services control panel and set Microsoft TCP/IP Printing Service to start automatically. Now when you select a port for your NT printers, the Add Ports tab includes an option for adding an LPR Port.

The server component, which installs with the TCP/IP Printing Service, is known as the Line Printer Daemon (LPD). LPD lets you submit jobs via LPR from UNIX, Windows NT, Windows 95, Macintosh, or any other client that runs TCP/IP and includes an LPR utility to a printer share on your NT print server.

Configuring a local printer: Plug 'n Pray

To access a printer's properties, right-click the icon for the Printers folder and choose Properties from the resulting pop-up menu. The Printers Properties window has six available configuration tabs: General, Ports, Scheduling, Sharing, Security, and Device Settings. These tabs each have some configuration options to know for the exam. The following sections present these options in detail.

General

The General tab has options for some of the more basic printer configuration requirements. See Table 12-3 for details.

Table 12-3	General Printer Properties
Property	*Description*
Driver	Select the print driver for the printer from a drop-down list. Only drivers installed on the system show up here.
New Driver	Installs or updates a print driver for a printer.
Separator Page	Opens a file selection box to specify a separator page for the printer to identify print jobs or toggle the printer between PCL and PostScript modes.
Print Processor	Opens a list box to select the data type for the printer to use. You should never need to change this option.
Print Test Page	This button produces a test page on the print device associated with the currently selected printer.
Comment	Text box that doesn't affect operation
Location	Text box that doesn't affect operation

Did you know that you could use a separator page to do more than just identify and separate different users' documents? You also can use a separator page to switch a printer between PostScript and PCL mode.

Ports

The Ports tab, shown in Figure 12-2, displays a list of available ports that your printer can print to. In addition, you can enable printer pooling from the Ports tab by checking the Enable Printer Pooling check box. If you enable printer pooling, you can select multiple ports for the printer to send print requests to. See the section "Diving in to Printer Pools" for more information.

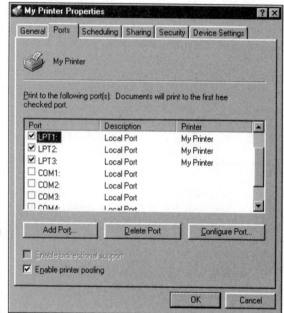

Figure 12-2:
The Printer
Properties
Ports tab.

Scheduling

The Scheduling tab, shown in Figure 12-3, controls the availability, priority, and spooler behavior of the printer. Table 12-4 presents the available selections from the Scheduling tab.

Table 12-4	Printer Scheduling Properties
Property	*Description*
Availability	Controls when the print device runs; the queue accepts documents until the printer is allowed to operate.
Priority	Select a value from 1 (the lowest priority setting) to 99.

(continued)

Table 12-4 *(continued)*

Property	Description
Spool print documents so program finishes printing faster	Saves pending print jobs in a directory on your server before forwarding them on to the print device. If you select this option, you have two additional choices, the next two options in this table.
Start printing after last page is spooled	Avoids delaying other print jobs while the print server waits for pages of a document.
Start printing immediately	Print jobs start as soon as the first page finishes spooling. If you have a fast print device that can print pages faster than a client can provide them, setting this option will cause a bottleneck as the device waits for spooled pages.
Print directly to the printer	Bypasses the spooler. Useful only for troubleshooting, because it limits your ability to manage documents and slows the speed of document completion in a multiuser environment.

The exam presents scenarios in which different functional user groups need to use the same print device. Your job is to find a method that allows access based on the types of jobs submitted. That's where the Print Priority and Availability options on the Scheduling tab come into play. The following list highlights some points you want to focus on for the scheduling questions that you may get on the exam:

✔ Your priorities can range from 1 to 99, with 1 being the lowest priority and 99 being the highest priority.

✔ You set priorities in the *printer properties* and then set user rights to define who can access the printer. You don't assign priorities to users, you assign them to printers.

✔ A single printer cannot have multiple priority assignments. For each new priority you want to assign to a print device, you must create a new printer definition and then set security and access privileges through that printer's security dialog box.

✔ Availability does not prevent a user from submitting a print job to a printer at any given time. Rather, availability settings cause submitted print jobs to be held in the spooler until the time falls within the availability constraints. The spooler then forwards the held jobs to the print device.

✔ You can define multiple printers with similar availability settings but different priorities. When the print jobs go active within the availability constraints, the system looks at the priorities of the multiple printers and completes all of the jobs in the print queue of the higher-ranked printer before starting on any of the jobs in the queue of the lower-ranked printer.

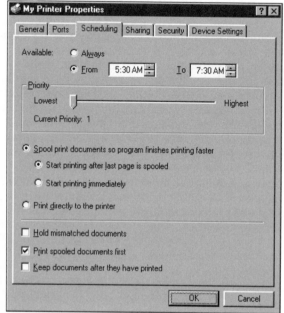

Figure 12-3:
The Printer
Properties
Scheduling
tab.

The way the Availability settings most frequently come up on the exam is in situation questions that involve large, non-time-sensitive documents. The key concept here is "non-time-sensitive." If you see the words "not" and "time-sensitive" together, you can eliminate answers that don't involve scheduling or availability.

Print Priority and Availability setting requirements typically show up together in questions on the exam. Here's an example:

Suppose you have two user groups, Accountants and Managers. The Accountants users print two types of documents: 200-plus page documents, which can tie up the printer for hours at a time, and brief one- or two-page memos. They print their large documents only for archival purposes, so printing the documents is only minimally time-sensitive. The memos, on the other hand, need to print shortly after hitting the print queue. All that the

Managers print are one-to-two-page memos, which they nearly always want to print immediately. In addition, management has requested that you give their print jobs priority over all other users. Your print server has only one physical print device. What would you do to optimize your printing environment?

You need to define three NT printers, all of which point to the same physical print device. Create a Managers Memo printer with a printing priority of 99. The priority of 99 will cause the memos to print ahead of lower priority documents. Point the members of the Managers group to this printer. Next, create two printers for the Accounting group, an Accounting Memos printer and an Accounting Archives printer. Give both printers a print priority of 1, and set Availability for the Accounting Archives printer to after 5:00 PM only. This will insure that no large documents occupy the printer during normal working hours. You would be able to do this since the large documents have minimal time sensitivity. Instruct your accounting users to send their large documents to the Accounting Archives printer and their memos to the Accounting Memos printer. Accounting memos are allowed to print at any time, but management memos are given priority in the print queue.

This solution applies scheduling by directing the large print jobs to a printer that you make available only after 5:00 PM, and it applies priority assignments that allow the manager's print jobs to print before the accounting print jobs.

Sharing

Sharing printers over the network allows multiple users to utilize a single hardware resource. Resource-sharing is, after all, one of the primary benefits of networking.

On the Printer Properties Sharing tab (refer to Figure 12-1), you can specify whether to share a printer. If shared, you can set the printer's share name on the network. Oh, and don't forget, if you want a shared printer but don't want everyone to be able to see it, adding a dollar sign ($) after the share name makes it invisible to a network browser. The Sharing option also lets you select and install additional drivers for automatic download from other Windows client platforms. Table 12-5 presents the options available within the Sharing properties tab.

Table 12-5	Printer Sharing Properties
Property	*Description*
Not Shared	Makes the printer available only to individuals logged in to the system on which the printer is defined.

Property	Description
Shared	Local users and users on the network can use the printer.
Alternate Drivers	Lists the additional client drivers that are installed for the printer. Installing additional drivers allows the listed clients to automatically download the server's version of the print driver upon initializing a print request.

Security

The Security tab has three options: Permissions, Auditing, and Ownership. Focus your attention on the Permissions option for the server exam. If you see any questions on auditing or ownership, they focus not on the relationship to printers, but on the general theories as they relate to any object in NT. You find more information on file services such as permissions and security in Chapter 16.

Permissions

You can assign printers group permissions just as you can files and folders, with one major difference: You can assign only four permissions to an NT printer. If not, Table 12-6 lists the available permissions. Figure 12-4 shows the default group permissions granted to a newly created printer on a domain Print Server.

Table 12-6	Printer Permissions
Permission	**Description**
Print	Allows users to print documents and manage queued documents that they have sent to the printer.
Manage Documents	Allows users to manage documents in the queue, regardless of who sent them. Document management includes pausing, restarting, resuming, and deleting existing documents.
No Access	Denies users access to the printer or print queue.
Full Control	Allows users to create, manage, and delete printers or documents.

Auditing

Auditing a printer allows you to track print events on a specific printer. For each event, you can tell the date and time an event occurred, who performed the event, and the computer from which the event was initiated. You can audit success or failure for the following events:

- ✔ Print
- ✔ Full Control
- ✔ Delete
- ✔ Change Permissions
- ✔ Take Ownership

To view audited print events in the System and Security log of the Event Viewer, choose Start⇨Programs⇨Administrative Tools⇨Event Viewer.

Ownership

The Take Ownership button allows a user who has the proper permissions to take ownership of a printer. The user may then change current permissions on the printer to any of the four available settings listed in Table 12-6 (memorize them).

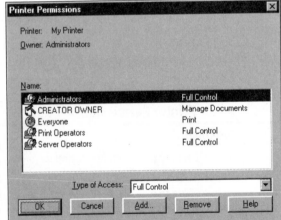

Figure 12-4:
Default
print
permissions.

Device settings

The Device Settings tab differs depending on what print driver the selected printer uses. You can set options such as the Form to Tray assignments, Installed Font Cartridges, and Halftone Setup. You do not need to know any specifics on the Device Settings tab for your exam.

Managing print jobs

For the exam, you need to know the available management functions that you can perform both globally and for single print jobs on an NT printer.

Again, look to the NT Printers folder for management tasks. Each printer that you define on your print server has an associated icon in the Printers folder. Double-clicking the icon for a given printer opens that printer's printer status window, which displays details for all jobs currently in the queue, as shown in Figure 12-5.

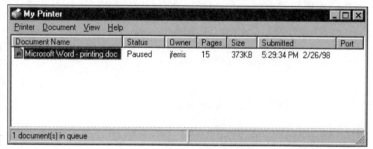

Figure 12-5:
A sample
printer
status
window.

After a print job reaches the queue, anyone who has the Manage Documents permission or the Full Control permission can modify the status of the print job. You can pause, resume, restart, and cancel specific print jobs from the Document menu. You can perform more global functions from the Printer menu, such as pausing or canceling all jobs for a printer, setting the printer as the default printer for your local system, selecting default document properties, or entering the Printer Properties screen for the printer.

Deleting jobs

To delete a print job from the queue (like a long document you know is wrong), simply select the job in the queue before it finishes forwarding to the print device and then press the Delete key.

You also can highlight the job and choose Document⇨Cancel.

Controlling print jobs

The options under the Document menu are specific to a print job in the main window for the printer you are working with. You can use the Document menu to perform the following actions on a particular print job:

- ✔ Pause
- ✔ Resume
- ✔ Restart
- ✔ Cancel

The Properties option under the Document menu allows you to view or change document specific settings for documents already in the print queue.

Adventures in moving print jobs from server to server

The exam may ask about transferring existing print jobs from one server to another. When would you want to perform this type of activity? If your printer fails for a hardware or networking reason, or some other issue that can't be corrected through software, you'll still need to be able to allow your users to print. For example, suppose you have a print device that suddenly stops producing output. You could tell all your users to redirect their print jobs to another similar printer, and then, after you correct the problem, instruct them to change the printer back to the original. Alternatively, you could make the redirection transparent and perform the change from the server end. To practice transferring print jobs, try Lab 12-2.

Lab 12-2   Transferring Print Jobs

1. Open the Printers folder.

2. Select the printer you want to redirect.

3. Choose Printer⇨Properties.

4. Click the Ports tab and then click the Add Port tab.

5. Select Local Port and then click the New Port button.

6. Enter the UNC path for the server and the Share Name of the printer to redirect the print jobs through, and then click OK.

7. Click Close and then click OK.

Additionally, if the print device that fails is part of a printer pool, simply deselect its port on the Ports tab; the printer pooling continues to distribute the print requests to the functioning print devices.

Diving in to printer pools

The exam most likely will include at least one question regarding printing pools. Know and understand the following definition: *Printer pooling* is associating multiple *print devices* (the physical machines that do the printing) with a single *printer* (the program acts as a go-between for the print devices and the operating system) — that's two or more print devices, only one printer. Don't confuse printer pooling with associating multiple NT printers to a single print device. You enable printer pooling from the Printer Properties Ports tab (refer to Figure 12-2) by activating the Enable Printer Pooling check box and selecting multiple ports in the port box.

To use printer pooling, the printers that you intend to use must meet two criteria:

 ✔ Can use a common print driver

 ✔ Are connected to the same print server

Ideally, from a network design standpoint, the print devices are also all located in close physical proximity. You don't want your users to have to wander around the building trying to find their print-outs.

On the other side of the spectrum, associating multiple printers with a single print device facilitates scheduling and priority assignments. This feature has no special name, but you certainly don't want to overlook it when you're preparing for the exam. Review the section on the Scheduling tab for more information.

Remote Printers

A *remote printer,* in contrast to a local printer, is any printer attached to a *different* computer on the network. Your computer forwards print requests to a printer share on a remote computer, which then spools the print job according to the local settings for the printer. Configuring and managing a remote printer on an NT client is identical to configuring and managing local printers.

Information on connecting to resources on a non-NT platform applies to printing in the same way it applies to file-sharing. Although I don't discuss connecting to resources such as NetWare printers and Macintosh printers, you should be aware that the process is the same as connecting to NetWare or Macintosh file resources. For example:

 ✔ To print to a NetWare Print Queue, you must first install Gateway Services for NetWare (GSNW) on your Windows NT Server.

 ✔ To print to Apple PostScript printers, you must first install the Services for Macintosh on your Windows NT Server.

Troubleshooting Print Problems

Troubleshooting questions on the Server exam usually focus on fixing printing problems for print jobs residing on a Windows NT Print Server. Print problems in the real world could, however, arise from any number of components in the printing process, such as:

> ✔ The application that submits the print request
>
> ✔ The client platform submitting the print request
>
> ✔ A print device's mechanical components
>
> ✔ The network configuration of a network interface print device

These issues are not a focus on the exam, and as such, I do not cover them in detail for this section. Most exam questions about printer troubleshooting concern the Spooler service.

Spooler service

If your printer produces documents intermittently or if you suddenly can't manage or delete documents in the print queue, but in either case your print device appears otherwise operational, the culprit may be the Spooler service. You need to know the two ways to stop and restart your spooler:

> ✔ From the Services Control Panel, select Spooler, click Stop and wait for the service to stop, and then click Start to restart the service.
>
> ✔ From the command line, you can issue the command NET STOP SPOOLER to stop the spooler service, and NET START SPOOLER to restart the service.

Just restarting your spooler often corrects your printing problems.

Resolving printing problems

If restarting the spooler doesn't fix your problems, check the following possible points of failure:

> ✔ Is the printer plugged in and powered up?
>
> ✔ Is the printer Online or Ready? If not, is it reporting an error condition?
>
> ✔ Are you using the proper type of cable for your printer connection? Is the cable attached securely at both ends?
>
> ✔ Do you have the latest version of the printer driver? Most manufacturers provide a Service and Support section on their Web sites where you can obtain updated device drivers.
>
> ✔ Are you printing to the correct printer port?
>
> ✔ Can you print a test page? If so, the application may be causing the print problem.
>
> ✔ Does the drive or partition you're spooling to have enough space? If not, you can use the Windows NT Registry to change the spooler location.

Prep Test

1 Your users have sent several jobs to the print server, but the print device hasn't printed out a single page. You enter the print queue, and discover that you cannot delete the print jobs. What must you do to correct this problem?

- A ○ Stop and restart the Spooler service.
- B ○ Manually delete the files in the spool folder.
- C ○ Create a new printer that points to the same print device, and drag and drop all of the jobs in the old print queue to the new print queue.
- D ○ Stop and restart the Server service.

2 Which option would you set in Printer Properties to make sure that large documents occupy a print device for the least amount of time?

- A ○ Start Printing Immediately
- B ○ Print Directly to Printer
- C ○ Print Spooled Documents First
- D ○ Start Printing After the Last Page is Spooled

3 You are adding an HP LaserJet 5 to your NT server. The printer uses an internal HP Network Interface Print Device to attach directly to your network. What must you do before you can see the HP port on your network?

- A ○ You only need to connect the printer to the network, and the NT browser service detects the network interface device automatically.
- B ○ You must install the included DLC print driver under the printer properties.
- C ○ You must install the DLC network protocol on your server.
- D ○ You cannot control a Hewlett-Packard Network Interface Print Device with NT.

4 You want to configure only one printer on your NT print server to handle print requests from UNIX, NT Server, NT Workstation, and Windows 95 clients. Your network uses TCP/IP as the only network protocol. What must you install on NT server to facilitate printing from all of these systems with a single printer?

- A ○ You must add the NWLink protocol.
- B ○ You must add the DLC printing service.
- C ○ You must add the Microsoft TCP/IP Printing service.
- D ○ You must add the Microsoft LPR Printing service.

5 You run a small domain with two user groups, Managers and Peons. Your boss asks you to make sure any documents that members of the Managers group submit will print before documents that members of the Peons group submit. Which of the following must you do to accomplish this task? (Choose all that apply.)

A ❏ Create a separate printer for users of the Managers group and configure the printer to start printing immediately.

B ❏ Create a separate printer for users of the Managers group and set the print priority to 1.

C ❏ Create a separate printer for the users of the Managers group and set the print priority to 99.

D ❏ Create a separate printer for users of the Peons group and set the print priority to 1.

E ❏ Create a separate printer for users of the Peons group and set the print priority to 99.

6 You have 25 users using Microsoft Windows NT Workstation, and 10 users using Microsoft Windows 95. All of these users print to the same print device attached to your NT Print Server. You download a new driver for this print device. What is the best way to update the driver for all of the clients that need to access this printer?

A ○ Update the print drivers on all client systems. You do not need to update the server, because it uses the client driver software.

B ○ Create a new printer under NT that uses the new driver and make all of the client computers print to the new printer.

C ○ Put the new driver in the NETLOGON share and add a command to the startup script for all users that updates the driver on the client systems.

D ○ Install both the NT and the 95 drivers on the NT Print Server and do nothing more.

7 A user in your Marketing department is trying to send a large print job to her local printer, but she has been unsuccessful. Her system has 64MB of RAM and a 1GB hard disk. She recently added an additional 1GB hard disk, because her first drive was nearing capacity. You suspect her system may not have enough space on the hard drive to successfully spool her print jobs. How can you change the location of the spool file folder to the newly added hard drive?

A ○ Set the Spool File Folder option under the printer's Spooler properties tab.

B ○ Set the Location property of the Spool File Folder under the Spooler Service properties in the Control Panel⇨Services window.

C ○ Modify the **HKEY_LOCAL_MACHINE\SYSTEM\CurrentControlSet\ Control\Print\Printers** Registry key.

D ○ Set the Spooler options to Start Printing After Last Page Is Spooled on the Scheduling tab.

8 What is the easiest way to switch a print device between PCL and PostScript modes?

A ○ Define multiple printers using different Separator pages.

B ○ Add a PCL driver and a PostScript driver under the Ports properties tab.

C ○ Set the Printing Format under the document properties option.

D ○ Set the printer to autodetect PCL job submissions.

9 You are creating a printing pool that includes two different print devices so that print jobs sent by users from the Accounting group can print on either device. Which of the following statements best describes a printing pool? (Choose all that apply.)

A ❑ All print devices must use the same type of printer port.

B ❑ All print devices must use TCP/IP Printing.

C ❑ All print devices must be able to use a common driver.

D ❑ You can direct certain print jobs to a specific print device in the printing pool without having to define a second printer.

E ❑ All print devices in the printing pool must be connected to the same print server.

10 You have defined the availability settings on the Scheduling properties tab of an NT printer to allow printing only between the hours of 1:00 A.M. and 7:30 A.M. Jeffrey in the IS department tries to print his resume at 11:00 A.M. so that he can have a fresh copy for his interview during lunch. Which of the following happens when Jeffrey submits his print job?

A ○ The printer does not accept the print job. Jeffrey has to wait until 1:00 A.M. and then resubmit the print request.

B ○ The printer accepts the print job, and the print server sends a message to Jeffrey's workstation notifying him that his print request will be handled during the hours of availability, 1:00 A.M. to 7:30 A.M.

C ○ The print spooler stores the job until the current time falls within the availability constraints, and then the job processes based on its priority as it relates to other print jobs in the spooler. Jeffrey does not receive notification of the delay from the print server.

D ○ An error is generated on the print server, because you should not send a print job to a printer during times marked as unavailable. You can view this error under the Applications log in the Event Viewer.

Answers

1 *A.* You must stop and restart the Spooler service. You can perform this task in two ways, either by choosing Control⇨Services, or by using the commands NET STOP SPOOLER and then NET START SPOOLER from the command line. You cannot drag and drop print jobs from one queue to another. *Review "Spooler service."*

2 *B.* The Print Directly to Printer option prevents delays while the print server waits for the client to render individual pages in a print job. *Review "Scheduling."*

3 *C.* The HP Network Interface Device requires that the DLC protocol be present on any system that needs to communicate with it directly. *Review "Network print devices."*

4 *C.* Adding the Microsoft TCP/IP printing service allows you to use the LPR utility to send print jobs from any TCP/IP printing client, such as the UNIX clients, to the IP address or hostname of your NT server. You must specify the host and the printer share name when sending your print requests through LPR. *Review "Using LPR."*

5 *C, D.* You set printer priority on the Scheduling tab for Printer Properties. The highest priority is 99 and the lowest is 1. *Review "Scheduling."*

6 *D.* NT and 95 clients automatically download the updated driver when they connect to the remote print server. *Review "Sharing."*

7 *C.* The Registry provides the only way to change the location of the spool file. You can use one of two included utilities to edit the Registry: Regedit or Regedt32. *Review "Print spooler."*

8 *A.* You can use separator pages to identify which print jobs belong to which users, but you also can use them to switch a printer between PCL and PostScript modes. The Separator Page files are located under the \WINNT\SYSTEM32 directory, and have an extension of *.SEP. *Review "General."*

9 *C, E.* To successfully implement a printing pool, all printers must be able to use a common driver and must be connected to the same print server. However, you can use different types of printer ports, such as one Local port (LPT1) and one Network port. When implementing a printing pool, all print devices act as a single physical unit, and you cannot direct a print job to a specific device without creating an additional NT printer. *Review "Diving in to printer pools."*

10 *C.* The availability settings affect when a print spooler can forward its print jobs to a print device. The process is automatic, and transparent to the user. A user does not get a message if they send a print request during a time when the printer is not marked as available. *Review "Scheduling."*

Chapter 13

User Accounts

Exam Objectives

▶ Understanding permissions

▶ Planning and setting account policies

▶ Understanding user rights

▶ Working with shares

▶ Creating and managing user accounts

▶ Working with logon scripts

▶ Creating profiles

*T*he heart of Windows NT Server is the idea of a single logon for access to all resources in the domain. To accomplish this simple goal, you must create a database of user accounts and distribute it to all domain controllers. The exam draws on many questions dealing with:

- ✔ User accounts
- ✔ Policies
- ✔ Rights
- ✔ Profiles

You must understand how to perform all tasks pertaining to users. In this chapter, I explain what you need to know.

Quick Assessment

Working with Logon Scripts

1 Network resources are connected at logon by using a _____.

Creating and Managing User Accounts

2 _____ is the primary tool for managing user accounts.

3 By default, Windows NT Server creates the _____ and _____ user accounts.

Planning and Setting Account Policies

4 You set minimum password length by using the _____ dialog box.

5 What objects can you audit in Windows NT?

Understanding Permissions

6 You assign local file access permissions the _____ permissive access.

7 You assign share access permissions the _____ permissive access.

Working with Shares

8 You use the _____ Manager to set up shares.

Creating Profiles

9 You can control the user environment via the _____ dialog box.

Creating User Profiles

10 A user's default folder is known as the _____ directory.

Answers

1   *Logon script.* Review "Editing user profiles: I'm okay, you're okay."

2   *User Manager for Domains.* Review "Managing User Accounts."

3   *Administrator; Guest.* Review "Administrator and Guest accounts."

4   *Account Policy.* Review "Policy planning."

5   *Files, folders, printers.* Review "Policy planning."

6   *Most.* Review "Security planning."

7   *Least.* Review "Security planning."

8   *Server.* Review "Policy planning."

9   *Mandatory Profile.* Review "Profiles."

10   *Home.* Review "Editing user profiles: I'm okay, you're okay."

Planning

A good plan almost always saves countless hours of retracing steps and cleaning up, whatever you try to do, but especially when you deal with user accounts and all that goes with them. You want to plan your user accounts database so that you can quickly and easily perform the following chores:

- ✔ Add user accounts
- ✔ Make changes to user accounts,
- ✔ Delete user accounts
- ✔ Build default templates
- ✔ Use scripts to batch user-related jobs

Remember, the user accounts database is the foundation of all access. Plan ahead and you can have an efficient and useful resource. Don't plan, and your professional life can become a living hell. This chapter offers a few tips on planning your user accounts. The exam asks questions about user accounts and all the properties associated with them. I go over all of them in this chapter.

Naming conventions

As long as usernames are unique and fall within a few other restrictions (see "Creating user accounts" later in this chapter), Windows NT is satisfied. A free form style is fine in small domains where you know everyone and can remember their usernames, but in larger, more spread-out domain structures, you need a *naming convention* to help identify users. There are as many naming styles as there are "experts." Just choose one that works for your situation and stick to it.

Consider other resources in the domain and what clients are connecting to the server. If you have MS-DOS or Windows 3.*x* clients, for example, you want to keep usernames to eight characters or less, so that you can assign the same name for the username and the user's home directory. Usernames that approach the 20-character limit require tons of typing and are a nuisance to users.

The exam uses several different naming conventions to illustrate a situation. Don't let a change in user naming throw you. Unless the question is about a specific naming convention or a username's correctness, don't worry too much about it.

Some common naming conventions:

- ✔ **First name plus last initial:** For example, KenM and SandraB. If you have duplicates, you can add numbers to the end (for example, KenM1 and SandraB2) or additional letters (for example, KenMaj or SandraBar).

- ✔ **First name plus a number:** For example, Mary2367 and Dave307. This scheme can annoy everyone if the numbers don't have some significance; you want to use something like a phone extension or employee number.

- ✔ **First initial and last name:** For example, Msmith. If you have multiple Msmiths, say you have a Mark Smith and a Melissa Smith, you can add numbers or extra letters; for example, MaSmith and MeSmith or Msmith1 and Msmith2.

It doesn't matter what naming convention you use, just so it accommodates all current users and lets you integrate future users.

Security planning

Planning a naming convention is important, but planning a security scheme is even more important. You want users to have access to all the files and folders they need for doing their jobs, but you also need to protect data from unauthorized access.

In Windows NT, you can set access permissions on every file, folder, and resource in the enterprise. Use NT Explorer to control the database of user accounts and the groups to which they belong.

Although you can grant or deny individual users access to specific resources, keeping up with changes quickly becomes a management burden if you have to individually grant and deny users access to every specific file and folder they need to do their jobs. That's a burden if you have to do it for just one user, let alone all of them. What you have to do is arrange users into groups and grant access based on group membership — plan, plan, plan.

The exam has many questions pertaining to group membership and access to specific files and folders. I find that writing out the groupings and then figuring the cumulative access permissions helps me keep everything straight. You can use the same method on the test to avoid getting confused and make the answer clearer.

File system permissions

You can set file system permissions on each file and folder on the server. In Chapter 2, I discuss the file and folder permissions that you can set. The key point to remember about file and folder permissions concerning user accounts management is that you should grant access based on group membership.

Conflicting permissions

Permissions usually are *cumulative,* in that users are granted the most permissive access. That is, a user who has more than one group membership may end up with unnecessary access to a particular set of files. It can happen both with share permissions and NTFS permissions. For example: A user belongs to both Cats and Dogs, and Cats have permissions to cat food files and Dogs have permissions to dog food files. No problem at this point, but members of Cats have permissions to Furniture, but members of Dogs don't. Now, the member of both Cats and Dogs has access to Furniture even though they're Dogs.

The only exception is the No Access permission. If a user is a member of a group that you have assigned the No Access permission, they simply have no access.

Both share and NTFS permissions apply for remote users, and the most restrictive permissions take precedence. Only NTFS permissions apply for local users and the least restrictive permissions take precedence. The default NTFS permission is always Full Control, and you should restrict access to the local system to Administrators and the various Operators groups. By setting access permissions on the server's shares to allow access only to the desired groups, applying the *most* restrictive permissions enforces the correct security.

Choosing permissions

You assign permissions by using the Security tab in the properties box. You can bring up the properties box by right-clicking the file or folder.

The default NTFS permissions on files and folders is the Full Access permission. Most users use the network to connect to the server, so you're better off setting permissions on the shared folders.

You should limit local access to the server to only those users who must perform administrative tasks.

Policy planning

You must make a variety of policy decisions for users in Windows NT Server, ranging from the times a user can log on to the length of their password. You can use *policies* to control:

- ✔ Desktop settings
- ✔ Screen savers
- ✔ Configuration settings

Because these policies apply to all users or groups of users, you want to be sure to plan a policy that works for each group.

Various exam questions cover all types of policies. You get exhibits, normally a screen shot of the utility being used for the scenario, with most of these questions. You need to understand the action of all the switches and fields of the different policy tools.

User Manager is your tool for setting:

- ✔ Account policies
- ✔ Audit policies
- ✔ User rights

To create and edit system policies, you use the Policy Editor. You set file and folder auditing and sharing via the file or folder's properties box.

Account policies

Account policies deal with passwords. Several questions on the exam relate to this area. You need to be familiar with all the options in the Account Policy dialog box (see Figure 13-1):

- ✔ **Maximum Password Age:** Sets the maximum amount of time a user's password can remain the same before the user must change it.

- ✔ **Minimum Password Age:** Sets the minimum time a user must use a password before changing it. This setting prevents a user from immediately turning around and changing a newly forced new password back to the old password.

- ✔ **Minimum Password Length:** Sets the minimum number of characters a password must contain. You should require at least six to eight characters; short passwords are easy to guess.

- ✔ **Password Uniqueness:** Specifies a minimum number of passwords a user must choose before reusing an old favorite. A value here requires a value in the Minimum Password Age block.

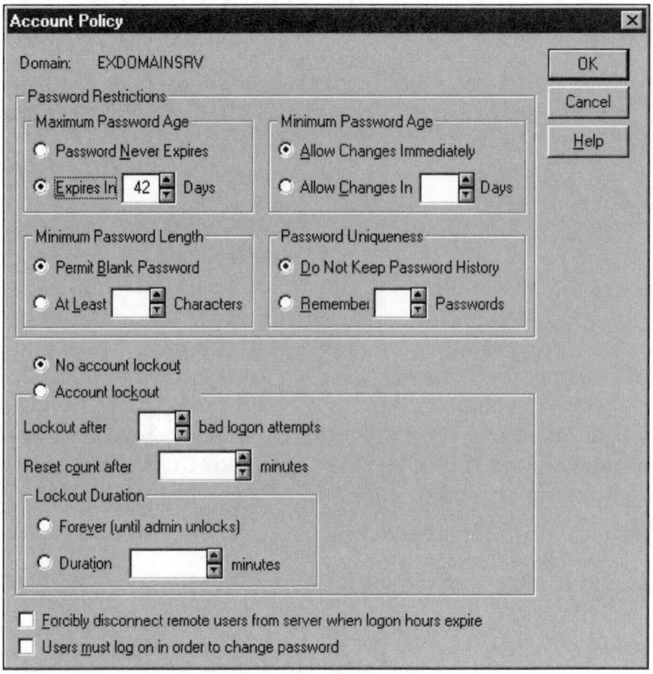

Figure 13-1:
The
Account
Policy
dialog box.

The remaining areas in the Account Policy dialog box deal with account lockout. Enabling the Account Lockout option is a good way to foil hackers attempting to log in by repeatedly trying to guess user passwords.

- ✔ **Lockout After:** Sets the number of failed login attempts a user can make before being locked out.

- ✔ **Reset Count After:** Sets the number of minutes the system waits after a bad set of login attempts before resetting the count. If a user uses up all of his attempts without successfully logging in, the account remains locked out until an administrator releases it.

- ✔ **Lockout Duration:** Sets the amount of time a user's account remains locked out before the system releases it. Using this option can save you many calls.

Additional policy control is available via the two check boxes at the bottom of the Account Policy dialog box. The first option, Forcibly Disconnect Remote Users from Server When Logon Hours Expire, is really a suboption of the Logon Hours setting, which specifies a range of hours during which a user can log in (see "Creating User Accounts" later in this chapter for information on the Logon Hours dialog box and creating new users). Setting this check box option forces users to log out when they reach the end of their assigned time range; otherwise, they can remain logged on as long as they want, even beyond the specific Logon Hours time range setting. This option affects Windows NT users only.

If you enable the second check box option, Users Must Log On in Order to Change Password, users must log in to the system before they can change their password. That way, when a user's password expires, the user can't change the password without your help.

The exam asks both general knowledge and scenario type questions that test your knowledge of the account policies. Many of these questions include exhibits of the Account Policy dialog box. If you know the different options here, you should be fine.

User rights

Users must be able to log in and get to resources they need. What users can or cannot do depends on what rights and permissions you grant them. Rights and permissions are not exactly the same thing. *Rights* generally apply to the system as a whole, whereas a *permission* is the access a user or group has to specific files or folders.

You set rights via the User Manager for Domains. The ability to back up files or to log on to a server are rights that you can give or take away. You can assign rights to individual users, but arranging users into groups and then assigning rights per group is a far more efficient strategy.

User rights basically fall in one of two categories: regular or advanced. Figure 13-2 shows the User Rights Policy dialog box. This is where you can assign rights to users or groups. *Regular rights* are the rights that most commonly affect what users are permitted to do. The built-in groups in Windows NT Server have whole sets of user rights assigned to allow them to perform their designated tasks. (I discuss NT Server's built-in user rights in Chapter 15.) You rarely need to edit these rights. The regular rights deal primarily with what a user can do to the system. Table 13-1 lists regular user rights.

Figure 13-2:
The User
Rights
Policy
dialog box.

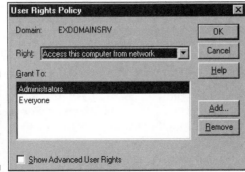

Table 13-1	Regular User Rights	
Regular Right	*Definition*	*Default Assignment*
Access this computer from the Network	Allows user to log on to this computer through the network.	Administrators, Everyone
Add workstations to domain	Allows a user to create computer accounts in the domain.	None
Backup files and directories	Grants a user the right to back up all files on this computer.	Administrators, Backup Operators, Server Operators
Change the system time	Allows a user to set the computer's time clock.	Administrators, Server Operators
Load and unload device drivers	Permits a user to install and remove device drivers on this computer.	Administrators
Log on locally	Allows a user to log on to the server.	Administrators, Backup Operators, Server Operators, Account Operators, Print Operators
Manage auditing and security log	Permits a user to manage the auditing policy.	Administrators
Restore files and directories	Permits a user to restore files and folders. Supersedes any permission restrictions.	Administrators, Backup Operators, Server Operators
Shut down the system	Allows a user to shut down a server.	Administrators, Backup Operators, Server Operators, Account Operators, Print Operators
Take ownership of files or other objects	Allows a user to take ownership of object owned by other users.	Administrators

Advanced rights apply more to programmers and applications than to users. Here are the two main ones you need to know:

- ✔ **Bypass Traverse Checking:** Allows a user to pass through a folder they do not have permission to access. They cannot change or read anything, they can only pass through to the subfolder.

✔ **Log on as a Service:** Permits a user account to log on as a service. Service accounts use this right. Examples of service accounts are the user accounts created to run the Replicator service.

You may get a question on the exam about a user who can access files and folders via the network and can log on from a workstation but cannot log on at the server. The question asks you what to do to allow the user to log on to the server at the console. You need to set the user right Log on Locally for this user.

Audit policy

You use the Audit Policy dialog box, shown in Figure 13-3, to set the basic audit policy for the server. You cannot extend it beyond what you can set in this dialog box, but you can refine the policy to audit specific files, folders, and printers.

Figure 13-3:
The Audit
Policy
dialog box.

Audit Policy			
Domain: EXDOMAINSRV			OK
○ Do Not Audit			Cancel
◉ Audit These Events:			Help
	Success	Failure	
Logon and Logoff	☐	☐	
File and Object Access	☐	☐	
Use of User Rights	☐	☐	
User and Group Management	☐	☐	
Security Policy Changes	☐	☐	
Restart, Shutdown, and System	☐	☐	
Process Tracking	☐	☐	

Auditing is a useful tool to log access to specific resources on your Windows NT server. Lab 13-1 steps you through setting up auditing. As you proceed, pay particular attention to what you can audit and why you might want to keep track of them. Try turning auditing on and off on various things, then access the audited item. Check the event log to see if you have been audited.

Lab 13-1   Setting Up Auditing

1. **Open User Manager for Domains.**

2. **Choose Policies⇨Audit.**

3. **Click Audit These Events and then select the event you want to audit on success or failure.**

   An entry is made in the event log each time the audited event occurs.

4. **Click OK.**

You set up file and folder auditing via the Properties dialog box for the individual file or folder. Figure 13-4 shows the Directory Auditing dialog box. To practice the process, try Lab 13-2.

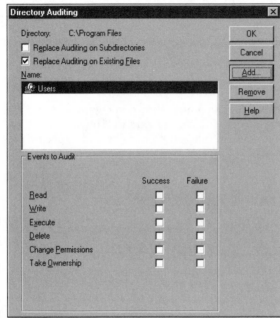

Figure 13-4:
The
Directory
Auditing
dialog box.

Lab 13-2   Setting Up File or Folder Auditing

1. **Right-click the file or folder you want to audit.**

2. **On the Security tab, click Auditing.**

3. **Select the user whose files or folders you want to audit.**

4. **Click Add.**

   The Add Users and Groups dialog box opens, as shown in Figure 13-5.

5. **Select the users or groups whose use of the files or folders you want to audit.**

6. **Click Add until you have all the names you want listed in the Add Names box and then click OK.**

7. **Select the events you want to audit and click OK to save the information.**

You can audit printers in much the same way as you audit files and folders, only you use the Printer Auditing dialog box, shown in Figure 13-6. Lab 13-3 illlustrates the process.

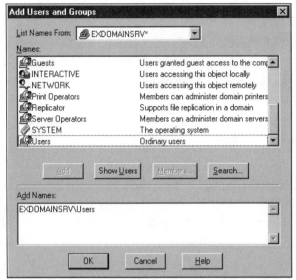

Figure 13-5:
The Add
Users and
Groups
dialog box.

Figure 13-6:
The Printer
Auditing
dialog box.

| Lab 13-3 | Starting the Auditing of a Printer |

1. **Right-click and select Properties.**

   The printer's properties box opens.

2. **On the Security tab, select Auditing.**

3. **Click Add.**

   The Add Users dialog box opens.

4. **Select the users or groups whose use of the files or folders you want to audit.**

5. **Click Add until you have all the names you want listed in the Add Names box and then click OK.**

6. **Select the events you want to audit.**

7. **Click OK to save the information.**

System policies

System policies control user environments and actions. To establish system policies, you use the System Policy Editor (located in the Administrative Tools folder: choose Start⇨Programs⇨Administrative Tools), shown in Figure 13-7.

Figure 13-7:
The System
Policy
Editor.

The System Policy Editor enables you to specify what programs are available in the users' Control Panel, specify network settings, control network access, customize user desktops, and set the Start menu program options.

You can set a default system policy for all users, computers, groups or individual users. Setting up policies modifies corresponding Registry settings in the HKEY_LOCAL_MACHINE and HKEY_CURRENT_USER hives.

To define a system policy as the default policy, you must save the policy in the \winnt\system32\Repl\Imoprt\Scripts folder, with the filename of NTCONFIG.POL. Windows NT shares this path by default as NETLOGON$. After replication commences, the PDC copies the default system policy to all BDCs in the domain.

If you define a system policy, you must choose between two modes: Registry mode and Policy File mode. To choose a mode:

1. Select the File menu in the System Policy Editor.

2. Choose either Open Policy or Open Registry.

   Open Policy lets you edit an existing policy. Open Registry leads you to the Registry hives, HKEY_LOCAL_MACHINE and HKEY_LOCAL_USER.

3. Make your changes and then save them.

Share planning

The primary method for connecting to Windows NT Server to utilize resources is through a share. A share plan is necessary so that users from different groups can use the files, folders, and printers to do their jobs.

You can share a folder under many different names at the same time and different groups can have a different set of permissions under each share name. The process for creating a share is easy, as I demonstrate in Lab 13-4.

Lab 13-4   Creating a Share

1. **Using Windows NT Explorer or My Computer, select the folder or resource you want to share.**

2. **Right-click the directory or resource and then select Sharing from the drop-down menu.**

   By default, folders are not shared.

3. **Click the Share As button.**

   A dialog box pops up and Windows NT displays a default share name (normally the first eight characters of the folder name).

You cannot access share names longer than eight characters from DOS-based clients.

You also can use the Sharing tab to limit access to the share to a maximum number of users; it's a good way to lessen the load on slower servers.

After creating the share, you can use the Permissions option on the Security tab to assign permissions to the share. By default, share permissions are set to Full Control, for Everyone.

A number of administrative shares are hidden from users but accessible to administrators. You can recognize these shares by the dollar sign ($) appended to their names. Table 13-2 shows the default administrative shares. You need to know the respective purposes of these shares.

Table 13-2	Default Administrative Shares
Share Name	*Description*
Admin$	The folder in which Windows NT is installed, and that you use to administer NT remotely.
Driveletter$	The letter of the drive on which a storage device is installed. Members of the Administrators, Backup Operators, and Server Operators groups can access this drive remotely.
NETLOGON$	The share that the logon server uses, set by default to %SystemRoot%\system32\Repl\Import. The NETLOGON service uses this share for processing domain requests.
Print$	Used for management and support of shared printers.
Repl$	The shared Export folder, used for replication, set by default to %SystemRoot%\system32\Repl\Export.

You also can use the Server Manager, shown in Figure 13-8, to set up and manage shares. To use Server Manager to monitor a share:

1. Launch Server Manager.

2. Highlight the desired machine and choose Computer➪Properties.

3. Select one of the following radio buttons:

   • **Users:** Use this option to see the number of users connected to the resource.

   • **Shares:** Use this option to see all of the shares on the domain, the number of users accessing shared resources, and the name of the resource being shared.

   • **In Use:** Use this option to see all the open resources on the domain, the users that have those resources open, the type of operation taking place on the resource, the number of locks on the resource, and the path for the open resources.

   • **Alerts:** Use this option if you want to build a list of all NT-based computers that you want to receive administrative alerts.

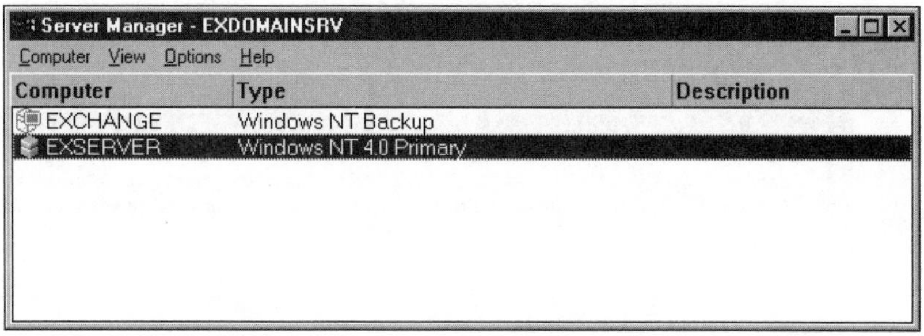

Figure 13-8:
The Server
Manager.

To use the Server Manager to create a share, perform the steps in Lab 13-5.

Lab 13-5	Creating a Share with Server Manager

1. **Launch Server Manager.**
2. **Highlight the server on which you want to create a share.**
3. **Choose Computers⇨Shared Directories.**
4. **Click the New Share button and enter the share name and path.**
5. **Click OK.**

Managing User Accounts

In most network operating systems, administrators manage users per user, which is cumbersome and administratively tasking. Windows NT Server offers the User Manager for Domains for user management. The User Manager, shown in Figure 13-9, is the primary access tool for administering users and groups.

Windows NT employs a group administration philosophy; that is, it subscribes to the notion that placing users into groups and assigning rights and permissions to the group is much easier than administering users individually. When you assign a user to a group, the user inherits all the rights and access permissions of that group. I discuss group management further in Chapter 14.

In this section, I tell you all about what you need to know about managing user accounts to pass the exam. You may want to go over this section carefully to make sure you understand everything. The exam tests you in many situations about user management.

User Manager - EXDOMAINSRV		_ □ ×

User   View   Policies   Options   Exchange   Help

Username	Full Name	Description
Administrator		Built-in account for administering the computer/domain
Exchange Service	Exchange Service Accour	
Guest		Built-in account for guest access to the computer/domain
IUSR_EXCHANGE	Internet Guest Account	Internet Server Anonymous Access
Test User	Test User	

Groups	Description
Account Operators	Members can administer domain user and group accounts
Administrators	Members can fully administer the computer/domain
Backup Operators	Members can bypass file security to back up files
Domain Admins	Designated administrators of the domain
Domain Guests	All domain guests
Domain Users	All domain users
Guests	Users granted guest access to the computer/domain
Print Operators	Members can administer domain printers
Replicator	Supports file replication in a domain
Server Operators	Members can administer domain servers
Users	Ordinary users

Figure 13-9:
The User
Manager.

Networked and local users

Windows NT Server can support two types of user accounts: local user accounts and domain user accounts.

Local user accounts can access the server from the local keyboard. Windows NT has two built-in default local user accounts: the Administrator account and Guest accounts. A local user account applies only to the machine the account is located in.

Domain user accounts belong to users on the network. These are the accounts that the domain controllers manage. All access permissions are based on this central database of user accounts. Only the PDC and BDCs hold a copy of this database.

The From box in the Login dialog box is the key to knowing which account database is being used for user log on; that is, whether the user is logging on locally or into the domain. If the From box contains the name of the specific server, you know that the local account database is being used; that is, that the user's logging on locally. If the From box contains the domain name, you know that the account database is being used; that is, that the user's logging on into the domain.

The exam could ask about the default user accounts on a Windows NT Server. The only two accounts on a Windows NT member server by default are the Administrator and Guest accounts. The Guest account is disabled by default. You should not create any more local accounts on a member server. Use the domain account database instead.

Administrator and Guest accounts

The Administrator account is the primary local account for a Windows NT computer. The Administrator account grants complete access to all

- ✔ Files
- ✔ Folders
- ✔ Resources
- ✔ Administrative functions on the local server

You cannot delete this account, but you can rename it.

The Guest account is the other default account on a Windows NT system. This account has Guest permissions (meaning, it doesn't have any special privileges) by default. The Guest account cannot perform any administrative functions. It is disabled by default, and you should leave it that way.

Virtually without exception, the Administrator and Guest accounts are the only local accounts you should ever have on a Windows NT Server. All other accounts should be domain accounts. You can grant all administrative user rights and permissions for the local server to a domain user account.

Creating user accounts

When you add a user account, you must provide a username (you can make it as long as 20 characters). It must be unique to the domain or computer that you're administering. The name can contain any uppercase or lower-case characters except the following:

```
"  /  \  [  ]  :  ;  |  =  ,  +  *  ?  <  >
```

A username cannot consist solely of periods (.) and spaces.

To create a new user account in User Manager, perform the following:

1. Open User Manager, then choose User⇨New User.
2. Complete the New User dialog box (shown in Figure 13-10). Fill in the Username, Full Name, Description, Password, and Confirm Password fields.
3. Enable the check box options that apply to your goals for the user account.

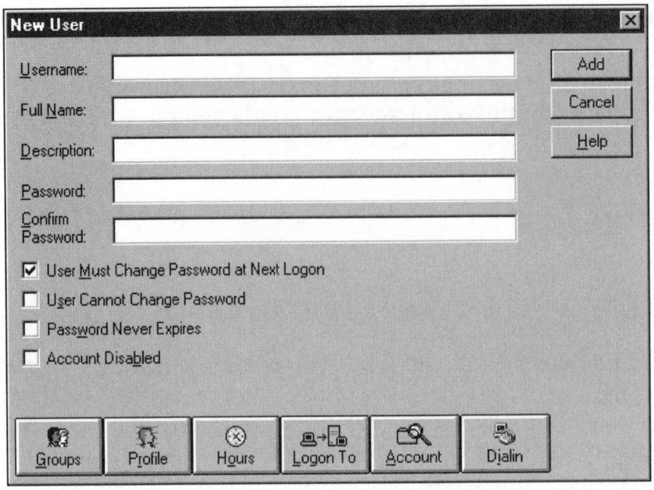

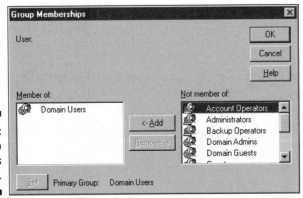

Figure 13-10:
The New
User dialog
box.

You should know when you need to use the six button options at the bottom
of the New User dialog box. You use these options to govern many of the
user's capabilities:

- **Groups:** This option (Figure 13-11 shows the Group Memberships
  dialog box) enables you to add a user to, or remove a user from, one or
  more groups.

- **Profile:** This option allows you to define a user's profile, logon script,
  and home directory.

- **Hours:** This option (Figure 13-12 shows the Logon Hours dialog box)
  allows you to set the times during which a user can log on to the network.
  By default, a user has 24-hour access to the network. If a user is logged
  on at the end of a restricted time period, the user may remain logged
  on; however, the user cannot log on outside of the allowed time range.

Figure 13-11:
The Group
Memberships
dialog box.

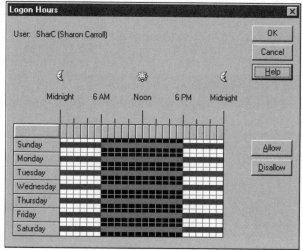

Figure 13-12:
The Logon
Hours dialog
box.

You also can specify that a user be forcibly logged off at the specified
time, using a check box setting in the Account Policies dialog box (see
"Account Policies" earlier in this chapter).

✔ **Logon To:** This option enables you to restrict a user to one or more
specific computers in the domain. By default, a user can use all workstations, as shown in Figure 13-13.

✔ **Account:** This option (Figure 13-14 shows the Account Information
dialog box) lets you set the length of time an account is active, a good
setting to use for temporary employees and contractors. The default is
Never. You also can assign an account as Local or Global.

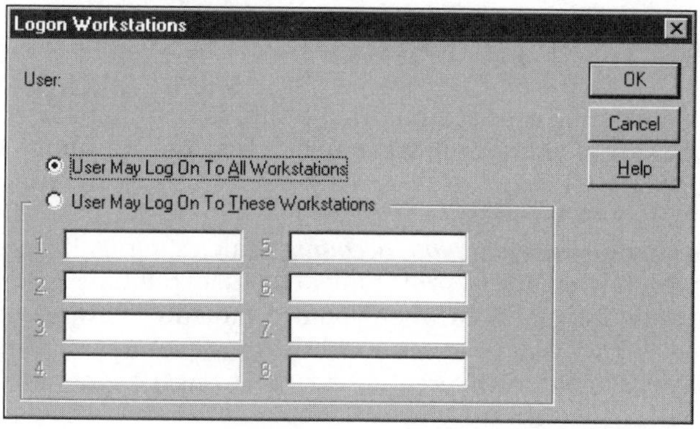

Figure 13-13:
The Logon
Workstations
dialog box.

✔ **Dialin:** This option (Figure 13-15 shows the Dialin Information dialog box) enables you to establish a user's right to dial in to the network. It also lets you establish callback security if necessary.

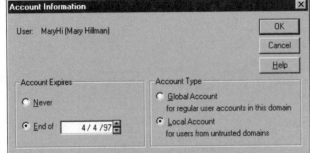

Figure 13-14: The Account Information dialog box.

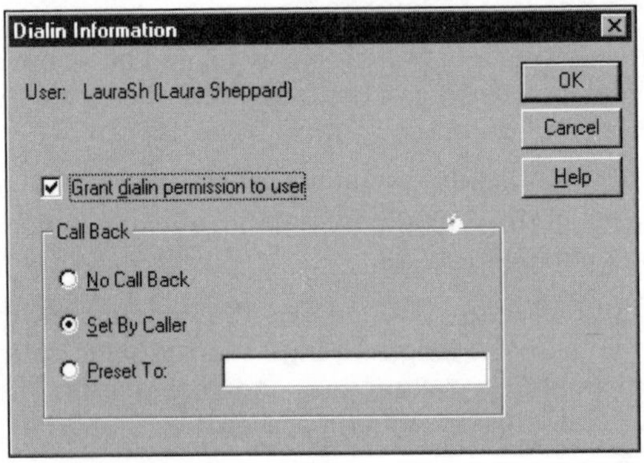

Figure 13-15: The Dialin Information dialog box.

Copying user accounts

If you have an existing user account that's substantially similar to a new account you want to create, you can copy the existing account and modify it as necessary.

Many administrators use *template accounts,* which are regular user accounts that are disabled. You build a prototypical user account for each type of user on the network, and then when you need to add a new user of that type, you just copy the account and add the new user name. Template accounts save tons of time in creating many new user accounts.

At least one question asks what is copied when you copy a user account. When you copy a user account, the copy contains all the information from the original except these three components:

- ✔ Username
- ✔ Full name
- ✔ Password

The fastest way to create a few users is to use the Administrative wizards, found in the Administrative Tools program group.

Lab 13-6 shows you how to copy a user account. This method is handy when using user templates. Notice which settings are copied and which ones are not.

Lab 13-6	Copying a User Account

1. **Open User Manager for Domains.**

2. **Select the user account you want to copy.**

3. **Choose User⇨Copy.**

4. **Type in the new information and make any necessary modifications to the Groups, Hours, Logon To, Profile, and Dialin settings, and then click Add.**

Disabling and deleting user accounts

Disabling a user account and deleting a user account may sound fundamentally the same, but these tasks are in fact quite different. The main similarity between disabling and deleting a user account is that either action prevents a user from logging on.

When you disable an account, the user can't log on, but the account is still alive. You can still view it, along with all the other enabled and disabled accounts, in the User Manager for Domains window, and you can re-enable it at any time. When you delete a user account, however, it's dead — it's gone, and it's never coming back.

When you create a user account, NT assigns that user a unique Security Identifier (SID). Internal processes in Windows NT Server refer to a user account's SID rather than its username. If you delete a user account that has Read access to a certain shared directory and then create another user account with the same username, the new account doesn't have access to the directory; you still have to reapply permissions to the shared directory.

Lab 13-7 shows you the two processes for disabling and deleting a user account. Notice that a disabled account still shows up in the User Manager for Domains user account list.

Lab 13-7	Disabling and Deleting User Accounts

Disabling a User Account

1. **Open User Manager for Domains.**

2. **Select the user account you want to disable.**

3. **Click the Account Disabled check box.**

4. **Choose OK.**

Deleting a User Account

1. **Open User Manager for Domains.**

2. **Select the user account you want to delete.**

3. **Choose User⇨Delete.**

4. **When NT prompts you with the warning confirmation box, select Yes.**

Renaming user accounts

When a new user replaces an existing one, renaming the existing account is easier than creating a new one. Only the username changes; the user's SID doesn't change, so all group memberships and access permissions remain.

You may get a question on the test about how a new user is taking over for another one. The old user has individual access privileges set all over the place. The question is "How do you give the new user the same access privileges as the old one?" The answer is "Rename the old user account for the new user and change the password."

Editing user profiles: I'm okay, you're okay

You define the specific properties of a user's working environment in the User Environment Profile dialog box.

The user profile contains the desktop and program settings for a user. The *user profile path* is the network path to the user's profile folder in the UNC form of the \\servername\profiles folder. A *logon script* is a batch file that runs when a user logs on to the network. The *home directory* is the user's default directory for opening and saving files (and can reside on either a server or a workstation).

Logon scripts

A *logon script* is simply a batch file that runs when a user logs on to the network. You can assign a single logon script to many users. You define the name and location of a user's logon script in the Profile window of the user's account. By default, logon scripts are stored on the PDC in the following folder:

```
%WINROOT%\system32\Repl\Import\Scripts
```

To ensure that the Replicator service distributes the logon scripts to all the domain controllers, you must place them on the PDC, in the following folder:

```
%WINROOT%\system32\Repl\Export\Scripts
```

Because logon scripts are batch files, you can use variables in them. Table 13-3 lists the variables that you can use in logon scripts.

Table 13-3	Variables Available for Logon Scripts
Variable	*Description*
%HOMEDRIVE%	The user's local workstation drive letter that is associated with the user's home drive.
%HOMEPATH%	Full path of the user's home directory.
%HOMESHARE%	The share name that contains the user's home directory.
%OS%	The user's operating system.
%PROCESSOR_ARCHITECTURE%	Processor type of the user's workstation.
%PROCESSOR_LEVEL%	Processor level of the user's workstation.
%USERDOMAIN%	Domain where the user's account is defined.
%USERNAME%	Account username.

To assign a logon script to a user, follow the steps in Lab 13-8. Pay attention to the dialog boxes.

Lab 13-8   Assigning a Login Script

1. **Open User Manager for Domains.**

2. **Double-click the user's account name.**

3. **In the User Properties dialog box, click Profile.**

4. **In the User Environment Profile dialog box, type the name of the logon script batch file in the Logon Script Name text box.**

5. **Click OK once to close the User Environment Profile dialog box, click OK again to close the User Properties dialog box, and then close the User Manager.**

Home directories

Each user on the network must have a home directory, usually located on a server. This directory can contain the user's personal files as well as certain user-specific files, as designated by the administrator. Users have control over their own home directories.

You can assign home directories to a user's local hard drive. That's fine to do, too, as long as the user always logs on from the same location. If a user must have access to their home directory from any client, you must put the home directory on the server and make it accessible via all clients. You may see questions with both scenarios.

You also may get a question about assigning a home directory with a user template. Substituting *%username%* at the end of the path to the home directory creates a folder that has the same name as the user's username. This technique is good for building user templates.

Assigning a networked home directory is shown in Lab 13-9. This is how a user can have the same home directory from any workstation.

Lab 13-9   Assigning a Home Directory

1. **Open User Manager for Domains.**

2. **Select the account to which you want to assign a home directory.**

3. **Choose User⇨Properties.**

4. **Click Profile.**

    The User Environment Profile dialog box opens.

5. **Under Home Directory, select either Local Path or Connect.**

    For a Local drive, you only need to type the path in the Local Path text box. For a server based home directory, select a drive letter and then type the path in the To text box.

6. **Click OK.**

Profiles

When a user logs on to their workstation for the first time, Windows NT creates a profile by recording any changes made to the profile during that session and storing them in that person's local user profile. Those settings are specific to that workstation. You can set up a *roaming profile* for the user so that their setting travels with them. Lab 13-10 gives you the details for creating a roaming profile.

Lab 13-10 Creating a Roaming Profile

1. Copy the user's profile from their workstation to a shared network path.

2. Open the Control Panel and double-click the System icon.

3. Select the user's profile entry, select Copy To, and type the full UNC pathname, including the server where the profile will reside.

4. In the User Profile dialog box, enter the full UNC pathname for the profile in the User Profile Path field.

You also can use *mandatory profiles* to force users to maintain settings. Lab 13-11 shows you how to create a mandatory profile.

Lab 13-11 Creating a Mandatory Profile

1. Establish a roaming profile for a user.

2. Copy that profile to a shared directory.

3. Assigning the appropriate users to the profile.

4. Change the name of the Ntuser.dat file to Ntuser.man.

5. Enter the profile path into the User Profile Path dialog box in the User Environment Profile screen for each user.

If the PDC is unavailable at logon, the user cannot receive the mandatory profile. If that happens, Windows NT uses the user's last locally cached profile or the default profile assigned to the workstation. NT uses the locally cached profile if the user has successfully logged on to the domain in the past. If the user has never logged on before, it uses the default profile.

Prep Test

1 Joe is leaving the company and they're replacing him with Sandy. What's the best way to give Sandy access to Joe's old resources?

A ○ Use Joe's account as a template account for creating an account for Sandy; then delete Joe's account.

B ○ Rename Joe's account in User Manager and tell Sandy to change the password when she logs on the first time.

C ○ Use Sandy's account as a template account for creating an account for Joe; then tell Joe to change his password the next time he logs on.

D ○ Use Joe's account as a template account for creating an account for Sandy; then disable Joe's account.

2 You have written a new logon script for all users in the domain. Which of the following has nothing to do with implementing the new script?

A ○ Save the new script in the \Winnt\System32\Repl\Export\Scripts folder on the PDC.

B ○ Set the Logon Script name in the User Environment Profile for the selected users.

C ○ Configure replication on all Windows NT Server domain controllers.

D ○ Save the new script in the \Winnt\System32\Repl\Import\Scripts folder on the PDC.

3 Which of the following tools is the best one to use to create a new shared directory on a domain server from your Windows NT Workstation computer?

A ○ User Manager for Domains

B ○ Server Manager

C ○ Windows Explorer

D ○ Share Manager

4 You want to force all Accounting users to use the same profile; you don't want them messing around with individual desktop settings. You would assign which of the following filenames in the User Profile Path box?

A ○ Ntuser.dat

B ○ Ntuser.man

C ○ Ntuser.usr

D ○ Ntuser.pol

5 BobA has no problem logging on to the network at his desk, but when he tries to log on at the Windows NT Server, he receives an access denied error. A possible cause could be:

A ○ BobA does not have the Log on Locally user right set.

B ○ BobA's account has been locked out.

C ○ BobA needs to change his password.

D ○ BobA is not a Power User.

6 SandyB tries to change her password. She receives a message that her new password isn't long enough. You use which of the following tools to set password length?

A ○ User Manager for Domains

B ○ Password Manager

C ○ Account Policy

D ○ Policy Editor

7 Someone has been using the printer excessively. To find out who, you should try which of the following tactics?

A ○ Turn on Auditing on the printer.

B ○ Turn on Security passwords for printing resources.

C ○ Set No Access permissions on the printer.

D ○ Use a system policy to limit access to the printer to only managers.

8 Which Registry hives do you affect when you use system policies? (Select two.)

A ❑ HKEY_LOCAL_MACHINE

B ❑ HKEY_CLASSES_ROOT

C ❑ HKEY_CURRENT_USER

D ❑ HKEY_LOCAL_USER

9 Which of the following is a valid username for a Windows NT user?

A ○ Sandra B Majors

B ○ Sandra;B;Majors

C ○ Sandra,B,Majors

D ○ Sandra*B*Majors

10 At 5:00 P.M., KeithM's computer suddenly logs him out and he cannot log on again. A possible reason:

A ○ The Account Policy in User Manager

B ○ A setting in the Hours dialog box in User Manager

C ○ A setting in the Account dialog box in User Manager

D ○ A user profile

Answers

1 B. Renaming Joe's account doesn't change the SID associated with that account, but it does give Sandy exactly the same access and ownership of all of Joe's resources. *Restudy the "Renaming user accounts" section.*

2 D. All login scripts are placed in the \winnt\system32\Repl\Exports Scripts folder on the PDC. You must set up replication to distribute the scripts to all domain controllers, and you must configure the user environment to use the script. *Check the "Editing user profiles: I'm okay, you're okay" section.*

3 B. Server Manager is the best tool for creating and managing shared folders. *Check the "Policy planning" section.*

4 B. Ntuser.man. The MAN extension designates a profile as mandatory. *See the "Profiles" section for more details.*

5 A. User rights are settings that delimit what users can and cannot do. Only members of the Administrators and the Backup, Server, Account, and Print Operators groups have the right to log on locally to a server. *Recheck the "Policy planning" section.*

6 C. Look over the "Policy planning" section for more details.

7 A. You can audit several events on printers, files, and folders. *Study the "Policy planning" section on auditing for more details on what you can audit.*

8 A, C. System policies affect the local machine and current user Registry hives. *The "Profiles" section has more details.*

9 A. You can use as many as 20 characters (and spaces) in a username. *See "Creating user accounts" for parameters on usernames.*

10 A. The Account Policy tool is what lets you activate the setting for forced logout. I admit, it's a bit of a trick question. You do, however, need to know where you can set the different options. *See the "Policy planning" section again for a refresher on what you can control via the Account Policy tool.*

Part V
Resource Management

The 5th Wave   By Rich Tennant

BEAL & WASP
Network Consultants

"OUR GOAL IS TO MAXIMIZE YOUR UPSIDE AND MINIMIZE YOUR DOWNSIDE WHILE WE PROTECT OUR OWN BACKSIDE."

In this part . . .

1 talk about how to manage resources by using user and group accounts. I explain how to manage user accounts, groups, user rights, administer policies, and audit resources. I also cover creating and managing profiles and policies, managing disk resources, and administering remote servers from client workstations.

In addition, I help you study managing user accounts in your NT domains and examine group management for local and global groups — these topics are regulars on the Server exam (Enterprise too, FYI!).

Chapter 14

User Groups

● ●

Exam Objectives

▶ Creating local groups

▶ Creating global groups

▶ Understanding built-in groups

▶ Assigning users to groups

● ●

Group management is a key topic on the Windows NT Server exam. You need to fully understand the concept of groups. You need to know the built-in groups and what rights and permissions each group inherits. The exam has many questions that pertain to local and global groups and how they interact within a domain. There are many labs in this chapter to help you understand the difference between local and global groups. You will better understand when to use the different types of groups after reading this chapter.

Quick Assessment

Creating
Global
Groups

1 By default, all members of the domain are members of the _____ global group.

2 Global groups can contain _____.

Creating
Local
Groups

3 Members of the _____ and _____ local groups on a domain controller can create user accounts.

4 Who belongs to the Everyone group?

5 Local groups can contain _____ and _____.

Assigning
Users to
Groups

6 When you assign a user to a group, the user _____ the user rights of that group.

Under-
standing
Built-in
Groups

7 How many users should you assign to the Replicators group?

8 By default, members of the _____ and _____ groups can add work-stations to the domain.

9 The _____, _____, and _____ built-in groups can perform backups.

10 You use _____ to create global groups.

Answers

1 *Domain Users.* See "Built-in global groups."

2 *User accounts.* See "Global groups."

3 *Administrator; Account Operators.* See the sections by the same names.

4 *Everyone.* See "Everyone."

5 *User accounts and global groups.* See "Global versus local groups."

6 *Inherits.* See "Planning Groups."

7 *None.* See "Replicator."

8 *Account Operators; Administrators.* See the sections by the same names.

9 *Administrators; Backup Operators; Server Operators.* See the sections by the same names.

10 *User Manager for Domains.* See "Account operators."

Planning Groups

The best way to manage access to resources is to use group memberships. Planning out how to group your users is of the utmost importance.

Because maintaining permissions for a group is easier than maintaining permissions for many user accounts, you generally want to use groups to manage access to resources, such as directories, files, or printers:

- ✔ Assign permissions to a group, and then add user accounts to that group as desired.
- ✔ Users assigned to a group inherit the rights and permissions assigned to that group.
- ✔ Change the permissions provided to a set of users or add or remove the permissions assigned to the group, but do not change each account.

When you assign user abilities, remember to take advantage of the built-in groups that Windows NT provides. These built-in groups offer useful collections of default rights and permissions.

Managing Groups: Round 'em Up

Rather than forcing you to work with each individual user to grant the appropriate rights and permissions, Windows NT manages groups.

- ✔ Group accounts are collections of user accounts.
- ✔ Giving a user account membership in a group gives that user all the rights and permissions granted to the group.
- ✔ Group membership provides an easy way to grant common capabilities to sets of users.
- ✔ Managing user accounts in groups makes managing and tracking users' access to resources (that is, your job) easier.
- ✔ In a large, multiple server domain, using groups makes the account domain administrator's job significantly easier.
- ✔ Using both groups and account templates, discussed in Chapter 13, you can set up new users and grant them access rights and permissions quickly and efficiently.
- ✔ In smaller single domains, building global and local groups eases management of users.
- ✔ As the domain grows or as you incorporate a different model, the framework is already in place and you can migrate with a minimum of reconfiguration.

The Windows NT Server exam doesn't focus too much on trust relationships, but you should know a bit about them.

🖊 Global groups are best used in the account domain.

🖊 If a resource domain trusts an account domain, you can use the account domain's global groups in the resource domain's local groups.

Well, now that we know why we need groups, let's add some users to a
group. Lab 14-1, "Assigning Users to a Group," steps you through the process. Follow the steps and try both adding a single user as well as multiple
users. You want to do this lab until you are comfortable with the process of
adding users to groups.

Lab 14-1   **Assigning Users to a Group**

1. **Start User Manager for Domains (choose Start⇨Programs⇨
   Administrative Tools⇨User Manager for Domains.**

2. **Select the group to which you want to assign the user by double-
   clicking the group name in the list near the bottom of the window.**

   The Group Properties dialog box opens, as shown in Figure 14-1.

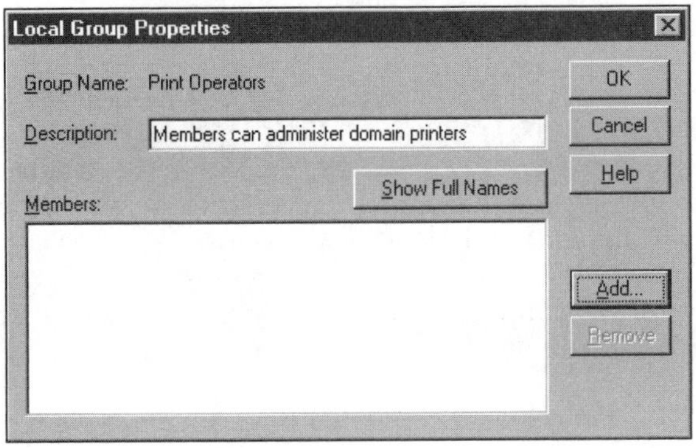

Local Group Properties

Group Name: Print Operators

Description: Members can administer domain printers

                                    Show Full Names

Members:

[OK] [Cancel] [Help] [Add...] [Remove]

Figure 14-1:
The Group
Properties
dialog box.

3. **Click the Add button.**

   The Add Users and Groups dialog box opens, as shown in Figure 14-2.

4. **Select the user to add to the group and click the Add button. You can
   select multiple users by using the CTRL and SHIFT keys with your
   mouse clicks.**

5. **Click OK to accept the changes and close the dialog box.**

The users are now members of the group. You can see the names of the users you added in the Group Properties box.

6. **Click OK to close the Group Properties dialog box.**

Global groups versus local groups

When you create groups in Windows NT Server, they belong to one of two categories: global (domain) groups or local groups.

Deciding which type of group to use isn't always simple. Consider the following points when you need to decide on group type:

- ✔ A group of users who require rights within a single domain must be a local group.

- ✔ A group that contains users from more than one domain must be a local group.

- ✔ A group that can contain both users and groups must be a local group.

- ✔ A group that contains users who need resources in other domains must be a global group.

- ✔ A group that you can grant local permissions on Windows NT Workstations must be a global group.

Plan ahead on group names. After you create a group, you cannot rename it. Try to make the group name indicate the group's purpose or location. You also may want to use the Description field to keep track of the groups' purposes.

Global groups

A *global group* contains a number of user accounts, all from one domain, grouped together under one group account name. A global group can contain only user accounts from the domain in which you create the global group.

You can grant a global group permissions and rights

- ✔ in its own domain
- ✔ on member servers in trusting domains

You should always grant rights and permissions to local groups and use the global group as your means of adding users to local groups.

Global groups contain domain user accounts only. You cannot create a global group on a computer running Windows NT Workstation or on a computer running Windows NT Server as a member server.

You can add global groups to

- ✔ Local groups in the same domain
- ✔ Local groups in trusting domains
- ✔ Member servers in the same or a trusting domain
- ✔ Computers running Windows NT Workstation in the same or a trusting domain

You create global groups at the account domain and they can contain only user accounts from that domain. Global groups are convenient for managing large or diverse groups of users.

Now it is time to create a global group. Lab 14-2, "Creating a Global Group," will show you how easy this is. After completing the exam you will find many ways to use global groups in the Windows NT Servers you will administrate.

Lab 14-2	Creating a Global Group

1. **Start User Manager for Domains (choose Start⇨Programs⇨ Administrative Tools⇨User Manager for Domains).**

2. **Choose User⇨New Global Group.**

   The New Global Group dialog box opens, as shown in Figure 14-3.

Figure 14-3: The New Global Group dialog box.

3. **Enter the name and description of the new global group. You can also select any initial members of the global group.**

4. **Click OK.**

Local groups

A *local group* contains user accounts and global groups from one or more domains, grouped together under one local group account name. You can add users and global groups from outside the local domain to the local group only if they belong to a trusting domain. Local groups enable you to quickly assign rights and permissions for the resources on one domain (that is, the local domain) to users and groups from that domain and other domains that trust it.

Local groups also exist on member servers and computers running Windows NT Workstation, and can contain user accounts and global groups. A local group cannot contain other local groups.

Local groups are created in much the same way as global groups. Lab 14-3, "Creating a Local Group," shows you the differences. Remember that local groups can contain global groups and users. In practice it is better to only assign global groups to the local groups.

Lab 14-3   **Creating a Local Group**

1. **Start User Manager for Domains (choose Start⇨Programs⇨ Administrative Tools⇨User Manager for Domains).**

2. **Choose User⇨New Local Group.**

    The New Local Group dialog box opens, as shown in Figure 14-4.

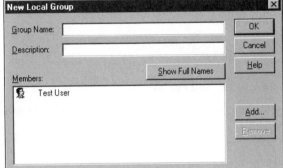

Figure 14-4: The New Local Group dialog box.

3. **Enter the name and description of the new local group. You also can select any initial members of the local group by clicking the Add button.**

    The new global groups show up in the Add dialog box. Refer to Figure 14-2 to see the Add Users and Groups dialog box.

4. **Click OK.**

Here's an easy way to remember the roles of the different type of groups:

- ✔ Global groups contain domain users only.

- ✔ Local groups contain global groups and any user.

- ✔ Nothing contains a local group.

Put users into global groups and global groups into local groups, and grant rights and permissions to the local group.

If you need to create several similar groups, follow these steps:

1. Create one group.

2. Assign the right to this group.

3. Copy the group.

4. Assign members.

Lab 14-4, "Copying a Group," demonstrates this feature. After performing the lab, you may want to read back over the text and think about how this feature can be used in a real situation. Remember: The test contains many situational questions.

Lab 14-4	Copying a Group

1. **Start User Manager for Domains (choose Start⇨Programs⇨ Administrative Tools⇨User Manager for Domains).**

2. **Select the group to copy.**

3. **Choose User⇨Copy.**

    The New Local Group dialog box appears.

4. **Type in the new name and change the description.**

5. **Click Add to add or remove users from the original group.**

6. **Click OK.**

Special and built-in groups

Windows NT Server has several built-in groups. Each of these groups have specific capabilities as well as restrictions. You must understand these built-in groups and when to use each of them. In this section we will look at each built-in group and its capabilities.

Built-in global groups

On a domain's primary and backup domain controllers, three global groups are built in:

- ✔ Domain Admins
- ✔ Domain Users
- ✔ Domain Guests

You cannot delete any of these groups.

Domain Admins

The Domain Admins global group is initially a member of the Administrators local group for the domain and of the Administrators local group for every computer in the domain running Windows NT Workstation or Windows NT Server. The built-in Administrator user account is a member of the Domain Admins global group and a member of the Administrators local group, and you cannot remove it. Because of these memberships, a user logged on as an administrator can administer the following:

✔ The domain

✔ The primary and backup domain controllers

✔ All other computers running Windows NT Workstation and Windows NT Server in the domain

To give a new account administrative-level abilities, add the account to the Domain Admins global group. Members of this group can administer the following:

✔ The domain

✔ All domain servers and workstations

✔ Any trusted domains that have added the Domain Admins global group from this domain to the Administrators local group in the trusted domain

Domain Users

The Domain Users global group initially contains the domain's built-in Administrator account. By default, all new accounts created thereafter in the domain are added to the Domain Users group, unless you specifically remove them. The Domain Users global group is, by default, a member of the following groups:

✔ The Users local group for the domain

✔ The Users local group for every computer in the domain running Windows NT Workstation

✔ The member servers running Windows NT Server

The Domain Users group is the default primary group for each user. Because of these memberships, users of the domain have normal user access to, and abilities for, the domain and the computers in the domain running Windows NT Workstation and Windows NT Server as member servers.

Domain Guests

The Domain Guests global group initially contains the domain's built-in Guest user account. If you add user accounts that you intend to have more limited rights and permissions than typical domain user accounts, you may want to add those accounts to the Domain Guests group and remove them from the Domain Users group. The Domain Guests global group is a member of the domain's Guests local group.

Built-in local groups

The built-in local groups differ depending on the server's role. You need to be aware of the differences and know what members of all the local groups may do.

For servers that act as domain controllers, the local groups are

✔ Administrators

✔ Account Operators

✔ Backup Operators

✔ Print Operators

✔ Server Operators

✔ Replicator

✔ Users

✔ Guests

For servers that act as member servers, the local groups are

✔ Administrators

✔ Backup Operators

✔ Power Users

✔ Replicator

✔ Users

✔ Guests

Notice the difference in the local groups based on server roles. The Power Users group exists only on member servers. The only "Operators" group that exists on member servers is the Backup Operators group.

Administrators

The Administrators group is the most powerful local group. It gives the user complete control over the domain and the domain controllers and servers. It is the only local group automatically granted every ability and every right in the system. When Windows NT is installed, the Domain Admins global group is automatically a member of the Administrators local group.

Account Operators

Account Operators can use User Manager for Domains to create user accounts and groups for their home domain. They can modify or delete most user accounts and groups. They also can add workstations to the domain. They cannot change or modify any of the following groups:

✔ Domain Admins

✔ Administrators

✔ Backup Operators

✔ Print Operators

✔ Server Operators

✔ Account Operators

Backup Operators

Members of this group can back up and restore files and folders on servers and domain controllers. They cannot change security settings.

Print Operators

The Print Operators group member can manage every aspect of printing. They can share and stop sharing printers.

Power Users

The Power Users group is a local group that exists only on member servers and workstations. Members of the Power Users group can modify only user accounts and groups they create. They also can add and remove users from the Power Users group, as well as share and stop sharing folders and printers.

Replicator

The Replicator group isn't like other local groups. No one is automatically a member of the Replicator group. You don't assign actual users this group; rather, you should establish a special account and assign that account to it. You use the Replicator group to manage the replication of files and folders on the domain controllers.

Server Operators

This local group is on domain controllers and its members can do most jobs on a server, except manipulate security options. Server Operators can

- ✔ Lock and override the lock on a server
- ✔ Format the server's hard drive
- ✔ Create common groups
- ✔ Share and stop sharing folders and printers
- ✔ Back up and restore files and folders
- ✔ Change the system time

The key to remembering the difference between the Account Operators group and the Server Operators group is in their names:

- ✔ Members of the Account Operators group can manage issues concerning user accounts. They can do most user account tasks; they can't modify security settings.

- ✔ Members of the Server Operators group can do almost anything concerning servers, but they have nothing to do with user accounts. They can create a group, but they can't mess with security settings, either.

Administrators are the only ones who can do it all, including manage security.

Users

The Users group is the default group for all users. It gives users rights to perform end-user tasks:

- Logging on to a workstation and accessing the network
- Running an application
- Printing
- Creating and managing their own local groups
- Keeping a personal profile
- Locking and unlocking their workstation

Users group members do not have the right to log on locally to a server.

Everyone

Anyone who has a user account in a domain is a member of that domain's Everyone local group by default. Granting access to a file or folder to Everyone means just that: Everyone can access that file or folder. The same applies to user rights. Be careful with this group.

Special built-in groups

Windows NT Server includes four special groups that serve only to show how a user is using the system at a particular time. These groups have no actual members, but membership is implied by access to a resource.

- **Interactive:** Any user who is logged on locally.
- **Network:** Any user who has gained access through the network.
- **System:** The operating system.
- **Creator/Owner:** Anyone creating a file, folder, or print job.

Get familiar with which groups can do what jobs. The exam presents situational questions that call on you to know what groups can perform what jobs. You need to know all the built-in groups and their capabilities.

Prep Test

1 Your company plans to bring in temporary employees to work on a project. Someone will need to create and rename several user accounts every day. The company wants fast response for these changes. The project leader is willing to take responsibility for managing these changes. Which built-in group should you place him in to perform only these tasks?

A ○ Server Operators

B ○ Administrators

C ○ Account Operators

D ○ Replicators

2 A department in your company has a local group assigned, using the name of their department as the group name. After reorganization, the department name changes. The department head wants you to change the name of the local group to reflect the current name of the department. How do you accomplish this task?

A ○ Create a new global group, then pull the old local group into it as a member.

B ○ Copy the old local group, assign a new name, and delete the old local group.

C ○ Rename the local group.

D ○ Create a new local group and pull the old local group into it as a member.

3 TabithaM has no problems logging in to the network and attaching to her resources. When she was in the computer room, she tried to log on to one of the servers and was denied access. What could be the cause?

A ○ She is a member of the Print Operators global group.

B ○ She is a member of the Domain Users global group.

C ○ She is a member of the Backup Operators global group.

D ○ She is a member of the Server Operators global group.

4 The following group memberships apply:

Joe S is a member of the Administrators group.
BettyM is a member of the Server Operators group.
KeithM is a member of the Backup Operators group.
DavidC is a member of the Account Operators group.
BobA is a member of the Print Operators group.

JoeS and KeithM are out of town. A user has accidentally deleted some critical files and the files must be restored. Which user should perform the task?

A ○ BobA
B ○ BettyM
C ○ DavidC
D ○ None of the above

5 The following group memberships apply:

JoeS is a member of the Administrators group.
BettyM is a member of the Server Operators group.
KeithM is a member of the Backup Operators group.
DavidC is a member of the Account Operators group.
BobA is a member of the Print Operators group.

DavidC has to leave for a business trip and wants to leave his duties to his assistant. Who can place his assistant into the Account Operators group? (Choose all that apply.)

A ❏ JoeS
B ❏ BettyM
C ❏ DavidC
D ❏ BobA
E ❏ KeithM

6 The following group memberships apply:

JoeS is a member of the Administrators group.
BettyM is a member of the Server Operators group.
KeithM is a member of the Backup Operators group.
DavidC is a member of the Account Operators group.
BobA is a member of the Print Operators group.

BobA is out for the day. Who can accomplish the task of sharing a new printer to the network? (Choose all that apply.)

A ❑ JoeS
B ❑ BettyM
C ❑ KeithM
D ❑ DavidC

7 The server has been locked for security purposes. Which group can override the lock on the server?

A ○ Print Operators
B ○ Backup Operators
C ○ Server Operators
D ○ Account Operators

8 While using the User Manager for Domains tool, you notice the Power Users group. The server must be a _____.

A ○ Primary domain controller
B ○ Backup domain controller
C ○ Member server
D ○ Account server

9 Who can make changes to the Domain Users global group?

A ○ Backup Operators
B ○ Server Operators
C ○ Account Operators
D ○ Replicators

10 By default, who is a member of the Replicator group?

A ○ All valid users
B ○ Only users who have local accounts
C ○ Only the Administrator
D ○ No one

Answers

1   C. The Account Operators group enables him to manage the user accounts and not much else. *Review the "Special and built-in groups" section for more information.*

2   B. You cannot rename groups, but you can copy them. Just copy the old group and assign a new name; then remove the old group. *Review "Global groups versus local groups."*

3   B. She is just a member of the Domain Users group. The others all have the Log on Locally right, so they can log on locally to a server. *Review "Special and built-in groups."*

4   B. Server Operators have the right to back up and restore files. *Review "Special and built-in groups."*

5   A. Only a member of the Administrators group can assign a user to the Account Operators group. *Review "Special and built-in groups."*

6   B. Server operators can share and stop sharing printers. The exam has several questions about group rights. *Review "Special and built-in groups."*

7   C. Server Operators and Administrators can override the lock on a server. *Review "Special and built-in groups."*

8   C. Member servers are the only server type that will have this local group. *Review "Special and built-in groups."*

9   C. Account Operators and Administrators are the only two groups that can create a user account. *Review "Special and built-in groups."*

10   D. No one is assigned to the Replicator group by default. This is a special group. *Review "Special and built-in groups."*

Chapter 15

Server Management

Exam Objectives

▶ Managing Windows NT Servers remotely using Windows 95 and Windows NT Workstation

▶ Understanding and administering Windows NT disk resources

▶ Understanding and administering Windows NT file auditing

▶ Understanding the concepts of Windows NT replication

▶ Understanding the advantages of the Windows NT SNMP Agent

*W*hether you design complex networks full-time for a multinational corporation or set up NT environments for local nonprofit organizations on a volunteer basis, your understanding of the basic principles of server management will define your ability as an MSCE. Microsoft wants to make sure that you can demonstrate your knowledge of these "hands on" tasks during the NT Server exam.

You can count on about 3 or 4 questions dealing with server management on the 70-67 exam and another 4 or 5 on exam 70-68.

Before you read this chapter, make sure that you have a firm grasp of the concepts in Chapters 10 and 14.

If you read no further, make sure that you're comfortable with the finer points of the following topics:

✔ Setting up and using NT Shares

✔ Setting up and using NTFS permissions

✔ Setting up and using NT auditing

✔ Knowing which server tools to use for what jobs

Quick Assessment

Disk Resources

1 What directory does the administrative share, ADMIN$, point to?

2 What applications can you use to create and manage a server's net work shares?

3 Workstations and servers are added and removed from a Windows NT domain by using the _____ server tool.

File Auditing

4 You grant user Sally the No Access right to the directory C:\Data and you grant the group Datamaster the Full Control right over the directory C:\Data. Sally is a member of the Datamaster built-in group. What rights does Sally have in the directory C:\Data?

Managing Servers Remotely Using Windows 95 and NT Workstation

5 If user Barney has List permissions to the directory C:\Access, can he navigate into the subdirectory C:\Access\Secrets?

6 The Windows NT Event Viewer can be used to view and manage *System*, _____ and _____ event logs.

7 In order to enable auditing of the file system, you need to set the _____ and _____ Access policy for Success and Failure via User Manager.

8 What tools that ship with Windows NT Server 4.0 permit an administrator using a Windows 95 computer to manage Windows NT systems?

SNMP Agent

9 What is SNMP?

Replication

10 What Microsoft operating systems can participate as import servers in directory replication?

Answers

1 *The Windows NT directory; C:\WINNT by default.* See "File Service Overview."

2 *Windows File Manager, Explorer, NT Server Manager.* See "File Service Overview."

3 *Windows NT Server Manager.* See "Remote Administration."

4 *NO ACCESS.* Read "File Service Overview."

5 *Yes.* Review "File Service Overview."

6 *System, Application,* and *Security.* Review "Remote Administration."

7 *File and Object Access.* See "File Service Overview."

8 *User Manager for Domains, Event Viewer, Server Manager, and extensions for the Windows 95 Print Manager and Explorer t to manage NT Print Queues and NTFS permissions.* See "Remote Administration."

9 *Simple Network Management Protocol.* Review "Remote Administration."

10 *Computers running Windows NT Server and Windows NT Work station.* See "Directory Replication."

File Service Overview

Before you even think about opening the virtual doors to the data vault, you need to get organized. That means grouping data into directories and segregating it into finite sets that can be managed as a single entity. By keeping similar data grouped together under a single directory structure, an administrator will simplify the process of:

- ✔ Accessing the data both locally and from the network
- ✔ Sharing the data to other users
- ✔ Securing the data from unauthorized persons
- ✔ Auditing who access the data

Most of the permission questions on the exam come in the form of "what is the best answer" type questions. Remember that setting permissions on the directory is always a better answer than setting the permissions on an individual file.

Sharing resources

Ever since Mrs. Nugent and my kindergarten class, I love to share. When your servers are up and running and your data is organized into directories, it's time to gather everyone around the file server and let them have a look.

By default, all fixed drives and a few key directories on an NT system are automatically shared by the operating system. These shares are known as administrative shares and include C$, D$, and ADMIN$. Shares that end with a $, such as C$ or ADMIN$, are not visible (hidden) from the network browse list. The C$ and D$ shares are created on the drives C and D, respectively, while the ADMIN$ share points to the directory in which Windows NT is installed (C:\WINNT by default). Only local Administrators and Server Operators can mount these shares. You may come across this on the test so don't forget it.

To create a share on the local file system, you can use Windows NT Explorer or Windows NT File Manager. To create or manage a share on a remote computer, you can use either Windows NT File Manager (see Figure 15-1) or Windows NT Server Manager (see Figure 15-2).

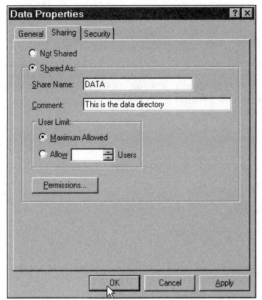

The next three labs, 15-1, 15-2, and 15-3, walk you through setting up and configuring shares via Explorer (Lab 15-1), Windows NT File Manager (Lab 15-2) and Windows NT Server Manager (15-3). While you have probably done these dozens if not hundreds of times, it is often helpful to walk through it again. While the exams generally will not expect you to remember the location of a specific dialog window, they do expect you to be intimately familiar with the process.

Lab 15-1   Sharing a Directory Using the Explorer

1. **Click on the directory folder to share.**

2. **Choose File⇨Properties and then click the Sharing tab.**

3. **Select the Shared As option.**

   Note: To stop sharing a directory, select Not Shared from the folder's Properties page.

4. **Fill in the Share Name and Comment fields.**

   Use a logical share name so that others can identify the type of data kept in the directory.

   Share names that don't meet the 8.3 naming standard (no more than 8 characters followed by a dot and no more than 3 more characters) are not visible to MS-DOS clients!

   (continued)

Lab 15-1 *(continued)*

5. **Select the Maximum Allowed option.**

Specifying this option automatically sets the user limit to maximum.

6. **To limit access to the shared directory, click the Permissions button and add the users and groups with whom to share the resource.**

Lab 15-2   Setting Up a Network Share from the Windows File Manager

1. **Select the directory folder that you want to share.**

2. **Choose Disk⇨Share As.**

Note: To stop sharing a directory, choose Disk⇨Stop Sharing.

The New Share dialog box opens, as shown in Figure 15-2.

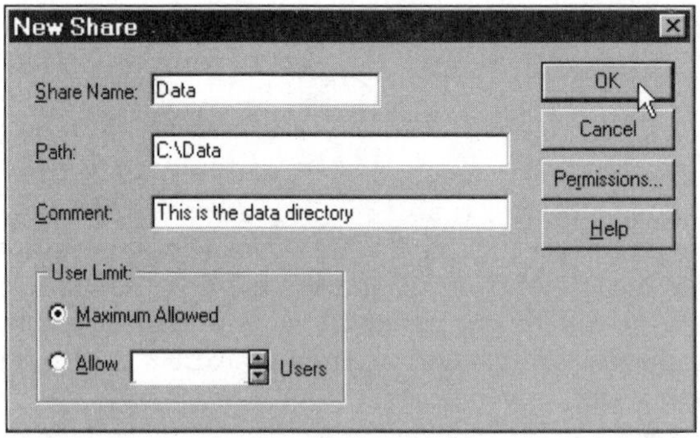

Figure 15-2:
Setting up a
network
share.

3. **Fill in the Share Name, the Path (if different), and Comment fields.**

4. **Select the Maximum Allowed option.**

5. **To limit access to the shared directory, click the Permissions button and add the users and groups with whom you want to share the resource.**

Lab 15-3   Setting Up a Network Share Using Server Manager

1. **Run Server Manager and select the computer on which you want to add the share.**

2. **Choose Computer⇨Shared Directories.**

The Shared Directories dialog box opens.

3. **Click the New Share button.**

The New Share dialog box opens, as shown in Figure 15-3.

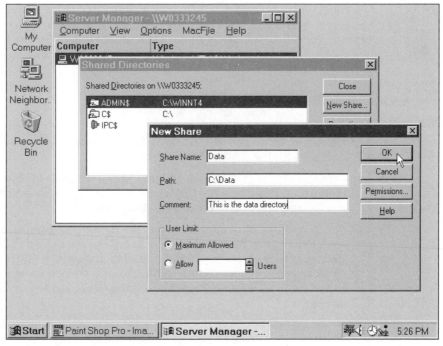

Figure 15-3:
Running
Server
Manager to
add a
share.

Note: To stop sharing a directory, select Stop Sharing in the Shared Directories dialog box.

4. **Fill in the Share Name, Path, and Comment fields.**

   When entering the path, be sure to reference it as if you were local to the server.

5. **Specify Maximum Allowed as the user limit.**

6. **To limit access to the shared directory, click the Permissions button and add the users and groups with whom you want to share the resource.**

Permissions and security

Even in a kindergarten class, someone (namely, the teacher) needs to moderate sharing. The teacher needs to control who has access to what toys; otherwise, you get little tikes swinging baseball bats at one another quicker than you can say "emergency room." In the NT world, you manage access control via the use of permissions on the share and file system level.

You can apply permissions only to files and directories on NTFS partitions; if security is required for files on a FAT partition, you must use shares. It is easy to overlook permissions when preparing for the NT Server exams, but you should expect to see one or two questions so you should understand how they work.

To make your life a little easier, try to remember the following points relating to NT permissions:

- ✔ Users who try to access data on an NTFS volume via a network share operate with the least rights that the share and file system grants.

- ✔ Permissions are cumulative, and they sort from most to least access (with the exception of the No Access permission — No Access is always interpreted first and overrides all other permissions).

- ✔ The Owner of a file or directory has the right to change permissions, even if they have been assigned No Access to the data. If Fred is the Creator Owner of the directory C:\Freddata; he can modify the permissions on the directory to remove the No Access right assigned to the group Workers and assign himself the rights needed to use the directory.

- ✔ By default, members of the Administrators group can take ownership of files and directories, even if those files and directories have been assigned the No Access permission.

- ✔ When you create new files or folders in a subdirectory, they inherit permissions from the parent directory.

- ✔ Microsoft recommends that you assign permissions to groups rather than to individual users to ease future administration.

The following list describes the rights that you can set via the Permissions tab. Know these rights for the test:

Full Control	User can read, write, delete, and change the permissions of a file.
Change	User can read, write, and delete the item.
Add & Read	User can write new files to a directory and can read all files. User cannot modify existing files.
Add	User can create new items in a directory. Does not apply to files.
Read	User can read the contents of a file or directory.
List	User can list the filename and read directory contents but cannot read or modify the file.
No Access	User has no access in the directory or to the file.

File auditing

To prepare for file auditing, make sure you can answer these three questions:

- ✔ How do you enable auditing?
- ✔ Where is auditing recorded?
- ✔ What actions are audited given specific settings?

All auditing events are recorded in the Security log viewable via the Event Viewer. To enable file and directory auditing, follow the following steps:

1. Log on to the server as an administrator or an account operator.

2. Run User Manager and select Policies⇨Audit.

3. Select the Audit These Events button.

4. Enable success and/or failure for File and Object Access.

5. Run Explorer and select the file or directory to audit.

6. Select choose File⇨Properties⇨Auditing.

7. Select the Add button and add the user and groups you wish to audit. To audit all access to the directory, add the special group Everyone.

8. Select what events to audit. A description of the events are outlined below.

The following list tells you which actions are audited given a particular audit setting. It is important to be familiar with these for the exam.

Action	*Audit Setting*
Opening a file or displaying a file name	Read
Displaying a file or directory's attributes	Read or Execute
Displaying a file or directory's permissions	Read, Write, or Execute
Changing a file or directory's data	Write
Changing a file or directory's attributes	Write
Running (executing) a file	Execute

(continued)

(continued)

Action	Audit Setting
Deleting a file or directory	Delete
Changing permissions on a file or directory	Change Permissions
Taking ownership of a file or directory	Take Ownership
Navigating into a directory's subdirectories	Execute

Distributed File System (Dfs)

The Microsoft Distributed File System for Microsoft Windows NT Server (Dfs) is a free add-on to Windows NT 4.0 Server that presents multiple distributed file shares on the network as a single directory tree. Accessing volumes in a Dfs tree or searching for data becomes as simple as traversing directories or using NT's built-in file search tools.

The NT Server exam does not have any questions concerning Dfs so don't waste your time studying this product.

Remote Administration

If you feel comfortable using the tools and you're aware of the features of the tools, you should do fine on these questions.

Windows NT Workstation server tools

I list these tools in order of likelihood to appear on the exam. The best way to ensure doing well on this portion of the exam is to use these tools enough to feel comfortable talking about them.

Windows NT Server Manager

Windows NT Server Manager is a Windows NT utility that permits an Administrator or Server Operator to manage domains and computers on the network.

Windows NT Server Manager can perform the following tasks in the domain:

- ✔ Promote a backup domain controller to the primary domain controller. You cannot demote a primary domain controller with Server Manager; you can only promote a backup domain controller. The act of promoting a backup domain controller automatically demotes the primary.

- ✔ Synchronize the account database on backup domain controllers with the primary domain controller.

- ✔ Add or remove domain controllers, member servers, or workstations from the domain.

Additionally, you can use NT Server Manager to perform the following tasks on any Windows NT computer:

- ✔ Manage directory replication

- ✔ Manage installed services

- ✔ Manage the list of alert names

- ✔ Send messages to users connected to a server

- ✔ View a list of connected users and open resources

- ✔ View and manage shares

User Manager for Domains

User Manager for Domains (shown in Figure 15-4) is a Windows NT utility that permits an Administrator or Account Operator to manage a user and group security for the domain. Specifically, you can use User Manager for Domains to perform the following tasks:

- ✔ Create and modify user accounts on a computer or the domain

- ✔ Create and modify group membership on a computer or the domain

- ✔ Manage a computer or domain's account security policy

- ✔ Manage user rights within a domain

- ✔ Configure a computer or domain's audit policy

- ✔ Establish and manage trust relationships with other domains

Remote Access Administrator

Remote Access Administrator is a Windows NT utility that permits the management of Windows NT Remote Access Services, including:

- ✔ Identifying what servers within a domain are running Windows NT Remote Access Services

- ✔ Starting and stopping the remote access service

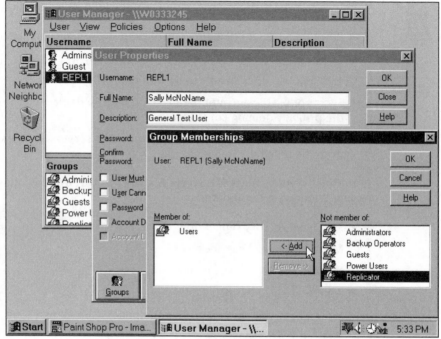

Figure 15-4:
User
Manager
for
Domains.

✔ Checking the status of the communication ports

✔ Setting user access permissions and configuring callback security

✔ Viewing and sending messages to connected users

Registry Editor

Windows NT 4.0 ships with two versions of the Registry Editor, REGEDIT.EXE and REGEDT32.EXE. These utilities permit the user to manage the settings of the Registry both on a local Windows NT computer and a remote computer. Here are the key facts about these tools for the exam:

✔ The directory of the Registry is known as the Key. The name of the entry is known as the Value. The information stored in the Value is known as the Data.

✔ The Registry Editor tools do not automatically refresh when you use them on remote computers.

✔ The REGEDIT.EXE tool can search in Keys, Values, and Data, whereas the REGEDT32.EXE tool can search only in Keys and Values.

Windows NT Event Viewer

Although the exam isn't likely to test your knowledge of the specific operation of the Windows NT Event Viewer, you will need to know it is used to view the logs on the local and remote computer. Specifically, you should know that the three Windows NT Event Logs are:

- ✔ Security
- ✔ System
- ✔ Application

User Profile Editor

The User Profile Editor is a Windows NT utility that enables you to determine what portions of your users' Windows NT desktops they can control. Using the User Profile Editor, you can control the appearance of the desktop and a number of other features. I don't recall any exam questions involving this tool.

Remoteboot (RPL) Manager

The Remoteboot (RPL) Manager is a Windows NT utility that you can use to manage remote program load (RPL) or remote boot profiles. Although the exam does ask a few questions about the RPL service, none of the questions focus on the specifics of operating the tool.

WINS Manager

WINS Manager is a Windows NT utility that enables you to manage the Windows Internet Server Service (WINS). There are several questions on the WINS service on the 70-68 exam but I don't recall any specific questions on 70-67.

DHCP Manager

DHCP Manager is a Windows NT utility that you can use to manage the Dynamic Host Configuration Protocol (DHCP) server. The DHCP Manager isn't covered at all on the 70-67 exam.

Services for Macintosh Manager

Services for Macintosh Manager is a utility for managing the Macintosh File and Print services on Windows NT Servers. The exam doesn't even mention this tool.

Windows 95 server tools

This section of the exam is kind of tricky if you have never managed a Windows NT Server network from Windows 95 computers. Most people I know use Windows NT Workstation computers (or NT Server itself) to do

NT systems management. If you want to know more about these tools than is covered on the exam, check out the Windows NT 4.0 Server Concepts and Planning Manual (see Chapter 14) that ships with Windows NT Server. For the sake of the exam, here is a quick overview of each tool.

The Network Client Administrator toolkit contains three primary applications for managing your Windows NT environment. These tools have all the same functionality as their Windows NT counterparts listed in "Windows NT Workstation Server Tools."

- ✔ Windows NT Server Manager

- ✔ Event Viewer for Windows NT

- ✔ User Manager for Domains

Additionally, the toolkit contains extensions for the Windows 95 Explorer and the Windows 95 Print Manager that permit you to manipulate NTFS security and manage NT and FPNW print queues.

Simple Network Management Protocol (SNMP)

People have written entire books on SNMP, but the exams keep the topic simple. All you need to know is what it is and what it provides to you as an administrator.

SNMP stands for *Simple Network Management Protocol* and is used on TCP/IP and some IPX networks around the world to manage network devices.

SNMP serves as a means of communications between an *agent* and a *host computer* running the SNMP management software. Some examples of SNMP management software packages include HP Openview and IBM's Netview. SNMP defines the formatting and meaning of the messages flowing between the agent and the host computer.

The SNMP management software can issue three commands:

- ✔ **get:** Requests a specific piece of data.

- ✔ **get-next:** Requests the next piece of data in the table.

- ✔ **set:** Inserts an item into the table.

The SNMP agent can issue only one command:

- ✔ **trap:** An event message sent from the agent to the host computer when a particular event has occurred.

Before you can monitor TCP/IP or other accessible counters on a Windows NT computer, you must first install SNMP on the computer you want to monitor. And you can't install SNMP unless TCP/IP is installed on the computer.

After you install SNMP, you can access a wealth of network utilization statistics in Performance Monitor. You do not have access to these counters unless you have installed SNMP.

Directory Replication

Microsoft provides a rudimentary directory replication service with Windows NT that permits administrators to push certain files, such as login scripts, around the domain. The exam usually has one or two questions on directory replication.

If you can remember these five points, you can coast through these questions on the exams.

- ✔ Only Windows NT Servers can import and export replication folders. Windows NT Workstations can import replication folders only. Windows 95 doesn't participate in replication.

- ✔ The default export directory used for NT replication is C:\Winnt\System32\Repl\Export\Scripts. The default import directory used for NT replication is C:\Winnt\System32\Repl\Import\Scripts. This directory is the NETLOGON share on NT domain controllers.

- ✔ The account used for replication (a) must be a member of the special built-in Replicator group and (b) must be granted Logon as Service rights.

- ✔ Replication across multiple domains requires that the replicator account used in the export domain have the same user name and password as the *replicator* account used in the import domain.

- ✔ When NT replicates from an NTFS to a FAT partition, only files with 8.3 names are replicated. Files without 8.3 names will have new 8.3 names generated on the FAT partition.

Configuring servers

Configuring replication involves three basic steps.

1. Creating a replication account

2. Configuring the export server

3. Configuring the import server

To set up the replicator account, compete the following two steps:

1. Run User Manager for Domains and new account, **repl**, in the target domain.

   I like to use **repl** as it clearly identifies this account as the replicator account.

2. Add the **repl** account to the Local group Replicator.

   You do not need to assign special rights to this group because it is done automatically when you set up the server.

Lab 15-4 and Lab 15-5 illustrate how to set up an export server and an import server.

Lab 15-4   Setting Up an Export Server

1. **Run Services from the Control Panel.**

2. **Choose the Directory Replicator service.**

   Set Startup to Automatic. Set Log On As to the replicator account for that domain. Enter the Password for the replicator account.

3. **Run Server Manager and select the export server.**

4. **Choose Computer⇨Properties.**

5. **Select Replication.**

   In the Replication dialog box, select Export Directories. The default location is %SYSTEMROOT%\SYSTEM32\REPL\EXPORT.

   Click Add. Specify the name of the import servers or domain. If you select a domain, NT configures all domain controllers as import servers.

   Click Manage. Specify what subdirectories you want to export. If you click Entire Subtree, NT replicates all subdirectories.

   If you click the Add Lock, NT will not replicate the directory until all file and directory locks have been removed. If you click Wait Until Stabilized, NT doesn't replicate until more than two minutes pass since the last change.

6. **Click OK.**

   NT starts the Replicator service. All events relating to the Replicator service now appear in the event log.

Lab 15-5   Setting Up an Import Server

1. **Run Services from the Control Panel.**

2. **Choose the Directory Replicator service.**

   Set Startup to Automatic. Set Log On As to the replicator account for that domain. Enter the Password for the replicator account.

3. **Run Server Manager and select the export server.**

4. **Choose Computer⇨Properties.**

5. **Choose Replication.**

   In the Replication dialog box, select Import Directories. The default location is %SYSTEMROOT%\SYSTEM32\REPL\IMPORT.

   Click Add. Specify the name of the export servers or domain. If you leave the field blank, the import service will attempt to import from all domain controllers in the domain.

   Click Manage to display the status for imported directories.

6. **Click OK.**

   NT begins replication.

Prep Test

1 Who has permissions to access the C$ share on a Windows NT Workstation?

A ○ Administrators

B ○ Server Operators

C ○ Power Users

D ○ Supervisors

2 You grant Sally the No Access right to the directory C:\Data. Sally is a member of the group Administrators on the computer that contains C:\Data. What must Sally do to obtain Read access to the file C:\Data\Myfile.txt?

A ○ Nothing. Sally already has access to C:\Data\Myfile.txt because she is a local administrator.

B ○ Look at the permissions set for C:\Data\Myfile.txt and give herself rights.

C ○ Take ownership of the directory C:\Data and C:\Data\Myfile.txt and grant herself Read access.

D ○ Sally cannot do anything to access the file C:\Data\Myfile.txt because you assigned her No Access.

3 Barney is a member of the local group Administrators and has taken ownership of the file A-file.doc. How should you configure file and directory auditing to record this event in the NT security log?

A ○ You cannot. NT Administrators are not subject to NT auditing policies.

B ○ Audit the file A-file.doc for Read access.

C ○ Audit the file A-file.doc for Execute access.

D ○ Audit the file A-file.doc for Take Ownership access.

4 What support do you add when you install the SNMP agent on your Windows NT computer? (Choose all that apply.)

A ❏ Access to WINS and DHCP performance statistics on the local computer via the SNMP get command.

B ❏ Access to the TCP/IP performance counter statistics on the local computer.

C ❏ Access to network performance counter statistics on the local computer.

D ❏ The ability to capture and view SNMP traps from other computers on the network.

5 What Microsoft operating systems can participate in directory replication? (Choose all that apply.)

A ❑ A primary domain controller running Windows NT Server 4.0

B ❑ A backup domain controller running Windows NT Server 3.51

C ❑ A Windows NT 4.0 Workstation residing in a workgroup

D ❑ A Windows 95 computer authenticating from a Windows NT Domain

6 Files in the common directory C:\Alldata are being deleted. How do you identify who is removing the files?

A ○ Create a network share point to C:\Alldata and check when the files were deleted; then use Server Monitor to see who was connected at that time.

B ○ Run Performance Monitor and look at the counter File System: FILE DELETE for any reference to C:\Alldata.

C ○ Enable User File Auditing for Everyone on the directory C:\Alldata.

D ○ Take ownership of all files in C:\Alldata.

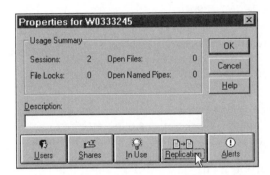

7 Auditing is configured as shown in the above figure. If administrator Sally takes ownership of the directory C:\Data, would the Event Log contain an audit for the action?

8 Which tool(s) would an administrator use to search the registry for all keys that contain the word DOMAIN in the value?

9 What tool would be used to send a message to all users connected to a particular server in a domain

10 In order to create a share on your local computer, you can use either the

_____, the _____, or _____ .

Answers

1 *A.* On Windows NT Workstation computers, only members of the local Administrators group have access to the administrative shares (C$, D$, or ADMIN$). On Windows NT Server computers, members of the Administrators and Server Operators groups may connect to the administrative shares. *See "Permissions and security."*

2 *C.* As an administrator, Sally must first take ownership of the directory and file before she can even view the permissions on Myfile.txt. Once Sally owns the file, she can view and set the permissions necessary to grant herself access. *See "Permissions and security."*

3 *A.* The file A-file.doc needs to have Take Ownership auditing configured to record this action. *See "Permissions and security."*

4 *A, C.* Installing the SNMP agent gives you access to MIB data for WINS and DHCP, as well as access to the network performance counters. TCP/IP counters are installed with the TCP/IP protocol and you need an SNMP management station if you want to receive SNMP traps from other computers. *See "Simple Network Management Protocol (SNMP)."*

5 *A, B, C.* Windows 95 computers cannot participate in replication regardless of how they are configured. Windows NT Workstations can participate as import servers and Windows NT Servers can participate either as import or export servers. All NT systems participating in directory replication must have a common Replicator account and password between the two systems. *See "Directory Replication."*

6 *C.* File Auditing for Everyone is the best answer for this circumstance, because it can clearly identify the culprit. *See "File Auditing."*

7 *No.* The audit policy for the directory would have to explicitly audit for Take Ownership. Auditing for Write or Delete is not sufficient. *Review "File auditing."*

8 *Regedit.exe.* The Registry Editor REGEDIT.EXE is the only registry editing tool that is capable of searching thru the Value. *See "Registry Editor."*

9 *Server Manager.* If you need to send a message to users connected to a Remote Access Server, the correct tool is RAS Administrator. *See "Configuring servers."*

10 *Explorer, File Manager, or Windows NT Server Manager.* Explorer and File Manager offer the easiest user interface but you can still use Server Manager. *See "Sharing resources."*

Part VI
Connectivity

The 5th Wave   By Rich Tennant

Network Help Desk at Disney Corp.

In this part . . .

1 help you study how to configure Windows NT Server for interoperability with NetWare servers. I also cover the Remote Access Service (RAS). Microsoft stresses your understanding of RAS configuration options and procedures on the certification test. Read on to prepare for all the connectivity questions the exam might toss your way.

Chapter 16
Remote Access Service

● ●

Exam Objectives

▶ Configuring RAS communications

▶ Configuring RAS protocols

▶ Configuring RAS security

▶ Configuring Dial-Up Networking clients

● ●

*O*ne of the most powerful and versatile technologies included with Microsoft's Windows NT Server is the Remote Access Service, more commonly known as *RAS*. RAS is designed to make network resources available to remote clients through a variety of dial-up options, such as standard phone lines, ISDN lines, and packet-switched networks like X.25. There are many configuration options and at least two different dialog boxes where RAS must be configured. Also, from a security perspective, if you configure RAS improperly, you face the potential for serious consequences.

To ensure proper implementation of this RAS technology, Microsoft stresses understanding RAS configuration options and procedures on the certification exam.

If you're already familiar with RAS in the Windows NT 3.51 implementation, you want to pay close attention to additional functionality available in the Windows NT 4.0 implementation, such as Multilink and the Point-to-Point-Tunneling Protocol (PPTP).

Quick Assessment

Installing and Config-uring Remote Access Service (RAS)

1 The _____ dial-up protocol was designed as an enhancement to the original SLIP specification and is an industry standard framing and authentication protocol that allows clients and servers to interoperate in a multivendor environment.

2 RAS includes a _____ that allows clients to gain access to NetBIOS resources such as file and print servers on a network, regardless of which transport protocol is installed on the server.

3 Microsoft RAS provides routers for the _____ and _____ network transport protocols.

4 _____ domain security provides for organization-wide security using a single network logon model, eliminating the need for duplicating user accounts across a multiple-server network.

5 The _____ API provides a standard way for communication applica-tions to control functions for data, fax, and voice calls.

6 You install RAS via the _____ tab, which you find by starting the _____ application from the Control Panel.

7 Windows NT Server 4.0 supports _____ simultaneous inbound RAS connections, whereas Windows NT Workstation 4.0 supports _____ inbound RAS connections.

8 RAS supports the following three LAN transport protocols: _____, _____, and _____.

9 _____ is installed on a Windows NT Workstation or Windows 95 machine that needs to act as a client to a RAS server.

Answers

1 *PPP.* Review "Making a Dial-Up Connection."

2 *NetBIOS Gateway.* Review "Configuring Network Protocols."

3 *IP; IPX.* Review "Configuring Network Protocols."

4 *Integrated.* Review "RAS Security."

5 *Telephony (TAPI).* Review "Remote Access Service Overview."

6 *Services, Network.* Review "Installing RAS."

7 *256, 1.* Review "Supported Operating Systems."

8 *NetBEUI, IPX, TCP/IP.* Review "Configuring Network Protocols."

9 *Dial-Up Networking.* Review "Installing RAS Client Software."

Remote Access Service Overview

One of the most challenging portions on any of the Windows NT certification exams is Remote Access Service (RAS) and Dial-Up Networking. The depth of knowledge required to successfully negotiate the exam questions ranges from analog modem signaling to network security operations.

Passing the exam doesn't require you to be an expert in all of these areas. A general operational knowledge of modems and LAN/WAN protocols helps you make intelligent configuration choices. As with many other Microsoft technologies, you only get credit for the Microsoft way on the MCSE exams!

This chapter assumes that you understand the basics of analog communications and LAN communications. You need to know that a modem is responsible for converting the digital signals in a computer to analog signals that can travel over phone lines and back to digital signals that another computer can process. You need to understand how to configure a modem in Windows NT and you need to know how to handle configuration problems. *Interrupt conflicts* and *modem speed mismatches* are two configuration problems that you may encounter in exam questions. You also need to have a good feel for the differences between LAN protocols such as TCP/IP, IPX/SPX, and NetBEUI before you can fully appreciate the different RAS configuration options relating to each protocol. If you feel at all shaky about any of these subjects, now might be a good time to check out Chapters 9 and 10 of this book, grab your modem reference book, or even review *Windows NT Administration Guide.* Come back when you're ready. This chapter isn't going anywhere without you.

Questions referring to calling cards, locations, or drivers are probing about the Telephony Application Programming Interface (TAPI).

New with Windows NT 4.0, Microsoft provides two new pieces to the RAS puzzle, and you need to know how to install and configure them both:

> ✔ **Multilink:** Gives you the ability to use multiple modems for the same communication session

> ✔ **Point-to-Point-Tunneling Protocol (PPTP):** Provides for secure networking over the Internet

The security-related questions require an understanding of integrated domain security, the different encryption options available for logon, auditing, callback security, and PPTP filtering.

Server and RAS: What you can expect

Those reference books can be maddening! I know about the stress level involved in studying for certification tests. I've taken fifteen of them myself. I always wondered why all of the study guides I used didn't just spell out what was on the test. I vowed that I'd do that if I ever wrote a test guide. So, here it is!

First, know the definitions for all acronyms you meet in this chapter. Don't be surprised if you see a question or an answer that includes PPP, SLIP, TCP/IP, NetBEUI, IPX/SPX, or PPTP.

Remote Access Service breaks down into two main categories: the server side and the client side. In the following two sections, I tell you the areas that the certification exam stresses most about RAS clients and RAS servers, respectively.

RAS Clients

On the client side, the new kid on the block is an option called AutoDial. AutoDial allows you to map a network resource to a Phonebook entry, thereby allowing automatic dialing and connection when you access that resource. AutoDial is definitely useful, but using it does involve some gotchas. AutoDial supports TCP/IP connections only, and if you have many shortcuts to network resources on your desktop, using it is infuriating. Every time the desktop is refreshed, at logon for instance, the system will try and dial the phone number associated with the connection used by each shortcut.

The RAS Server

Understand the differences between RAS protocols like PPP, SLIP, and PPTP. You also should review X.25 and ISDN. Each protocol provides a different level of functionality and Microsoft wants to make sure that their Certified Professionals can pick the right protocol for a given situation.

Knowing how to configure networking protocols such as NetBEUI, TCP/IP, and IPX is a top concern. Configuring NetBEUI and IPX is straightforward; configuring TCP/IP is another matter. When you configure TCP/IP, you have quite a few options concerning how a RAS server handles IP addresses.

Troubleshooting RAS is a major exam area. Be familiar with

- Modem troubleshooting
- Windows NT Event Viewer
- Dial-Up Networking Monitor
- Logging (you have to make an entry in the Registry, not merely enable a check box option)
- Spotting authentication problems
- Multilink and Callback security issues

Analog modems

Analog modems use standard telephone lines. Sometimes you may hear these telephone lines referred to as *POTS* lines. POTS is an acronym for *Plain Old Telephone Service.* Don't be surprised if you see the acronym PSTN, too. Public Switched Telephone Network is simply the fancy name for the phone company. You need to be aware of several relevant features of modems. Here's a list of basic modem information for you to take into the test with you:

✔ Maximum modem speed right now is about 56 Kbps. Actual modem speed normally ranges between 28.8 Kbps and 38.4 Kbps.

✔ To configure a modem in Windows NT, you may need to define a port with the Control Panel Ports applet.

✔ To configure a port, you need an available interrupt.

Modems are *synchronous* or *asynchronous.* Synchronous modems are much more expensive than asynchronous modems, and usually provide higher throughput. On the certification exam, you should assume that *modem* refers to an asynchronous communication device (external or internal) that converts digital signals to analog signals and analog signals to digital signals for transmission over standard telephone lines.

Remember that modems make RAS a *point-to-point connection.* Modem communications occur in a *one-to-one relationship.* You need a modem at each end of the communications link to complete the connection.

ISDN

Integrated Services Digital Network (ISDN) is a digital system specification that offers higher throughput than the PSTN. ISDN was designed to eventually replace all analog telephone lines now in use by most telephone companies across the country. ISDN comes in two flavors: *Basic* and *Primary,* also sometimes called *BRI* and *PRI.* All you need to worry about for the exam is BRI.

The BRI specification allows you to configure two B channels for voice or data and one D channel for link management. Each B channel is a 64 Kbps digital transmission. If you use the channels separately, each channel has an individual, independently dialed telephone number. With most ISDN offerings, you can combine the two B channels to form one 128 Kbps channel (most often used for data).

Here are the ISDN basics to remember for the test:

✔ ISDN data transmission speed is either 64 Kbps or 128 Kbps.

✔ ISDN lines must be installed at both the server site and the remote site.

✔ An ISDN adapter must be installed in both the server and the remote client.

✔ Windows NT treats the ISDN adapter as a network adapter.

Supported operating systems

The certification exam tests whether you can distinguish between RAS server operating systems and RAS client operating systems. The server operating system list is easy to remember. It consists of Windows NT Server and Windows NT Workstation, although bear in mind that the basis for all test questions on the NT Server exam is, ultimately, NT Server.

RAS on NT Server allows 256 inbound connections. RAS on NT Workstation allows for only one inbound connection.

The client operating system list isn't much longer: It includes Windows NT Server, Windows NT Workstation, and Windows 95. (You only need to know about these three for the certification test.)

To determine whether an operating system is a viable client operating system, ask whether you can install and configure Dial-Up Networking on it. If you can, it qualifies as a RAS client.

Supported network interfaces

When thinking about network interfaces from a RAS perspective, try to remember that, for all intents and purposes, these interfaces are *Wide Area Networking (WAN)* interfaces. A WAN interface extends Local Area Networking (LAN) functionality over some type of point-to-point connection, such as a leased telephone line, or over a privately owned network. (Examples of privately owned networks include X.25 or Frame Relay networks.) All WAN interfaces, such as X.25 and ISDN adapters, appear as network interfaces under Windows NT.

Supported protocols

For the exam, you need to be able to keep two types of protocols straight. Figure 16-1 shows the client configuration option that enables you to specify a RAS protocol. Figure 16-2 shows the supported LAN protocols.

RAS protocols

✔ Serial Line Internet Protocol (SLIP)

✔ Point-To-Point Protocol (PPP)

✔ Multilink PPP

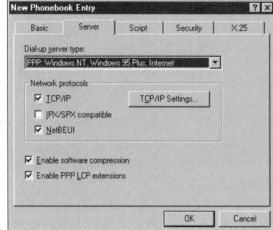

Figure 16-1:
The client
option used
to select
the type of
server.

Windows NT LAN protocols

✔ NetBEUI

✔ IPX

✔ TCP/IP

The *Serial Line Internet Protocol (SLIP)* is an old industry standard for establishing TCP/IP connections over serial lines. The Dial-Up Networking client still supports SLIP, but Microsoft dropped support for SLIP at the server level in Windows NT 4.0. For SLIP, remember

✔ Requires a static IP address

✔ Requires a text-based logon session that often requires scripting

✔ Supports TCP/IP only

✔ Transmits authentication passwords as clear text

PPP was designed to overcome some of the limitations of the SLIP standard. The PPP specification provides a set of standard framing and authentication protocols that enables RAS clients and servers to interoperate in a multivendor environment.

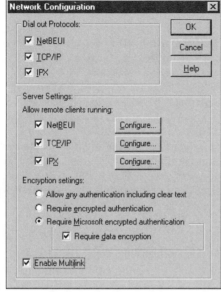

Figure 16-2:
The
available
LAN
protocols.

The PPP architecture allows clients to connect with LANs running TCP/IP, NetBEUI, and IPX. That means that client applications written to the Windows Sockets Interface (WinSock), NetBIOS, or IPX can all use the same communication method to connect to server applications.

PPP also allows clients that are running Client Services for NetWare (CSNW) to dial in and connect to NetWare servers.

Any answers that suggest configuring SLIP on the RAS server for either Microsoft- or UNIX-based clients are wrong. SLIP is not available as a RAS server dial-in protocol in Windows NT 4.0.

WAN connection

For the exam, any connection you create with RAS is a WAN connection. If a question asks specifically about a WAN connection, however, consider whether the question is about an X.25 connection or an ISDN connection.

Don't let "WAN connection" throw you. Aside from some configuration options, a WAN connection is just like a network adapter for your LAN.

RAS limitations

Microsoft tends to emphasize the features and benefits of their technologies and to downplay the limitations. That doesn't let you off the hook for knowing problems with RAS.

Remember the connection limits of NT Server and NT Workstation. Server allows up to 256 connections and Workstation allows just one connection.

Another limitation of RAS is *bandwidth*. The certification exam may hit you with a situational question that requires you to choose whether to implement RAS or some other form of connection, such as a leased line. Following are some guidelines for choosing RAS as your communication method.

Choose RAS when

- ✔ Your bandwidth requirement is less than 128 Kbps.
- ✔ You do not require a full-time connection (the system dials when the connection is demanded).
- ✔ Low cost is the driving factor.

Don't choose RAS when

- ✔ You need higher bandwidth than an asynchronous-modem-based communication method can provide.
- ✔ You require a dedicated, full-time communication pathway.
- ✔ Leased lines already exist, or cost is not an issue.

The one caveat to using leased lines is Microsoft's backup connection recommendation. Microsoft suggests that you implement RAS as a backup communication pathway for a leased line connection. For example, you might have a T1 connection between a branch office and the home office. To provide a backup connection should the T1 go down, you could configure a RAS server at the home office and a client running NT Server and Dial-Up Networking at the branch office. If the T1 went down, you could then use the RAS connection to reestablish communications.

The final limitation involves Multilink. You may not be able to achieve a 128 Kbps connection with an ISDN adapter, and you cannot achieve your full throughput potential with callback security.

Installing RAS

When installing RAS, take a few moments to gather some information before you begin the actual installation. Here's the information that you should have available to you:

- ✔ The model of the modem and driver
- ✔ The type of communication port you need to configure
- ✔ Whether to use the computer for dial-out, dial-in, or both
- ✔ The client protocols, and the correct options
- ✔ Modem settings, such as baud rate
- ✔ Security settings

When you install RAS as a service on an NT Server, you use the Services tab in the Networking Configuration dialog box, shown in Figure 16-3.

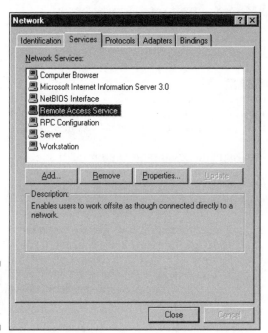

Figure 16-3:
Installing
RAS.

PSTN modems

If you can find the device on the NT Hardware Compatibility List, you can use it as a RAS communications device.

A modem is a serial device, so it needs a COM port, and a COM port needs an available IRQ. Figure 16-4 shows the RAS configuration screen for a PSTN modem.

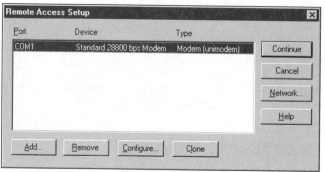

Figure 16-4:
The con-
figuration
screen for a
PSTN
modem.

ISDN adapters

You can use two types of ISDN hardware devices to connect your computer to an ISDN line: *internal ISDN cards* and *external ISDN adapters.*

Internal ISDN cards can take full advantage of your ISDN line. You can install an internal adapter, however, only if your computer has a slot available to support the same type of bus (for example, ISA, EISA, or PCI) as the card you want to install.

External ISDN modems are easy to install, but they do not have the level of performance of internal modems. An external ISDN modem plugs into a computer's serial or parallel port. These ports impose speed limitations. Most computer serial ports do not transmit information faster than 115 Kbps, which is less than the ISDN maximum data speed of 128 Kbps.

Configuring network protocols

RAS server enables multiple clients to connect by using multiple protocols. The server also allows the same client to connect using more than one protocol. You want the RAS server and the LAN to run the same protocols, so that RAS clients can connect to network resources using any combination of configured protocols.

You configure protocols via the Network Configuration dialog box, which you open by choosing Network from the Remote Access Service dialog box. The Network Configuration dialog box gives you several options, as shown in Figure 16-2. Table 16-1 explains the four major categories of options.

Table 16-1	RAS Server Configuration Options
Options	*Use To . . .*
Dial-out protocols	Select dial-out protocols.
Server settings	Configure dial-in protocols.
Encryption settings	Set the authentication level required for logon.
Enable Multilink	Enable PPP Multilink protocol on the server.

TCP/IP

The most complex protocol to configure is TCP/IP. Also, the most thoroughly tested protocol on the certification exam is TCP/IP.

You set the TCP/IP protocol configuration for the RAS server in the RAS Server TCP/IP Configuration dialog box (shown in Figure 16-5), which you invoke by selecting the TCP/IP check box in the Network Configuration dialog box and clicking the Configure button.

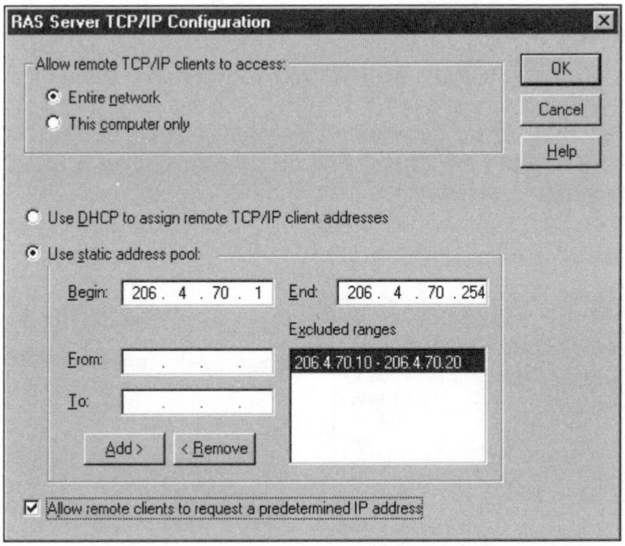

Figure 16-5:
The TCP/IP options.

✔ **Allow remote TCP/IP clients to access:** You use this option to grant clients access to resources located anywhere on the network or to restrict clients to accessing only resources located on the RAS server. This option enables or disables the IP router function included in the RAS server. Choose the Entire Network radio button option to enable the router; choose the This Computer Only radio button option to disable the router.

✔ **Use DHCP server to assign remote TCP/IP client addresses:** You use this option to allow remote clients to request a DHCP-assigned address from a DHCP server located on the RAS server or elsewhere on the network. All TCP/IP configuration information normally available through DHCP becomes available to remote clients.

✔ **Use static address pool:** Watch out for this option! It may look like DHCP, and it might taste like DHCP, but it's not DHCP. The real trouble begins when you inadvertently overlap the range of IP addresses defined to the RAS server with the scope of addresses defined on a DHCP server. Before you know it, you have IP address conflicts spreading like wildfire! I saw a question relating to this problem on a couple of the vendor exams, and on my certification exam.

✔ **Allow remote clients to request a predetermined IP address:** You use this option to allow users to request a specific address; for example, your clients require a specific IP address to function on your IP network. Now, don't mistake requesting an IP address for reserving an IP address on a DHCP server — that's something else altogether.

NWLink IPX/SPX

When Novell NetWare clients need access to NetWare servers through the RAS server, IPX support is a must. Use the RAS Server IPX Network Configuration dialog box to grant network access permissions and to assign network numbers to dial-up clients. Bring up the RAS Server IPX Network Configuration dialog box by activating the IPX check box in the Network Configuration dialog box. Figure 16-6 shows the IPX configuration options.

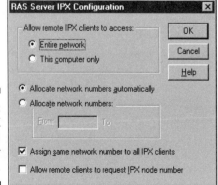

Figure 16-6: The IPX options and their functions.

The following options configure the IPX protocol for RAS client access.

- ✔ **Allow remote IPX clients to access:** Enables or disables the IPX gateway. *Entire Network* allows clients to access resources anywhere on the network. *This Computer Only* allows clients to access only resources on the RAS server.

- ✔ **Allocate network numbers automatically:** This radio button tells the server to randomly generate and assign the client an IPX network number. The network number is analogous to the station's address.

- ✔ **Assign same network number to all IPX clients:** This option specifies a range of network numbers for dial-up clients.

- ✔ **Allow remote clients to request IPX node number:** This option allows IPX clients to request a node number or IPX address.

NetBEUI

When you run the RAS setup program on a server on which the NetBEUI protocol has been installed, the RAS setup program automatically enables NetBEUI as a dial-in protocol. The setup program also enables the NetBIOS gateway. NetBEUI is a small, fast protocol that you should enable whenever you need to provide support only for small workgroups.

You only need to configure one option for the NetBEUI protocol, and you do it in the RAS Server NetBEUI Configuration dialog box, shown in Figure 16-7. (You open the RAS Server NetBEUI Configuration by checking the NetBEUI check box in the Network Configuration dialog box.) Choose the Entire Network option to allow clients to access network resources located anywhere on the network; choose the This Computer Only option to give clients access only to resources located on the RAS server.

Figure 16-7:
The
NetBEUI con-
figuration
dialog box.

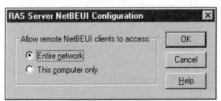

RAS security

Security is a big deal to Microsoft. Industry acceptance of their operating systems and software depends in part on offering secure products and training technicians to deploy those products properly.

You cannot pass any Microsoft exam without correctly answering a few security-related questions.

RAS is no exception to security scrutiny. When you configure a RAS server, it's an access point to your LAN or enterprise network that anyone who has a RAS client can use to gain access to your private information.

Permissions

To install and configure the RAS server, you must be an Administrator in the Windows NT domain that contains the RAS server or in the local Administrators group for the server.

Before a user can access a network via RAS, the user must have a valid Windows NT account on the RAS server or in the NT domain. You must grant that account the Dial-In permission by using one of the following utilities:

- ✔ User Manager
- ✔ User Manager for Domains
- ✔ Remote Access Administrator

The Remote Access Administrator Permissions, shown in Figure 16-8, is the tool of choice because it provides the most flexible interface.

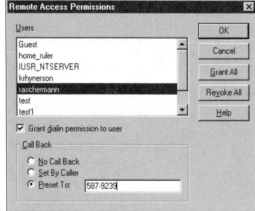

Figure 16-8: The Remote Access Administrator Permissions interface.

Callback

RAS offers a Callback feature that ensures that a user can access the network only from a specific location. It can also save users toll charges. When using callback, the user initiates a call and connects with the RAS server. The RAS server then drops the call and calls back a moment later.

Under the Remote Access Administrator utility, the Remote Access Permissions dialog box contains three callback options, described in Table 16-2.

Table 16-2	RAS Callback Security Options
Option	*Use To . . .*
Preset To	Specify the callback number for the user.
Set By Caller	Allow the user to specify the number for each call.
No Callback	Disable callback security.

No Callback is the default setting. Set to this default, the RAS server establishes the communications session with the client immediately.

To set maximum security, choose the *Preset To* option and type the telephone number for the user's modem. Use this option only for stationary remote computers. When the user's call reaches the RAS server, the server takes the following steps:

1. Determines whether the user name and password are correct.

2. Responds with a message that the user will be called back.

3. Disconnects and calls the user back at the preset number.

Use the *Set By Caller* option for clients who call from various locations and phone numbers. Besides letting these users call from different areas, it minimizes telephone charges. When the user's call reaches the RAS server

1. The server determines whether the user name and password are correct.

2. If the username and password are correct, the Callback dialog box appears on the user's computer.

3. The user enters the callback number and waits for the return call.

Passwords

RAS security features include password encryption using different forms of authentication protocols. The users have the same accounts and password combinations for the RAS server as they do at their desk in the office connected to the LAN. You can't give a separate password for RAS access.

RAS uses the Challenge Handshake Authentication Protocol (CHAP) to negotiate the most secure form of encrypted authentication that both server and client support. CHAP uses a challenge-response mechanism with password encryption. CHAP allows the RAS server to negotiate downward from the most secure to the least secure encryption mechanism, and it protects passwords transmitted in the process.

Data encryption

Data encryption is a way of maintaining security by ensuring that the data is unreadable even if it is intercepted during transmission. To configure data encryption, clients configure each Phonebook entry to use data encryption.

Remember two key facts about data encryption for the test:

✔ Information is encrypted from the RAS server to the RAS client.

✔ You can configure data encryption from the client or the server.

Multilink

A Windows NT Workstation can connect to a Windows NT Server by using Multilink PPP connections. Multilink enables you to combine the bandwidth of two or more physical communications links to increase RAS throughput. RAS Multilink lets you easily combine analog modem paths and ISDN paths.

When used with two or more modems or ISDN B channels, Multilink PPP supports simultaneous data transfer across multiple connections. (For the test, assume it works.) The aggregate bandwidth or throughput of a Multilink connection is the sum of the bandwidths of the individual connections.

Point-to-Point Tunneling Protocol (PPTP)

PPTP is a new networking protocol that supports multiprotocol virtual private networks (VPNs). PPTP allows remote users to access private networks securely across the Internet by dialing into an Internet service provider (ISP) or by connecting directly to the Internet.

Following are the key benefits of PPTP that you should remember

✔ Saves money (because you can connect to a local ISP).

✔ Enables encapsulation of other protocols in IP packets for Internet routing.

✔ A private point to point network is created between the RAS server and the RAS client by encrypting the data packets.

If you install and configure PPTP on both the RAS server and the remote client, you can establish a secure connection over the Internet. Use Lab 16-1 to practice establishing connections.

Lab 16-1   Installing PPTP

1. **Start the Network application, found in the Control Panel.**

2. **Click Add and select Point to Point Tunneling Protocol.**

3. **Enter the number of connections to make available to PPTP.**

4. **Select the port on which you want to install PPTP.**

5. **Restart your computer for the PPTP configuration to take effect.**

One way to protect your private network if you have PPTP enabled on the RAS server is to configure PPTP filtering. When you enable PPTP filtering, only PPTP packets may enter the private network. Lab 16-2 enables PPTP filtering.

Lab 16-2   Enabling PPTP Filtering

1. **In the Control Panel, double-click the Network icon and then click the Protocols tab.**

2. **Select TCP/IP Protocol and then click Properties.**

3. **On the IP Address tab, click Advanced.**

4. **In the Adapter box, select the network adapter for which you want to specify PPTP filtering.**

5. **Select the Enable PPTP Filtering check box.**

RAS Clients

When you study RAS for the certification exam, concentrate on the RAS server material. You need to know the answers to a few client questions (that's what this section is about), but focus on server functionality.

Installing RAS client software

The RAS client on Windows NT or Windows 95 is called Dial-Up Networking. Client knowledge is confined to 32-bit Microsoft operating systems.

Client software is also available for Windows 3.1, Windows for Workgroups, and DOS, but the exam doesn't test your knowledge of configurations for these older operating systems.

Dial-Up Networking is automatically installed on systems running Windows NT Workstation or Windows NT Server if the Remote Access To The Network option is selected during setup.

Making a dial-up connection

A phonebook entry stores all of the configuration information for a connection to a server. You can make phonebook entries specific to a user or available to all users on a system. System-wide phonebook entries are stored in the system phonebook.

The following list examines tabs and their configuration options. Knowing which options are found on which tab can help you beat the test.

- ✔ **Basic:** On the Basic tab, you must provide a name for your new connection. You specify the primary telephone number and any alternative telephone numbers for the connection. Alternative telephone numbers are dialed if dialing the primary number fails to establish a connection. You also specify dialing properties, such as long distance and credit card number numbers, on the Basic tab. Perhaps the most important thing to remember about the Basic tab is that you use this tab to enable Multilink connections.

- ✔ **Server:** On the Server tab, you must indicate whether you're connecting to a SLIP server or a PPP server. The rest of the configuration options differ based on which RAS protocol you choose. If you select PPP, you can select the LAN protocol you want to use and you can enable software data compression.

- ✔ **Script:** Use the Script tab to specify a script file to run to assist logon or logoff operations. For the test, just know what scripting is and what you can use it for; don't worry about needing to write or interpret a script.

- ✔ **Security:** Use the Security tab to set the level of authentication encryption you want to use. Also, remember that you come here when you need to enable data encryption.

- ✔ **X.25:** No exam questions relate specifically to X.25.

Client protocols

The client protocols are the same for Dial-Up Networking as they are for the server configuration: TCP/IP, IPX, and NetBEUI. Review the TCP/IP configuration options before going into the test. Remember that the same DHCP options available on a LAN are available to remote clients.

Security

Use the phonebook Security tab to configure the level of authentication and encryption for the client to use to connect to the server.

RAS security features include password encryption and authentication, data encryption, and callback security. RAS uses the Challenge Handshake Authentication Protocol (CHAP) to negotiate the most secure form of encrypted authentication that both server and client support. CHAP uses a challenge-response mechanism. The Password Authentication Protocol (PAP) uses clear-text passwords and is the least sophisticated authentication protocol.

The Microsoft RAS server has an option that you can use to block transmission of clear-text passwords. The No clear-text passwords option gives you the power to enforce a high level of security.

On installations that require total security, you can set the RAS server to force encrypted communications. Users who connect to that server automatically encrypt all data sent. Dial-Up Networking also provides the user a way to request data encryption. To maintain security in case of unauthorized interception of remote access transmissions, users configure each Phonebook entry to use data encryption.

As an additional measure of security, RAS offers a Callback feature. The Callback feature ensures that only users from specific locations can access the RAS server. It also saves toll charges for the user. To use Callback, the user initiates a call and connects with the RAS server. The RAS server then drops the call and calls back a moment later to the preassigned callback number.

Multilink

Before you can use the Multilink capability, you must have multiple communications devices, such as modems, installed and configured on your system. To enable the Multilink protocol, find the Dial Using list on the Basic tab of the phonebook entry and select Multiple Lines. Then click Configure. Select the devices that you want to use.

Scripting

You can use the Script tab of the phonebook entry to specify logon or logoff scripts to be run while starting or terminating a connection with the server. A script is often set for SLIP connection. A script usually waits for a sequence of characters, then sends a response, then waits again for another sequence. This process continues until the script is complete.

Troubleshooting RAS Connections

RAS troubleshooting questions fall into one of the following categories:

- ✔ Using the Event Viewer
- ✔ Enabling PPP logging
- ✔ Authentication problems
- ✔ Multilink and Callback incompatibility
- ✔ AutoDial

When you get a RAS troubleshooting question on the certification exam, remember that you're dealing less with RAS than you are with Windows NT — and Windows NT includes some top-notch troubleshooting tools.

Always make the Windows NT troubleshooting tools your first stop on the road to RAS problem determination and resolution. Windows NT includes a tool called the Event Viewer. Veteran system administrators can testify to the usefulness of this tool. You should think of the Event Viewer as the first place to go for information about a RAS-related problem if you want to score points on RAS troubleshooting questions.

You use the Event Viewer to monitor three separate logs: system, application, and security. The important log for RAS is the system log.

If you can't solve the issue at hand with the Event Viewer, you may need to dig a little deeper. The next logical step is to ensure that you're getting a good PPP connection. You can't just look at the Event Viewer for this one — you actually have to do a Registry edit! To enable PPP logging, you need to set the value of the following Registry key to 1:

```
\HKEY_LOCAL_MACHINE\SYSTEM\CurrentControlSet\Services\Rasman\PPP\logging
```

When you update this Registry entry, a *Ppp.log* file is created in the systemroot\System32\Ras folder. The file contains detailed information about PPP connections. You need to know how to enable PPP logging for the certification test!

Authentication problems represent another area of RAS troubleshooting you may face on the test. Users that don't use the same implementation of the encryption algorithms as the server will not be able to authenticate and gain access to network resources. To resolve this issue, select the lowest level of authentication at each end. (Low-level authentication often requires clear-text passwords.) If authentication is successful, increase the level of authentication. Continue this process until you find the highest level of authentication that both the client and the server support.

Multilink and Callback are two new RAS features included in Windows NT 4.0. Watch out on the certification test for a question that involves both Multilink and Callback. The issue is that you can configure only one callback number for a client. If you have four 28.8 Kbps modems connected to both your server and workstation enabled for Multilink, and you're using callback security, your throughput is only 28.8 Kbps because the server can call back only one number for the client.

The last area of troubleshooting is the new client feature, AutoDial. When Windows NT Explorer starts up, any persistent network connections or shortcuts on the desktop that point to network resources cause AutoDial to try to make the appropriate connections — yes, very annoying, to say the least. You have two options for resolving this problem:

- ✔ Disable AutoDial completely
- ✔ Remove the shortcuts from the desktop and eliminate any persistent connections

RAS Monitor

There are two programs often referred to as RAS Monitor, one a server-side application, the other a client-side application. Only one is the true RAS Monitor: the server-side application. The actual name of the client-side application is the Dial-Up Networking Monitor. You must keep these straight for the exam — and the only way to do that is to check the context of the question. Even Microsoft seems to have trouble keeping them straight!

The Dial-Up Networking Monitor starts automatically when the RAS client starts. The most common use of the Dial-Up Networking Monitor is to verify that a client is actually transmitting information to the server. If you ping the server from the client, you see the transmit light on the Dial-Up Networking Monitor flash four times, once for each successful transmission.

When a connection is made to a RAS port, the RAS service searches for the next available port. If a port is available, it queries the device to verify that its status is okay. If an error is returned, the port is listed as Line Non-Operational in the RAS Monitor. Figure 16-9 displays the Port Status screen of the RAS Monitor.

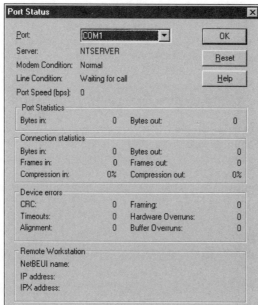

Figure 16-9:
The Port
Status
screen of
RAS
Monitor.

Prep Test

Prep Test

RAS

1 Which of the following network resources can a RAS client access? (Choose all that apply.)

A ❑ Printers
B ❑ File shares
C ❑ Databases
D ❑ Mail and Scheduling

2 Which of the following is not considered a WAN protocol?

A ○ PSTN
B ○ X.25
C ○ ISDN
D ○ T1

3 Which of the following protocols does RAS not support?

A ○ DLC
B ○ TCP/IP
C ○ NetBEUI
D ○ IPX

4 Which RAS protocol supports TCP/IP, NetBEUI, and IPX?

A ○ SLIP
B ○ PPP

5 Which of the following is not a security feature of RAS?

A ○ Auditing
B ○ PPTP
C ○ Callback
D ○ Multilink

6 Which of the following is not included as part of a TAPI location?

A ○ Area code
B ○ Outside line access codes
C ○ RAS server phone number
D ○ Calling card

7 RAS on Windows NT Server supports how many connections?

A ○ 1
B ○ 10
C ○ 255
D ○ 256

8 Which of the following is not a RAS port usage setting?

A ○ Dial-out only
B ○ Dial on demand
C ○ Receive calls only
D ○ Dial-out and receive calls

9 Where would you go first to troubleshoot a RAS problem? (Choose all that apply.)

A ❑ Performance Monitor
B ❑ Event Viewer
C ❑ PPP logging file
D ❑ RAS Monitor

10 You use which application for enabling PPP logging?

A ○ Dial-Up Networking
B ○ Network application under the Control Panel
C ○ Registry Editor
D ○ RAS Monitor

Prep Test Answers

1 *A, B, C, and D.* All answers are correct. I hate to start off with a trick question, but you need to remember that any resource that is not resident on the client or on the RAS server is a network resource. To gain access to network resources, you will need to enable access to the entire network. Do you remember how to do that? *If not, check out the client protocol configuration section "Client Protocols."*

2 *D.* A T1 line is a leased digital line. At least within the context of the test, a T1 line is not considered to be a WAN connection although a T1 line may be involved as an intermediate connection. *Review "RAS Limitations."*

3 *A.* Client protocols are TCP/IP, IPX, and NetBEUI. *Review "Supported Protocols" and "Remote Access Service Overview."*

4 *B.* SLIP is the older of the two remote access protocols. Its primary design purpose was to extend TCP/IP networks over phone lines, so it doesn't support the NetBEUI or IPX protocols. *Review "Supported Protocols."*

5 *D.* Multilink is a feature of RAS, but not a security feature. Remember that Multilink and Callback don't always play well together. *Review "RAS Security."*

6 *C.* This may seem picky, but this kind of question can trip you up on the exam, especially if you read too fast. The actual phone number that the client dials is part of the Phonebook entry, not the Location definition. *Review the "Server and RAS: What You Can Expect" sidebar.*

7 *D.* RAS on NT Server supports 256 inbound connections, and RAS on NT Workstation supports one inbound connection. *Review "Supported Operating Systems."*

8 *B.* Dial on demand is kind of a general term used to indicate that a connection is not a full-time connection. When you are configuring RAS ports, the ports will be designated to Dial Out, Receive calls only, or Dial out and Receive calls. *Review "RAS Limitations."*

9 *B, D.* I personally don't like this question, but I include it anyway because I've seen it pop up on a number of vendor exams with either answer being correct. The correct answer depends on the context of the question. If you're investigating the RAS server, you start with the Event Viewer. If your focus is the RAS client, you probably want to start with the Dial-Up Networking Monitor (also referred to as the RAS Monitor). *Review "RAS Monitor."*

10 *C.* A trick question. Remember that turning on logging requires a Registry edit. *Review "Troubleshooting RAS Connections."*

Chapter 17

NetWare

• •

Exam Objectives

▶ Installing Gateway (and Client) Services for NetWare (GSNW) and Client Services for NetWare (CSNW)

▶ Configuring Gateway (and Client) Services for NetWare (GSNW) and Client Services for NetWare (CSNW)

▶ Windows NT Connectivity with NetWare

▶ File and Print Services for NetWare (FPNW)

▶ Directory Services for NetWare

▶ Migration Tool for NetWare

▶ Gateway (and Client) Services for NetWare and Client Services for NetWare

▶ Understanding Interoperability with NetWare

• •

*W*elcome to the chapter that most people *think* that they can skip. After all, you're going to be an MCSE, not a Novell CNE, right? Many people go into the NT Server exam thinking just that. They're surprised when they get at least a half-dozen questions on NetWare.

Novell commands about 60 percent of the networking market, and that makes NetWare an important issue to Microsoft. In the real world, you run pretty good odds of having to deal with a combination of NetWare and NT on one network somewhere along the line. I can guarantee that a Microsoft exam will make you deal with it. Therefore, passing the NT Server exam includes knowing how to use NT to tame the Big Red Beast.

This chapter gives you what you need to meet this challenge. You don't need an expert understanding of NetWare to pass the exam. What you do need to master are the concepts and procedures that allow Windows NT to interact with Novell. You'll also need to know how to replace NetWare with Windows NT. After all, if there wasn't something about bumping the other guy out of the market, it just wouldn't be Microsoft.

Quick Assessment

Windows NT Connectivity with NetWare

1 You use _____ to set up NetWare file shares in NT Server.

2 You use _____ to migrate from NetWare servers to NT Server.

3 Microsoft's version of the IPX/SPX transport protocol is called _____, and NT uses it to communicate with NetWare.

4 You use the _____ application to map NetWare resources.

Configuring GSNW

5 To attach to a NetWare 3.12 server, you must supply GSNW with the _____'s name.

6 To attach to a NetWare 4.1 server, you must supply GSNW with the _____ and the _____.

7 GSNW provides access to NetWare _____ and _____ resources.

Windows NT Connectivity with NetWare

8 _____ is an add-on utility that lets NT Servers function as a NetWare 3.12 file and print servers.

9 _____ is an add-on utility that allows a single login for NetWare clients.

Installing GSNW

10 Before setting up GSNW, a user account and a group account named _____ must exist on the NetWare server.

Windows NT Connectivity with NetWare

11 _____ and _____ must be running on your NT Server before you can run Migration Tool for NetWare.

Answers

1 *GSNW.* See "Sharing NetWare Files."

2 *Migration Tool for NetWare.* See "Migration Tool for NetWare: Paving with Good Intentions."

3 *NWLink.* See "Configuring NT Server for NetWare."

4 *Network Neighborhood.* See "Mapping NetWare Resources."

5 *preferred server.* See "NetWare 3.12."

6 *default tree* and *context.* See "NetWare 4.1."

7 *file* and *print.* See "Gateway Services for NetWare (GSNW): The Bridges of Santa Clara County."

8 *FPNW.* See "File and Print Services for NetWare (FPNW)."

9 *DSMN.* See "Directory Service Manager for NetWare (DSMN)."

10 *NTGATEWAY.* See "Gateway Services for NetWare (GSNW): The Bridges of Santa Clara County."

11 *NWLink; GSNW.* See "Sharing Network Files."

Migrating from NetWare to NT

In the Beginning, there was NetWare, and the networks were good. Then a serpent named Microsoft came into this garden of cable to overthrow Novell from its reign. So NT was born. Microsoft included a number of tools that allow you to switch over from NetWare to Windows NT:

- ✔ NWLink
- ✔ Migration Tool for NetWare
- ✔ Gateway (and Client) Services for NetWare
- ✔ Client Services for NetWare

In addition, NetWare enthusiasts can purchase a software package from Microsoft called Services for NetWare. This package includes

- ✔ File and Print Services for NetWare (FPNW)
- ✔ Directory Services for NetWare (DSNW)

All of these provide a means of connectivity with NetWare networks, or a way of switching over a network from Novell to Windows NT. For the NT Server exam, you'll have to understand each of these.

The NT Server exam includes a number of questions on getting Windows NT and Novell NetWare to work together. You will also need to know how to change a network from being a NetWare environment, to being completely Windows NT (what they call "migration").

In the real world there is only one effective way of migrating from Novell NetWare to Windows NT: *slowly*. This is because doing so is an expensive process, time consuming, and a bit of a pain for a network administrator.

Real world aside, a Microsoft exam forces you to deal with the technical aspects faced from these real world situations. NWLink is the protocol used by Windows NT to communicate with NetWare. Gateway (and Client) Services for NetWare on an NT Server, and/or Client Services for NetWare on NT Workstations allow interaction with NetWare servers. FPNW and DSNW respectively allow NetWare clients to access NT Server resources, and enjoy a single logon to all servers in the network. After slowly incorporating these services, there's the final step of switching over NetWare servers to NT Servers with the Migration Tool. While these are the basic elements of a migration, each of these are covered in the detail you'll need to successfully complete the NetWare portion of your NT Server exam.

Configuring NT Server for NetWare

A common factor in NT Server's many services for NetWare is the use of the *NWLink* protocol, Microsoft's version of the Internet Packet Exchange/ Sequenced Packet Exchange (IPX/SPX) transport protocol. The NWLink protocol allows NT Server to communicate with NetWare servers and clients.

Although NWLink does allow these two disparate network systems to communicate, it does nothing to integrate the two environments. It just paves the road you'll travel during the migration. Microsoft provides the following services to allow NT and NetWare to interact efficiently:

- ✔ Gateway (and Client) Services for NetWare (GSNW)
- ✔ File and Print Services for NetWare (FPNW)
- ✔ Directory Service Manager for NetWare (DSNW)
- ✔ Migration Tool

You must have the NWLink protocol in place before you can use any of these services. In addition, each service has specific installation and configuration features. The common configuration on NT Server for each is NWLink.

If the NWLink protocol isn't running, neither GSNW, FPNW, DSNW, or the Migration Tool can run. If an NT Server has had NWLink removed, and can't run these services, then the problem is that NWLink isn't running. If the service involves NetWare, the NetWare compatible protocol must be running.

Microsoft Services for NetWare

Services for NetWare provides Novell networks with luxuries that Windows NT clients tend to take for granted. With it, NetWare clients can logon to the network. In NetWare, you log have one to each server separately.

Services for NetWare combines two previously separate services: File and Print Services for NetWare (FPNW) and Directory Service Manager for NetWare (DSNW). It doesn't come with the NT Server installation CD, so you must purchase it separately.

Don't get hung up on questions that ask for solutions that are offered with NT Server. If asked for a solution that is included with NT, you can easily disqualify Services for NetWare — and as a result, FPNW and DSNW. These aren't included with the NT Server installation disk.

FPNW is for *files* and *resources,* DSNW is for *access,* and Services for NetWare is the amalgamation of both into one package.

File and Print Services for NetWare (FPNW)

This add-on utility lets NetWare access resources on NT Servers. FPNW lets NetWare clients use the following services on an NT Server:

- ✔ File services
- ✔ Print services
- ✔ Application services

The NetWare client perceives the NT Server as a NetWare server the whole time it uses these services. Basically, it masks the NT Server. All the while, the NetWare client thinks it's accessing a NetWare server

Directory Service Manager for NetWare (DSMN)

The DSMN add-on utility enables NetWare users to perform the single network logon that Microsoft network clients enjoy. This service copies NetWare user and group accounts and synchronizes them across all NetWare servers. Consequently, users only have to remember an account name and a password to access file, print, and application resources. They only have to log on once, to access any of the resources to which they have proper permissions.

Because DSMN can copy NetWare accounts, you can copy the accounts to a domain controller, which, in turn, enables you to manage NetWare users from User Manager for Domains. It also makes these users subject to the NT Server domain's account policy.

Gateway Services for NetWare (GSNW)

Gateway (and Client) Services for NetWare gives NT Server, and computers that use NT Server, the capability to access NetWare file and print resources. The client doesn't access a NetWare server directly; instead, the client's requests go first to GSNW and from there pass on to the NetWare server.

GSNW uses its own account to access NetWare servers; all requests pass through that account. That eliminates the need to purchase multiple NetWare client licenses for users who access the server through this gateway. Everything passes through one account, so you only need one license.

Before you can set up Gateway Services for NetWare, you must first

1. Set up a user account with the appropriate rights to NetWare's file system.

2. Set up a group account named NTGATEWAY with appropriate rights to file and print resources.

Minus these two basic steps, GSNW cannot connect to NetWare.

After you set up the necessary accounts on NetWare, you're ready to set up GSNW on your NT Server. Lab 17-1 covers gateway service installation.

Lab 17-1   Installing Gateway (and Client) Services for NetWare

1. **From the Network applet in the Control Panel, click the Services tab.**

2. **Click the Add button and then select Gateway (and Client) Services for NetWare from the list.**

3. **NT Server then prompts you for the NT Server CD, and the software is installed.**

GSNW requires the NWLink protocol to run. If NWLink isn't already installed on NT Server, don't worry; GSNW just autoinstalls it.

NetWare 4.1

In NetWare 4.1, NetWare Directory Services (NDS) is used to store the location of resources on the network. This database, shared by all NetWare 4.1 servers, contains information on users, groups, printers, and other resources. NDS replaces the bindery of previous NetWare versions. Attaching to such a server, therefore, requires more information than attaching to a server running a previous version of NetWare.

NDS requires two important pieces of information — the default tree and context — which you must configure in GSNW (or CSNW). NDS has a hierarchical structure, made up like a tree. Because of that, NDS requires that you provide an NDS name (your user name), and the context (or position) of that name in the NDS tree. Basically, the context is a pointer to the location of an object (in this case, a user). If the NetWare network you're connecting to uses NDS, you must provide the default tree and context information to NDS. Lab 17-2 covers gateway service installation.

Lab 17-2   Configuring Gateway (and Client) Services for NetWare for use with NetWare 4.1

1. In the GSNW applet in the Control Panel, select Default Tree and Context.

2. Enter the tree name of your NetWare 4.1 server, as well as the context of your user account.

   After you supply this information, you can attach to the server.

NetWare 3.12

With NetWare 3.x, you don't need to worry about seeing the forest through the NDS trees. NetWare 3.12 predates NDS, which makes attaching to a NetWare 3.12 server simple. Because NDS isn't used, you don't need to specify such things as Default Tree or Context. You do however have to specify which is the preferred server you'd like to attach to. Lab 17-3 illustrates the configuration.

Lab 17-3   Configuring Gateway (and Client) Services for NetWare for use with NetWare 3.12

1. In GSNW in the Control Panel, select Preferred Server.

2. From the drop-down list, select the server you want to attach to, or, if you don't see the server you want on the list, type in the server's name.

Mapping NetWare Resources

Mapping NetWare resources is basically the same as attaching to a Windows NT resource. If you know how to attach to Windows NT resources, you pretty much already know how to map NetWare resources. Whereas attaching to a resource on an NT network involves browsing the Microsoft Network hierarchy, mapping NetWare resources requires you to choose NetWare or Compatible Network. The only difference between the two is where you go in Network Neighborhood. Lab 17-4 illustrates mapping.

Lab 17-4   Mapping NetWare Resources

1. In Network Neighborhood, double-click Entire Network and then select NetWare or Compatible Network.

2. Browse through the tree until you find the server you want to attach to, and then right-click the volume to map.

3. Select Map Network Volume and enter your NetWare account name in the Connect As text box.

Sharing NetWare Files

Gateway (and Client) Services for NetWare (GSNW) enables Microsoft network clients to access NetWare files. The way it works: An NT Server with the GSNW service uses a single account to attach itself (as a client) to a NetWare server. The Microsoft network computers then pass their requests through that NT Server to access the NetWare resources.

However, GSNW isn't the only means of sharing NetWare files to Microsoft network clients. You also can deploy Client Services for NetWare (CSNW), which can be installed on NT Workstation. Whereas GSNW passes requests from the client to an NT Server through to the NetWare machine, CSNW lets a client directly access a NetWare server (no middleman).

The service called Client Services for NetWare can only be installed on Windows NT Workstations. However, there is a client portion to GSNW. Remember that the full name for GSNW is Gateway (and Client) Services for NetWare. The client portion of GSNW is used to connect to the NetWare server, and is used when an NT Server is being used as a workstation and connecting to a NetWare server. Although you can't install the service CSNW on NT Server, you don't need to. It's included as part of GSNW.

CSNW accesses NetWare directly, while GSNW acts, as its name says, as a gateway with a single account. You can have 40 NT Workstations using CSNW, and 40 accounts are used to access the NetWare file server. If these same 40 NT Workstations pass their requests through an NT Server with GSNW, only one account accesses the NetWare server.

You install CSNW on NT Workstation almost exactly the same way as you install GSNW, but you must have a separate NetWare account for each person who uses CSNW. Again, GSNW passes requests to NetWare through just one account, but NT Workstations using CSNW access NetWare directly, which means that you need individual accounts for those users.

Don't spend much time trying to figure out if CSNW is referring to NT Server accessing NetWare. Although CSNW installs along with GSNW (as the client portion), Client Services for NetWare generally refers to the package installed on NT Workstations. Many people put CSNW as an answer for what GSNW uses to connect to a NetWare server, and are wrong. If it's NT Server, the answer is GSNW!

Gateway (and Client) Services for NetWare makes sharing NetWare files easy. When you install GSNW, a new GSNW icon appears in your Control Panel. In this new applet, you set up gateways to NetWare resources, which Microsoft clients can then access.

The CSNW for Workstation and GSNW for NT Server applets are identical, except for the Gateway button that appears when you open the GSNW applet. Clicking the Gateway button brings up the Configure Gateway dialog box. You use this dialog box to enable your gateway, by checking the Enable Gateway check box (when you install GSNW, the gateway doesn't become active until you check this box).

NT Server uses the information in the Gateway Account field to attach to the NetWare server. In the Password field immediately below the Gateway Account field, enter the password for this account (then use the extra box to confirm it). GSNW uses this account and password to log you on to NetWare.

For the GSNW account and password, you must have a matching account and password in NetWare. In NetWare, you need to

1. Set up a user account with the appropriate rights to NetWare's file system.

2. Set up a group account named NTGATEWAY with appropriate rights to file and print resources.

Lab 17-5 illustrates the process.

Lab 17-5   Creating a NetWare Share for Microsoft Network Users

1. **To create a NetWare share for users of a Microsoft network, click the Add button.**

   The New Share dialog box appears.

2. **Specify the Share Name that users can use to access a shared NetWare directory.**

3. **In the Network Path field, type the UNC name that specifies the location of the shared NetWare directory.**

4. **In the Use Drive field, select the drive letter that this directory will be mapped to.**

5. **You are given an option that allows you to limit the number of users that can use the shared directory. Choose either "Unlimited" or select a set user limit.**

Remember that as the number of users increase, the performance of the gateway decreases. If the gateway bogs down, decrease the user limit.

If you receive an error that the gateway could not be created (when you click OK and your configuration is saved), you may have exceeded the maximum number of users that can be logged on at one time to the NetWare server. Try again when fewer users are using the NetWare server. Otherwise, the new gateway share should appear in the Gateway Shares list box.

Migrating clients from NetWare to NT

Gateway Services for NetWare allows *gradual* migration. NT Workstations and other Microsoft-based systems can access NetWare servers, while NetWare users continue working without even knowing that you're making these changes. The gradual migration over time that GSNW enables you to deploy results in superior training for, and higher production quality from, your Windows NT users.

A common problem when you migrate from one NOS to another is something called *version control problems.* That is, you get two different versions of the same file. Each file has duplicate and dissimilar data, which causes problems when you finally migrate the network to the new system. By using GSNW, allows a slow migration, but also avoids version control problems.

These version control problems emerge something like this: You bring a new server with a nifty new NOS online and copy information (everything from account information to shared files) over to it. You migrate users over to this server that has the new network system, and these users, expecting to lose their jobs if they don't do their work, make changes to the information on the new server. Unfortunately, at the same time, users on the old system continue to do their jobs, making changes to information on the old server. What you get are two different versions of the same file.

Gateway Services for NetWare lets you bypass this migration gadfly. Because GSNW lets you access your original NetWare server, you can just leave the files on the NetWare server during the period of migration. Then, when you're ready to switch the servers over to NT Server, just copy the files to the NT server. No muss, no fuss.

Migration Tool for NetWare: Paving with good intentions

Migration Tool for NetWare makes the switch from NetWare to NT easy — well, at least easi*er*. It enables you to migrate a NetWare server to an NT domain controller in one fell swoop. However, even though Migration Tool is great for converting a server from NetWare to NT, it can't do everything. Items you can't migrate include:

- Workgroup and user account managers
- Login scripts
- Print server and print queue information
- Passwords

Some Netware information can't migrate to NT because

✔ Some data is encrypted.

✔ Some information serves different purposes in the two systems.

✔ NT does not use some of the information that NetWare needs.

You can't migrate passwords — they're encrypted in NetWare, and as such, NT doesn't understand them. The only way to migrate passwords (and other encrypted data) is to use a mapping file. A mapping file is used to specify which users and groups to migrate from NetWare to NT Server. You can also use this file to assign new user name and passwords, or to transfer passwords from NetWare to NT Server. While passwords are encrypted in NetWare, a mapping file is a simple ASCII text file (which Windows NT systems have no problem reading). The passwords can be specified in the mapping file, and migration of passwords can then take place.

What can you migrate? The Migration Tool enables you to select which directories and files to migrate, and then when it copies them to an NT Server, it retains the effective rights. It also lets you migrate user and group accounts and offers features for dealing with duplicate accounts.

Before you can run Migration Tool, you must have NWLink and GSNW running on your NT Server. If these are running, make sure you're logged on as an Administrator. You're now ready to start migrating.

The program name for Migration Tool for NetWare is NWCONV.EXE. It ships as part of the NT Server Installation CD and allows you to re-create a significant amount of information from a NetWare server into an NT Server. You don't have to do anything special to install the Migration Tool. When you install GSNW, it is installed automatically, and placed on the Administrative Tools menu.

Lab 17-6   Creating a NetWare Share for Microsoft Network Users

1. **Start Migration Tool.**

   You get a dialog box that presents a list of NetWare server and NT Server names. From this list:

   • Select the NetWare server to migrate from.

   • Select the NT Server to migrate to.

2. **Select the options — which are individual to your migration — by clicking the User Options and File Options buttons.**

3. **Check to see if your migration will work.**

   When you click the Trial Migration button, NWCONV.EXE (Migration Tool) performs a mock migration and checks for errors.

4. **If no errors occur, click the Start Migration button to start the actual migration.**

If you completely replace all NetWare servers with Windows NT Servers, you must replace some software on client computers, because after a complete migration, the NetWare clients are still using NetWare requestors (the NetWare term for redirectors). You have to replace those NetWare redirectors with Microsoft redirectors, because NT Server can't understand information sent from NetWare redirectors. You can replace client operating systems with such OSs as Windows NT Workstation, but simply changing the redirector is much cheaper — and sometimes is your only choice.

If a migration has taken place, but users can't interact with NT Server, NetWare requesters may still be on the client computers. Replace the NetWare requester with a Microsoft redirector.

Sharing NetWare Printers

NT Server makes sharing a NetWare *printer queue* (NetWare's word for what Microsoft calls a *printer*) easy. Because print jobs go through Gateway Services for NetWare, printing occurs through a gateway — which makes the NetWare printer seem (seamlessly so, no less) like a normal NT network printer. As with anything else in Windows NT, some configuration is required. Fortunately, it's no more difficult than setting up a local printer, or a printer on a Microsoft network. Lab 17-7 illustrates the process.

Lab 17-7   Sharing NetWare Printers through NT Server

1. **Double-click the Add Printer icon, in Printers in the Control Panel.**

   The Add Printer wizard springs into action.

2. **Select Network Printer Server and then click Next.**

3. **From the Share Printers list box, select the NetWare printer you want.**

   The Add Printer Wizard will prompt you to select or provide the printer driver, and ask if you want to make this your default printer.

4. **Right-click the printer to share and then select the Sharing tab.**

5. **Click the Shared radio button.**

6. **To change the name, click the Share Name field and type in the name to use for the share. Otherwise, skip this step, and keep the default share name, which is the same name of the NetWare Print Queue.**

After you complete the steps, you can use the shared NetWare printer queue. Because printing goes through GSNW, printer management occurs on the NT Server. Although the NetWare print server controls the printer, NT Server treats the printer like a Microsoft network printer.

Prep Test

1 You have set up GSNW and enabled the gateway. What else is required to access a directory on a NetWare server?

A ○ Set up a group account called NTGATEWAY.

B ○ Create a share.

C ○ Install NWLink.

D ○ Enable bindery emulation.

2 Which service allows migration to take place over a period of time?

A ○ Migration Tool for NetWare

B ○ GSNW

C ○ NWLink

D ○ Migration Services for NetWare

3 Which service allows NetWare clients to log on once to the network to access file, print, and application resources?

A ○ GSNW

B ○ CSNW

C ○ DSMN

D ○ FSNW

4 You use what to set up sharing NetWare printers in NT Server?

A ○ GSNW

B ○ CSNW

C ○ Printers

D ○ Syscon

5 To run Migration Tool, which of the following must be running on your NT Server? (Select all that apply.)

A ❑ GSNW

B ❑ CSNW

C ❑ Syscon

D ❑ NWLink

6 What must you use to migrate passwords from NetWare to NT Server?

A ○ GSNW

B ○ Mapping files

C ○ NWCONV.EXE

D ○ Mapping Tool for NetWare

7 You have set up GSNW on your NT Server. Before connecting to a NetWare 3.12 server through NT, what information must you supply? (Select all that apply.)

A ❑ Preferred Server
B ❑ Context
C ❑ Default Tree
D ❑ Version of NetWare you're connecting to

8 You have just set up GSNW on your NT Server. Before connecting to a NetWare 3.12 server through NT Server, what information must you supply? (Select all that apply.)

A ❑ Preferred Server
B ❑ Context
C ❑ Default Tree
D ❑ Version of NetWare you're connecting to

9 If you are completely replacing all NetWare servers on your network with NT Servers, what software must you place on the NetWare client machines?

A ○ NetWare requesters
B ○ NetWare redirectors
C ○ Microsoft requesters
D ○ Microsoft redirectors

10 After installing the GSNW service, you find that the gateway still isn't working. What is the most likely reason?

A ○ NWLink isn't installed.
B ○ Enable Gateway isn't checked in GSNW.
C ○ Enable Gateway isn't checked in Services.
D ○ The gateway hasn't been enabled from the NetWare side.

Answers

1 *B.* You must create a share in GSNW. *See "Sharing NetWare Files" for more information.*

2 *B.* Gateway Services for NetWare is the only possible answer that allows for migration to take place over a period of time. *See "Gateway Services for NetWare (GSNW): The Bridges of Santa Clara County" for more information.*

3 *C.* Directory Service Manager for NetWare (DSMN) allows NetWare clients to log on once to a network to access file, print, and application resources. *See "Directory Service Manager for NetWare (DSMN)" for more information.*

4 *C.* Sharing NetWare printers is set up in Printers on NT Server. *For further information, see the "Sharing NetWare Printers" section.*

5 *A, D.* You can't run Migration Tool if NWLink and GSNW aren't running on your NT Server. *See the "Migration Tool for NetWare: Paving with good intentions" section.*

6 *B.* Mapping files is the only way to migrate passwords from NetWare to NT. *See "Migration Tool for NetWare: Paving with good intentions" for more information.*

7 *A.* Before connecting the first time to a NetWare 3.12 server through NT, you must supply the name of the preferred server. *See the "NetWare 3.12" section.*

8 *B, C.* Before you can connect the first time to a NetWare 4.1 server through NT, you must supply the Default Tree and the Context. *See the "NetWare 4.1" section.*

9 *D.* When replacing all NetWare servers with NT Servers, you must supply Microsoft redirectors on all of the former NetWare clients so that they can interact with NT. *See the "Migration Tool for NetWare: Paving with good intentions" section.*

10 *B.* When you install GSNW, the gateway doesn't become active until you check the Enable Gateway check box in GSNW. *See the "Sharing NetWare Files" section.*

Part VII

Monitoring, Optimization, and Troubleshooting

The 5th Wave   By Rich Tennant

"Ah, we're in luck- the Director of IS is available for visitors."

In this part . . .

1 cover two sections of the Server exam: monitoring and optimization, and . . . yep, troubleshooting. I cover performance tuning and optimization using the Performance Monitor to identify and correct bottlenecks. I also cover troubleshooting, helping you study how to answer exam questions about installation, boot failures, configuration errors, printer problems, RAS problems, and connectivity problems. I discuss disaster recovery scenarios (including backup techniques and fault tolerance methods supported in Windows NT Server), as well.

Chapter 18
Reading the Gauges

Exam Objectives

▶ Running Performance Monitor

▶ Monitoring the Processor, Memory, Disk, and Network

▶ Understanding the Windows NT self-tuning process

*W*ant to know why your Windows NT Server runs so slowly? Interested in finding out just how much of your precious system resources are being soaked up by networked faxes? Does Windows NT Server have a program for you!

If you are into numbers, like details, or are just curious, then Performance Monitor is for you. It can tell you nearly everything about your server, and in many instances lend precious insight into the network itself. More important, Performance monitor is tested on many of the MCSE exams, including (of course) this one!

There are literally thousands of options in this program. If that is not enough, some programs install additional options for Performance Monitor. Take heart. This chapter shows you just what you need to pass the exam.

Quick Assessment

Running
Performance
Monitor

1 The four different views of Performance Monitor are Chart, Log, _____,
and Report view.

2 The _____ is a part of physical memory that holds recently used
information.

3 The _____ Object represents a running program.

Monitoring
the Processor,
Memory, Disk,
and Network

4 You may have a processor bottleneck if the System object: Processor
Queue length is often greater than _____.

5 You may also have a processor bottleneck if the Processor object: %
Processor time often exceeds _____%.

6 A _____ occurs when a program needs some data, and it can't find it
in the physical memory on the server.

7 The _____ bytes Counter is how much memory is left for the system
allocate. This is an instantaneous number, not an average.

8 If you do not have any activity when monitoring disk objects, you need
to issue the _____ command at the command prompt.

9 A constant disk queue of _____ or greater may determine a bottleneck
is occurring in the disk subsystem.

Understand-
ing Windows
NT's Self-
Tuning Process

10 The Windows NT _____ is responsible for determining the proper size
of the system cache.

Answers

1 *Alert*. Check out "Performance Tuning Overview."

2 *Cache*. Refer to Table 18-1 in "Performance Tuning Overview."

3 *Process*. See Table 18-1 in "Performance Tuning Overview."

4 *2*. Review "Processor bottlenecks."

5 *90*. See "Processor bottlenecks."

6 *Hard page fault*. See "Memory bottlenecks."

7 *Available*. Refer to Table 18-3 in "Memory bottlenecks."

8 *Diskperf -y*. Review "Disk bottlenecks."

9 *2*. See "Disk bottlenecks."

10 *Cache Manager*. Check out "Caching."

Performance Tuning Overview

The first thing you need to do in order to tune the performance of your Windows NT machine is to run Performance Monitor. Performance Monitor is located in the Administrator Tools section off of the Start menu.

Performance Monitor allows you to configure four different views:

- ✔ Chart view
- ✔ Log view
- ✔ Alert view
- ✔ Report view

Here's how Performance Monitor is organized. The things you can check are divided into categories called Objects. An object is a part of your Server that you can measure. Table 18-1 lists the default objects available in Windows NT Server 4.0. Each object is associated with counters.

For example, the Physical Disk Object has numerous counters that can be monitored. Using Performance Monitor on the Physical Disk Object, you can check on Average Disk Queue length, Percentage of Disk Time, and other items that will assist in your troubleshooting or optimization task.

In addition to Objects, and to Counters, you can also specify Instances. For example, if you have three Physical disks in your server, then you will have three instances of the Physical Disk. They are numbered 0, 1, and 2.

Table 18-1	Performance Monitor Objects
Object	*Description*
Cache	Part of physical memory that holds recently used information.
Logical Disk	Logical views of disk space, such as Disk partitions.
Memory	Random-access memory (RAM) used to store either program information or data.
Objects	Various software objects used by the system.
Paging File	Virtual memory. Like your Windows 95 swap file.
Physical Disk	The actual Hard disk or RAID device.
Process	Represents a running program.
Processor	Your actual CPU.
Redirector	The file system that diverts (redirects) requests that can't be satisfied locally to a network server.

Object	Description
System	System hardware and software.
Thread	The smallest part of a program or process that requires use of the processor.

The first thing you need to do is to "add a counter." There are counters for Processor, Disk, Memory, Page File, and many others. In addition to this, certain programs will add additional counters to Performance Monitor. For instance, when Proxy Server is installed, counters that allow you to monitor the number of users connected to the Proxy Server are activated. If you install the TCP/IP protocol, then additional counters for that protocol are added. Indeed, the extensibility of Performance Monitor is one of its greatest features.

Almost every Microsoft exam has questions on monitoring and optimizing your system. This is especially true for the Windows NT Server exam.

✔ Make sure you know the critical objects to monitor for each of the subsystems: disk, memory, processor, and network. The network counters are discussed in greater detail in the next chapter.

✔ Know the available views for Performance Monitor and when you should use them. You will most likely see a question on determining which view will give you the most information.

✔ Make sure you know how to turn on disk counters for monitoring.

✔ Also, make sure you know how to enable TCP/IP counters for monitoring.

Bottlenecks

On the exam, you may be presented with information gathered from Performance Monitor. Can you determine if a bottleneck exists with this information? So how do you answer these type of questions? You must have an idea of the objects and counters that are available in Performance Monitor. In real life you will establish a baseline of measurements as a guide for comparing your Performance Monitor results. For the exam, you won't have the luxury of a baseline to determine if you are being plagued by bottlenecks. You will have to understand the most important objects and counters for each of the major subsystems in your PC: processor, memory, disk, and network.

Processor bottlenecks

Usually, a processor bottleneck is really a memory problem. Occasionally, it may be a network problem, but seldom will it be a problem with the processor.

The symptoms of a processor bottleneck are easy. In fact, they are some of the few real guidelines available in working with Performance Monitor. These guidelines are as follows and should be memorized for the test.

- ✔ Processor object: % Processor time often exceeds 90%
- ✔ System object: Processor Queue length is often greater than 2
- ✔ On multi-processor systems, the System object: % Total Processor Time is often greater than 50%

You need to look at a few counters from the system object in Table 18-2, from the processor object (of course), and from the process object, and one from the thread object.

Table 18-2	Counters for Monitoring the Processor	
Object	*Counter*	*Description*
System	% Total Processor Time	This is a measure of the activity on all processors. In a single processor machine, it is equal to the Processor object, % processor time. In a multiple Processor machine, then it is equal to the sum of the % processor time for all processors in the machine, divided by the number of processors in the machine.
System Processor	Queue Length	This is an instantaneous count of how many threads are ready to be serviced, but have to wait for the processor to become available. Since this counter is not an average, it is best viewed in chart form.
Processor	% Processor Time	The percentage of time the Processor is busy.
Process	%Processor Time:_Total	This adds all the time all the threads are running on the Processor.

Processor bottlenecks occur when the processor is so busy responding to requests that it can no longer handle any more requests. When this happens, then the processor queue length continues to climb and no additional work is done by the Server. The trick in correcting a processor bottleneck is to find which process is hogging all the resources and balance the load on your servers. You may also be able to adjust the priority at which the application is running and therefore better allocate the resources. At any rate, you want to run the same set of counters after you make changes, to ensure you have in fact fixed the processor bottleneck.

Memory bottlenecks

If processor bottlenecks are rare, memory bottlenecks are common. In fact, a memory problem can often look like an underpowered processor, or a sluggish disk array.

Windows NT Server uses a memory system that combines physical memory and virtual memory (stores information on disk until needed). When the system has to retrieve information from disk and move it into physical memory, a slow, resource intensive process ensues. If this happens often enough, then you have a memory bottleneck. When the server *pages* (as it is called) data from the hard disk into memory, the processor, disks, and the controller are also involved. All of these resources are being pulled away from other activities, so the server slows down.

A sustained hard page fault rate of over 5 per second means memory bottleneck.

A hard page fault occurs when a program needs some data it can't find it in the physical memory on the server. Then it has to retrieve it from the disk.

Table 18-3 presents the most popular counters monitor memory-related events.

Table 18-3	Counters for Monitoring Memory
Counter	*Description*
Page Faults / Sec	How often data is needed for a process, and it is not available in physical memory
Pages Input / Sec	How many pages are coming from the physical disk to satisfy memory requirements of a process
Pages Output / Sec	How many pages are being written to the physical disk to free up space in memory for the faulted pages. If the process changes a page, then it has to be written to disk.
Pages / Sec	This is the sum of Pages In, and Pages Out
Available bytes	How much memory is left for the system allocate. This is an instantaneous number, not an average.

If you are looking for a memory bottleneck, then there are three counters to look at closely. These three counters are: Page Faults / Sec, Pages Input/Sec, and Page Reads / Sec. By examining these three counters, you can determine if you have a memory bottleneck. Figure 18-1 illustrates the three counters that should be added to determine if you have a memory bottleneck:

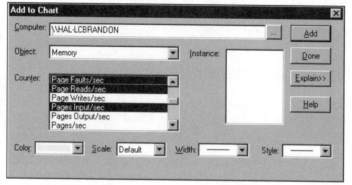

Figure 18-1:
The
Memory
counters
that should
be moni-
tored for
bottlenecks.

Lab 18-1 demonstrates performance monitoring your memory, in particular, the amount of Pages Input / Sec.

Lab 18-1	Using Performance Monitor Counters to Detect Page Faults

1. **Open up Performance Monitor by selecting Run from the Start menu, and typing** Perfmon **in the space provided.**

   This opens your friend Performance Monitor, which will not have any objects or counters present until you add them.

2. **Click the plus sign to add a counter.**

   A list of available counters will now be present.

3. **Select the Pages Input / Sec counter from the Memory object.**

4. **Click Add to add the counter.**

5. **Click Done to view the main Performance Monitor screen.**

   The counter has now been added, and is currently monitoring the page file.

6. **From the Start menu, select Run and type** Eventvwr.

   This will open the Event Viewer.

7. **Look at your Performance Monitor screen again.**

   Notice the spike in Pages Input / Sec at the time you opened the Event Viewer? That spike was due to Event Viewer being read from the hard disk, rather than from memory.

8. **Close Event Viewer.**

9. **Open Event Viewer again, just as you did in Step 6.**

10. **Look at your Performance Monitor screen again.**

   Notice there was no spike in Pages Input / Sec? This time Event Viewer was found in cache, and didn't need to be read from the hard drive.

Disk bottlenecks

The old saying, "Storage requirements always expand to meet the available disk space" certainly is true. However, in disk performance, we look at how long it takes to write and read from those storage bins.

Disk counters are not installed by default. They must be turned on separately. The reason for this is they do require a little bit of processor time, and could (on earlier models of 486 servers) adversely effect performance of the server. However, on modern servers, the effect is negligible.

To install Disk counters:

1. Go to a command prompt.

2. Type **diskperf -y.**

3. Restart the computer.

You must be a member of the Administrators group to issue this command.

Disk counters remain in effect until they are turned off. Even if you re-boot the system, they are in effect. If you need to see if they are in effect, the command is simply diskperf. To turn Disk counters off, follow these steps:

1. Go to a command prompt.

2. Type **diskperf -n.**

3. Restart the computer.

If you need to activate disk counters on a stripe set, follow these steps:

1. Go to a command prompt.

2. Type **diskperf -ye**.

3. Restart the computer.

Once you have the disk counters installed, which ones should you look at, and how would you interpret them? This is important for the exam, because you are asked which counters will determine whether a bottleneck exists in the system. Table 18-4 lists some of the more important disk counters, and gives you an idea of what they mean.

Table 18-4	Disk Monitoring Counters
Counter	**Description**
% Disk Time	How busy is the disk? A percentage of the time the disk is busy.
Ave. Disk Queue Length	The average number of operations waiting for the disk to become available.
Current Disk Queue Length	The current number of operations waiting for the disk to become available.
Ave. Disk Bytes / Transfer	The average number of bytes moved with each transfer. This is a measure of efficiency.
Disk Transfers / Sec	How fast are transfers being serviced? This counter does not consider the size of the transfers.

In order to recognize a disk bottleneck, there are some pretty good guidelines to keep in mind. They will appear as disk activity that is regularly above 85 percent, and disk queues that are greater than 2 while at the same time paging occurs at a rate of less than 5 per second. The paging value can be obtained from the memory counters of pages read / second and pages write / second.

High disk use is not a cause for alarm. It is not unusual for disk activity to remain at 40 input / output operations per second. But if you see constant use, and long disk queue lengths, then you have cause for concern.

Keep in mind that high disk use, and long queue lengths are typically signs of a memory shortage. First rule out memory as a problem before concluding you have a disk bottleneck.

Improving Network Performance

Network performance is largely a function of network bandwidth and network capacity. Network capacity is a broader term that takes into account the ability of the server and the network link to support the traffic and the resources using the network.

In examining bandwidth issues, you typically look at

- The rate at which bytes are transferred to and from the server
- The rate at which data packages (includes frames, packets, segments, and datagrams) are sent by the server
- The rate at which files are sent and received by the server

The counters examined in measuring Network capacity include

- Number of connections established by the server
- Number of connections maintained by the server

A likely exam question concerning network monitoring is what you need to install in order to monitor TCP/IP protocol information. In order to measure transmission rates with Performance monitor you would need to install the SNMP protocol through the protocol tab of network properties. You have access to the TCP counters, the IP counters, and the network interface performance counters if they are installed. Each of the installed protocols will have performance counters associated with the types detailed above.

Obstructed and non-obstructed views available

To work with the data collected over time, you have the option of creating a log. You often receive questions asking for the method to capture Performance Monitor data. You can examine the log in several different manners. If for instance, you wish open Performance Monitor, select input from where, and choose the log you had collected data into. At that point, you can choose which counter you wish to add from the previously collected data.

At times, however, you need to create a report from your data — perhaps to justify the expenditure for a system upgrade. In order to do this, choose report, and then tell it where the data is from. Remember that some types of data do not translate very well into reported data. These are typically the instantaneous types of data counters.

In addition to the two views mentioned above, you can choose to export the previously collected data into an Excel spreadsheet or into an Access database. Once you have the data there, then it is simple to manipulate the data and create the appropriate presentation method for the data.

Self-Tuning Tools

Once you have determined that you have a performance problem, you will then need to monitor the system with Performance Monitor to determine the true culprit. We have discussed the various disk, processor, and memory counters you should monitor for bottlenecks. You will also need to determine the amount of users, the types of applications, and how the operating system handles these applications.

Since this is a section on self-tuning tools, we will show just how Windows NT can keep things in balance through its own internal architecture. For example, you know that Windows NT will use the paging file (virtual memory) when the physical RAM has been depleted. Knowing this, you can configure your Windows NT system memory so that it is used more effectively, thus minimizing paging.

Multiprocessing

You learned earlier that Windows NT is fully scalable by taking advantage of multiple processors, otherwise known as *multiprocessing*. A Symmetric Multiprocessing (SMP) system can load balance processor requests across all the processors in the system. This will hopefully alleviate any processor bottleneck you may be experiencing.

Memory optimization

Once you have enough memory installed in your system, Windows NT will do the rest. There is no need to configure many memory related issues, with the exception of the page file. When the system uses the page file, it means not enough physical memory is available for use, so the system had to use the less efficient hard disk to store information. You are able to monitor your system for memory problems through the use of Performance Monitor and Task Manager. You should also have the correct page file settings in the System applet in the Control Panel.

Caching

Although cache is an overused term, will we be discussing the memory cache, which is where the system will first seek information. If the information is found in the cache, this is a *hit*. If the information is not found in the cache, this is a *miss,* and the system will have to retrieve the file from somewhere else in the system.

The Windows NT Cache Manager is responsible for determining the proper size of this cache, which is based on whether the system is functioning as a server or workstation. You will not need to configure these options because doing so is counterproductive. Basically, if the cache is too small, you need to add more memory to the system.

Here are four reasons why you may need to correct a performance issue yourself, because they cannot be automatically tuned by Windows NT:

- ✔ Resources not being used evenly
- ✔ A resource is not functioning properly
- ✔ One application is hogging a resource
- ✔ A resource is not correctly configured

Prep Test

1 Your boss has been on your back to add an additional processor to the server. However, you do not think it needs one. In order to prove the situation one way or the other, you decide to use performance monitor. Select the appropriate counters to prove your point to the boss. (Choose all that apply.)

- A ❑ Processor object: % Processor time
- B ❑ System object: Processor Queue length
- C ❑ Disk object: Disk Queue length
- D ❑ Memory: Pages per Second

2 You want to monitor Disk Object counters, but are unable to find them in Performance Monitor. Why?

- A ○ By default they are not installed.
- B ○ By default they are installed, but someone turned them off.
- C ○ It depends on which type of drives you have on the server as to whether or not they are available.
- D ○ You have a Disk Array installed, and Disk Object counters only work on single drives.

3 I am monitoring disk subsystem objects on my server with Performance Monitor. I feel I have a disk subsystem bottleneck. I open a few programs at the same time and the disk queue goes from zero to two. Does this indicate a disk subsystem bottleneck?

- A ○ Yes, because a disk queue of 2 means disk requests are waiting to be processed.
- B ○ No, because the disk queue should be *more* than two.
- C ○ No, because this is normal.
- D ○ Not enough information. You will need to monitor the page file to determine if there is also a queue for page file requests.

4 You want to quickly find a process using all the CPU resources. What do you do?

- A ○ Select the CPU object, and choose processes in Performance Monitor.
- B ○ Select the Process object in Performance Monitor, and choose "All."
- C ○ Start Task Manager, and select the processes tab, and look for a resource hogging process.
- D ○ Select the Processor object, and choose the Max process object.

5 You suspect you have a Memory bottleneck on your NT Server machine. To confirm your suspicion you select which of the following counters? (Choose all that apply.)

A ❑ Page Faults per Second

B ❑ Pages Input per Second

C ❑ Page Reads per Second

D ❑ Percentage of Processor Utilization

E ❑ Average Disk Queue Length

6 You want to check a number of TCP counters and a few IP counters in order to monitor Network protocol performance. When you start looking for the objects, they are not found. Why is this?

A ○ The counters will not be available if Network Monitor is not installed on the server.

B ○ The counters will not be available if SNMP is not installed on the server.

C ○ The counters will not be available if SMTP is not installed on the server.

D ○ The counters will not be available unless you have DLC protocol installed.

7 What Performance Monitor Object should be monitored for requests that can not be satisfied locally to a network server?

A ○ Network Object

B ○ Protocol Object

C ○ Redirector Object

D ○ Requestor Object

8 You are having high disk use and long queue lengths when you are running your Windows NT Server as an SQL database server. What is most likely the problem?

A ○ The processor can't keep up with the demand.

B ○ The hard drive is too slow.

C ○ You may not have enough physical memory on your system.

D ○ The paging file is not large enough.

9 You would like to gather Performance Monitor information to justify the need for more hardware for your file servers. Which type of view should you use?

A ○ Log view

B ○ Chart view

C ○ Report view

D ○ Alert view

10 I am done monitoring my disk subsystem, therefore I need to turn the disk monitoring counters off. However, I forgot how to do this. What should I do?

A ○ Use the diskperf command with no parameters

B ○ Use the diskperf -y command again

C ○ Use the diskperf -n command

D ○ Use the diskperf -ye command

Answers

1 *A, B, C, and D.* In addition to just monitoring the processor object, it is also import to look at memory and disk objects as well, to ensure they are not putting an additional load on the processor. *Review the section on monitoring performance.*

2 *A.* By default Disk Object counters are not installed. To install them you must install them from the command line. They are left out due to the load they can create on some older servers. *Refer to the section on monitoring disk performance.*

3 *C.* No, because this is normal. When opening several applications at once there may be a temporary queue of more than two. This is a normal operating condition, so it can be ignored. *Refer to the section on bottlenecks.*

4 *C.* Start Task Manager, and select the processes tab, and look for a resource hogging process. To quickly find a list of running processes, Start Task Manager, select the Processes tab, and look for the process consuming the most CPU time. *Refer to the section on the Task Manager.*

5 *A, B, and C.* To get a good overview of Memory performance, you would check Page faults per second. This is a total number of page faults and a good indicator of lack of memory. Additionally, you would check Pages Input, and Page reads per second to see where the paging is going. The other two do not provide direct input on memory performance. *Refer to the section on monitoring memory performance.*

6 *B.* The counters will not be available if SNMP is not installed on the server. In order to access certain Network counters, first the protocol has to be installed, and in addition SNMP has to be installed as well. *Refer to the section on monitoring network performance.*

7 *C. Redirector Object.* When information cannot be found on the local computer, it is the redirector's job to redirect the information to the proper destination. *Refer to the section on performance monitor objects.*

8 *C.* Even though these symptoms appear to be hard disk-related, this is a sign that you do not have enough physical memory installed in the system. If more memory was installed, the data could be found in memory more often, rather than being read from disk. *Refer to "Disk bottlenecks."*

9 *C. Report view.* Whenever you are asked to prepare a report or presentation on information obtained with Performance Monitor, you should use Report view. However, some of the instantaneous objects don't work well in Report view. *Refer to "Performance Tuning Overview."*

10 *C.* Use the diskperf -n command. Use this command to turn the disk counters off. You would use the diskperf -ye command to turn on disk counters for RAID systems. *Refer to "Disk bottlenecks."*

Chapter 19

Maximum Performance

. . . .

. . . .

*I*f you ever want to find out what's really going on with your Windows NT Server and the network, you certainly have the right tools at your disposal. Just like the exam will ask you questions about Performance Monitor, which we covered in the last chapter, the exam will also ask you about monitoring your server with Task Manager and monitoring your network with Network Monitor. Don't expect as many questions on these two topics though.

Task Manager gives you a quick overview of what applications are running on your system and how much memory those applications are consuming.

Network Monitor, a powerful tool that comes with Windows NT 4.0, enables you to look at the data stream on your network, as well as to (at a very low level) troubleshoot protocol and connectivity issues. You can also use Network Monitor to analyze the data (that it provides) in search of a wide variety of problems that may underlie bottlenecks or network congestion slowing the performance of your finely tuned network.

Quick Assessment

Monitoring with Task Manager

1   The three tabs in Task Manager are Applications, Processes, and _____.

2   In Task Manager, you can start a new task by selecting the _____ menu choice.

Understanding Network Monitor

3   You can't find Network Monitor in the Administrator Tools program group. Why not?

4   You are having network problems, and a consultant asks you to send him a network capture so he can diagnose the results. What is the easiest way to do so?

Collecting, Filtering, and Presenting data with Network Monitor

5   You suspect the IP protocol as the culprit concerning connectivity problems you're experiencing. How can you examine only this protocol in Network Monitor?

6   The default maximum buffer that Network Monitor allows is _____.

7   Your network card can capture packets from the network, even if it doesn't support _____ mode.

8   You suspect someone else might be running Network Monitor on your network. Can you find the person?

9   The two types of filters in Network Monitor are the capture filter and the _____ filter.

10 You can use logic expressions, such as AND, OR, and _____, when you create a capture filter.

Answers

1 *Performance.* See "Performance."

2 *File.* See "Applications."

3 *By default, Network Monitor is not installed.* Refer to "Network Monitor."

4 *The easiest way to get the data to a consultant is to save the capture as a CAP file.* Refer to "Saving Captured Data."

5 *To check on only one protocol, design a capture filter, and specify only that protocol.* Refer to "Filtering Captured Data."

6 *8MB less than the memory installed on the machine.* Review "Manually Executing a Capture."

7 *Promiscuous.* Check out "Network Monitor."

8 *Yes.* See "Network Monitor Installations: Detecting Others."

9 *Display.* See "Filtering Captured Data."

10 *NOT.* See "Filtering Captured Data."

Performance Monitoring

This chapter focuses on the main function of Windows NT Server: as a network file and application server. If you want Windows NT to perform network-related functions efficiently, you must use Performance Monitor (see Chapter 18) and Network Monitor to minimize network bottlenecks. Before I start talking about using Network Monitor to monitor system performance, I want to discuss another tool for monitoring the performance of your system: the Task Manager.

Although the Windows NT Server test doesn't focus much attention on Task Manager and Network Monitor, you should know a little bit about these two utilities. The following list tells you what you can expect to most likely make it onto the exam and what you can safely ignore:

- Don't spend every waking hour learning about Task Manager. Understand the basics; spend a few minutes playing around with it if you haven't already.

- Don't expect anything too deep concerning Network Monitor. You want to have a solid understanding of what Network Monitor enables you to do, as well as when and why to use it instead of Performance Monitor.

- Get a good handle on Network Monitor's filtering capabilities. You may get a question on the exam that presents a filter setup and asks you to identify what the filter is set up to collect.

In this chapter, I give you everything you need to ace these types of questions on the exam.

Task Manager

Task Manager provides a quick and easy way to get a look at what is going on under the hood of your server. By simply pressing Control+Alt+Delete and then selecting Task Manager, you bring up a very useful little utility. You also can bring up Task Manager by pressing Control+Shift+Esc. The following sections describe each of the three tabs available in the Task Manager, and explore a few ways to use it in day-to-day server management duties.

Applications

The Applications tab offers a quick view of the applications running on your server and their statuses (whether they're running, not responding, whatever), as shown in Figure 19-1. If you need to kill an application, you can do so by selecting the task and then pressing the End Task button at the bottom of the screen.

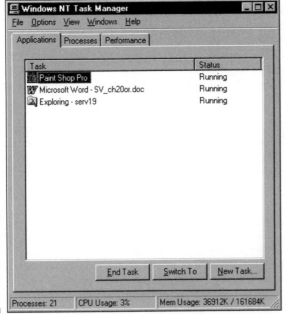

Figure 19-1:
The
Applications
tab in Task
Manager.

When I took the exam, I had a question that called on me to indicate (by checking items in a list) ways that you can start an application. Of course, the Run dialog box was one item, but so was Task Manager. Did you know that you can start applications with Task Manager? Yep. If you choose File⇨New Task in Task Manager, you get a dialog box like the Run dialog box.

To make sure you have this committed to memory, the next exercise will go through the steps required to start Task Manager, and then start an application, as shown in Lab 19-1.

Lab 19-1   Using Task Manager to Start an Application

1. **Open Task Manager by pressing Ctrl+Shift+Esc.**

2. **From the File drop-down menu, select New Task (Run).**

3. **In the Create New Task dialog box that just appeared, type** Eventvwr.

   Event Viewer opens.

4. **Close Event Viewer and Task Manager.**

Processes

The Processes tab (see Figure 19-2) lists processes running on the server. (*Processes,* as opposed to applications, run in their own memory space or use operating system services.) In addition to listing the current processes, this tab indicates the amount of memory usage, CPU usage, and processor time that each process is consuming.

To look at 16-bit tasks, you need to choose Options⇨Show 16 bit Tasks. Keep in mind that Task Manager shows the memory values in kilobytes, whereas Performance Monitor shows the values in bytes. If you compare values between the two, you need to multiply the values in Task Manager by 1024.

Performance

The Performance tab (see Figure 19-3) provides a real-time graph of the CPU utilization and Memory utilization. In four areas below the two graphs, it presents information about handles, threads, and memory on the server. To graph the percentage of processor time spent in Privileged or Kernel mode, choose View⇨Show Kernel Times. The Physical Memory section lists the amount of memory available.

Check the Performance tab first if you think you may be running out of physical memory or if you suspect excessive paging.

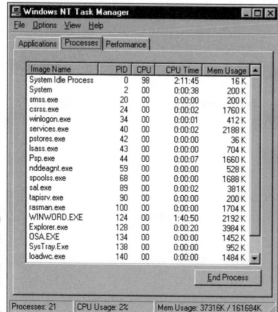

Figure 19-2:
The Processes tab in Task Manager.

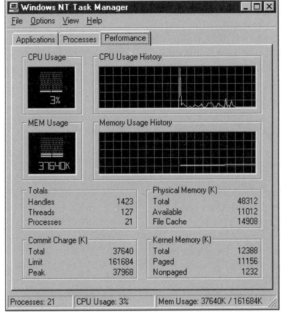

Figure 19-3:
The
Performance
tab in the
Task
Manager.

Network Monitor

For the exam, Microsoft may ask you what is required in order to use Network Monitor to capture packets of information from the network.

Nowadays, with Network Monitor, your network card does not have to support Promiscuous mode, because it uses the new NDIS 4.0 specification to copy all the frames that it detects into a *capture buffer* (a resizable area of memory). Consequently, however, Network Monitor can capture only as much information as can fit in available memory. Fortunately, insufficient available memory is rarely a problem, because you can select which part of the frame you need to see by designing a capture filter (works sort of like constructing a query on a database).

A filter lets you capture addresses, protocols, or protocol properties. I cover filtering in the "Filtering Captured Data" section.

Given Network Monitor's capability to capture data from your network, you cannot afford to ignore security concerns for this tool. You can take several steps to help protect your network from unauthorized use of Network Monitor (I deliver the goods in the "Network Monitor Security" section).

Installing Network Monitor

Network Monitor comes with Windows NT, but it doesn't come installed (by default). To install the program, choose Control Panel⇨Network⇨Services and then select Add Network Monitor Tools and Agent. Thereafter, you can launch Network Monitor from the Administrative Tools (Common) program group.

How to use Network Monitor

Network Monitor's primary function is to capture data. Your Ethernet card passes on a portion of the frames that it sees on the network to the capture buffer. If the capture buffer overflows, Network Monitor uses FIFO (first-in/first-out) to determine what to retain in memory. To prevent the capture buffer from overflowing, you can design a capture filter to refine what the card passes on to the capture buffer. You begin your capture session by choosing Capture⇨Start. Network Monitor displays statistics about the capture session as it runs, as shown in Figure 19-4. These statistics provide valuable information.

The exam may ask about which pane on the main screen of Network Monitor will display a certain type of information. With that in mind, you should know that the Graph pane (the upper left pane shown in Figure 19-4) provides an easy-see visual representation of your network's status. You can resize all of these panes to provide a better representation of the data you specifically want to view. This capability proves particularly useful when you monitor the progress of a capture in progress. This high-level overview can assist in troubleshooting by providing the following information:

- ✔ % Network Utilization
- ✔ Frames Per Second
- ✔ Bytes Per Second
- ✔ Broadcasts Per Second
- ✔ Multicasts Per Second

The Total Statistics pane (the upper right pane shown in Figure 19-4), gives you a numerical summary of the information displayed in the Graph pane. It also includes statistics regarding the captured data. It tells you how many frames you have in the buffer, how much of your buffer is in use, and whether you have dropped any frames owing to a full buffer.

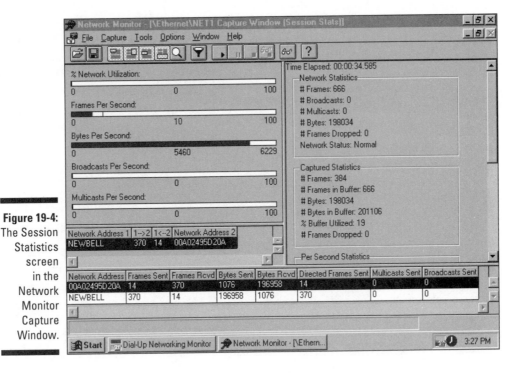

Figure 19-4:
The Session
Statistics
screen
in the
Network
Monitor
Capture
Window.

Figure 19-5 shows additional statistics that provide information about the
Network Card, and whether or not frames are being dropped.

The Session Statistics pane (just below the Graph pane) lists network
addresses of the computers talking in the current capture session. It details
the number of frames being passed about and the directions in which they
are going. Pay close attention to the arrow: It serves to indicate the direction of data flow (also, you use the arrow when you design capture filters).
The arrow always points toward the destination computer (the one where
the information is going). In Figure 19-5, for example, NEWBELL sends 370
frames of information to the computer at network address 2. NEWBELL
receives 14 frames from the other computer.

The Station Statistics pane (right below Session Statistics) breaks the
information from the Session Statistics pane down even further by listing
the number of bytes sent and received from each station represented in the
capture buffer. The information on broadcasts sent and multicasts sent, in
particular, helps you quickly pinpoint potential problems on your network.
You are able to determine if one computer is flooding the network with
broadcasts. In addition, you may want to investigate the direction of data
flow and sizes of the various exchanges taking place — all sources of
possible bottlenecks on the network.

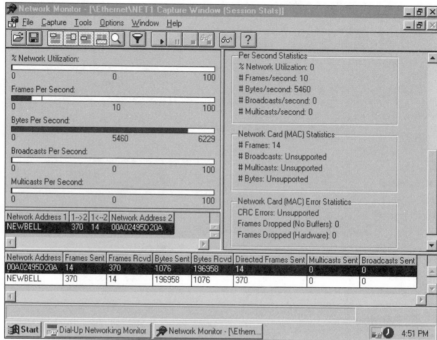

Figure 19-5:
The Total
Statistics
concerning
the network
card.

Manually executing a capture

Running Network Monitor is not difficult. To control a manual capture, you use the Capture menu, shown in Figure 19-6.

The nice Session Statistics Capture Window (I describe it in detail in the preceding section) actually puts a potentially unnecessary load on the CPU. If you choose Capture➪Dedicated Capture Mode, you can negate the load associated with updating the display and thereby provide additional re-sources for capturing frames. When you're in Dedicated Capture mode, you can switch to Normal mode to view real-time data, and vice versa (when you're in Normal mode, you can switch to Dedicated Capture mode — that item on the Capture menu toggles depending on which mode you're in).

Information captured

When you complete a capture session, what do you have? Network Monitor simplifies the task of analyzing the data by enabling you to organize the captured data into several different views. It also performs much of the protocol analysis for you. Figure 19-7 shows the Summary view, which helps you gain an overview of the information contained in the captured data.

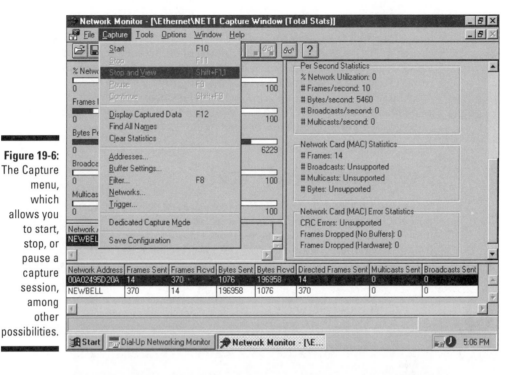

Figure 19-6:
The Capture
menu,
which
allows you
to start,
stop, or
pause a
capture
session,
among
other
possibilities.

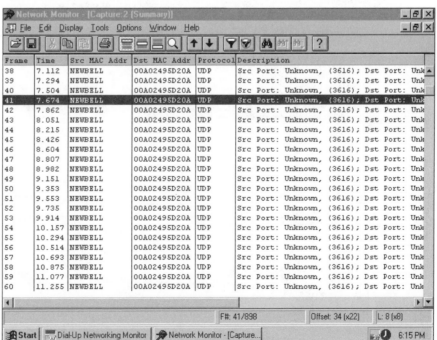

Figure 19-7:
The
Summary
view of
Network
Monitor.

You can find additional information, such as the source address, the destination address of the frame, and so on, by adding the Detail and Hex views, shown in Figure 19-8. You use the Window menu to access these additional views. Armed with the destination address of the offending computer, you can go to the machine and do a little investigative work to find out why the machine is flooding your network with useless broadcasts. This Detail view also gives you the detail you need about the protocols to change your buffer settings if you are focusing on one particular item.

Saving captured data

You can save data that you capture from the network. Perhaps you want to forward the information for expert analysis, or maybe use it as baseline information while you do some network tuning. At any rate, you save it as a CAP file that you can open in Network Monitor later. Network Monitor gives you the opportunity to choose the location and lets you indicate the range of frames you want to save.

The default is to save all the frames in the capture.

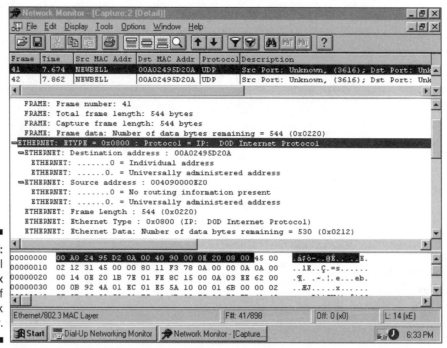

Figure 19-8:
The Detail
and Hex
view of
Network
Monitor.

Filtering Captured Data

If there was one thing I remembered about Network Monitor for my exam, it was the filters. You can use two kinds of filters with Network Monitor:

- ✔ Capture filters
- ✔ Display filters

Both types of filters work similarly. A filter works kind of like a query you would use on a database. It allows you to select a portion, or a subset, of the available data. For instance, if you have narrowed down a problem to a specific computer, you can filter out all other traffic and focus on that computer only. One other feature is that you can save your filters and reuse them later — this feature is especially helpful when you are trying to correct a particular problem. You save a data set, and after you make changes, you run the filter again, thereby enabling you to track your progress.

To design a capture filter, you choose Capture⇨Filter. You can filter data by Protocol, by Address, or by Data Pattern (or by a combination of all three), as shown in Figure 19-9.

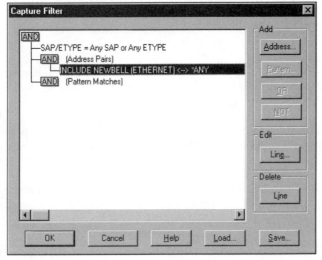

Figure 19-9:
Capture
Filter
functions
limit the
information
set for
capture.

If you want to filter by protocol, for example, you select the SAP/ETYPE line and then press the Edit Line button. You then get a menu that allows you to select the type of protocol to filter. To select one particular protocol, just disable all protocols and then enable the one protocol to examine.

If you are interested in just one machine, select the address pairs and again select the Edit Line button. Again, a menu opens, allowing you to select the address to examine, as shown in Figure 19-10. You can include an address or exclude an address. You also can specify the direction of information flow. You select the name for Station 1 in the left column, the direction arrow (remember, the arrowhead points in the direction of data flow), and then the recipient under the Station 2 column. For instance, in Figure 19-10, the filter includes data traffic from NEWBELL to any station on the network, as well as traffic from any station on the network to NEWBELL.

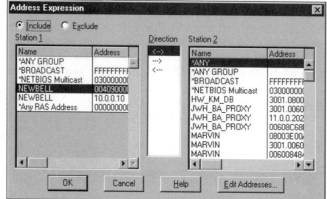

Figure 19-10:
Filtering
addresses
in Network
Monitor.

A *display filter* works much like a capture filter; however, because it works only on data already captured, it does not affect the contents of the capture buffer.

When you create a display filter, you can choose a particular protocol, address, or data property to help you sort through the data. Making the selections works the same as when you design a capture filter — with one important difference: You also can apply the logic expressions of AND, OR, and NOT. Being able to use logic expressions gives you a greater range of selectivity when you create your filter than you have in the Capture Filter mode.

Network Monitor Security

The power available via Network Monitor necessitates appropriate security measures to safeguard your network from those who would misuse the tool. Microsoft has already implemented one security feature for you — Network Monitor monitors only that traffic between the server it is running on and the rest of the network. However, the version that ships with Systems Management Server (SMS) can capture frames sent to any computer from any computer on the network, and it can capture frames over a remote network, as well.

Password protection

You can, using the Monitoring Agent icon in the Control Panel, set two different passwords for Network Monitor: the *display password* and the *capture password*. The display password permits you to access a saved capture (a CAP file). When you have the display password, you may only open previously saved capture files; you may not capture new data.

The *capture password* gives you unlimited access to Network Monitor. When you have the capture password, you may open saved capture files and create new captures.

If you install Network Monitor Agent on your computer and run the service without password protection, anyone who has the SMS version of Network Monitor can connect to your server and use it to capture data from your network.

Network Monitor installations: Detecting others

To protect your network from unauthorized snooping, Network Monitor can easily detect other instances of the program on your network, regardless of whether those other instances of the program are running. For instance, if the driver is installed on a machine, Network Monitor gives you the following information:

- ✔ Name of machine
- ✔ Name of user logged on to the computer
- ✔ Ethernet address of machine
- ✔ Version number of program
- ✔ Whether the program is capturing data or merely installed

To get this information, choose Tools➪Identify Network Monitor Users. ***Important:*** If you have network segments separated by a router that does not forward multicasts, you cannot detect Network Monitor installations on the other segment without being connected to that segment.

Prep Test

1 Your boss tells you that he thinks the network is sluggish, and he wants you to use Network Monitor to see if you can find any problems on the network. He asks you if the server Ethernet card supports Promiscuous mode. Why would he ask such a question?

A ○ Promiscuous mode is required in order to support Network Monitor.

B ○ Older sniffers required Promiscuous mode and he's unaware of the new NDIS 4.0 specification.

C ○ He's testing you with something that he made up.

D ○ If you want to monitor all traffic on the Network, your card must support Promiscuous mode.

2 You're looking over session statistics as you monitor a data capture session when, suddenly, your boss walks in. He points to the arrows under the network address section and says "What in the world do those arrows mean?" What do you tell him? (Tell him the truth, now.)

A ○ The arrows indicate the computer that I am currently monitoring.

B ○ The arrows indicate the direction of data flow; the arrowhead points away from the direction of flow.

C ○ The arrows indicate the direction of data flow; the arrowhead points in the direction of flow.

D ○ The arrows are placeholders; they hold a space for you to put data in later.

3 The Capture menu toggles between which two Network Monitor capture modes?

A ○ Detailed and Normal mode

B ○ Dedicated and Detailed mode

C ○ Normal and Filter mode

D ○ Dedicated and Normal mode

4 List the two types of passwords that you set on Network Monitor installations. (Choose all that apply.)

A ❑ Administrator

B ❑ Supervisor

C ❑ Display

D ❑ Capture

5 You suspect someone else is running Network Monitor on the network. What can you do to detect them?

A ○ Nothing.

B ○ Use Performance Monitor.

C ○ Using Network Monitor, choose Tools⇨Identify Network Monitor Users.

D ○ Using Network Monitor, choose Security⇨Find Other Installations.

6 You want to reduce the CPU load on the server that is running Network Monitor. What can you do?

A ○ Add more RAM.

B ○ Increase the paging file.

C ○ Run Network Monitor minimized.

D ○ Run Network Monitor in Dedicated Capture mode.

7 You ran a 40MB Network Monitor data capture session, but did not filter it. Now you have a rather large collection of data and are having trouble sorting it out. What can you do?

A ○ Save the data as a CAP (capture file), import it into an Excel spreadsheet, and then sort the data.

B ○ Save the data as a CAP (capture file), export it as a CSV (comma separated value) file, import it into an Excel spreadsheet, and then sort the data.

C ○ Save the data as a CAP (capture file), import it into an Access database, and then create your report.

D ○ Save the data as a CAP (capture file) and then create a display filter to select the data you want to examine.

8 You are troubleshooting an application that has been causing problems on your server. You press Ctrl+Alt+Esc to bring up Task Manager. What is the first thing you see?

A ○ The Applications tab

B ○ The Processes tab

C ○ The Performance tab

D ○ Nothing

9 You are using Task Manager to monitor applications on your server. You decide to bring up another application and watch the system resources as the application loads. When you right-click anywhere in the open area for current running tasks, what happens?

A ○ Nothing.

B ○ You can change only the icons of the currently running tasks.

C ○ You have the New Task option.

D ○ You have options such as End Task and Bring to Front.

Answers

1 *B.* Older sniffers required the Ethernet card to support Promiscuous mode; however, with the advent of NDIS 4.0 (which Network Monitor supports), support for Promiscuous mode is no longer required. *Refer to "Network Monitor."*

2 *C.* The arrowheads that you see in the Session Statistics pane as you monitor a data capture session point in the direction of data flow. The same principle applies when you create a capture filter. *Refer to "Filtering Captured Data."*

3 *D.* The two available options for capturing data are the Dedicated capture mode and Normal mode. The use of these capture modes will depend on how much system resources you would like to allocate to capturing data. *Refer to "Manually Executing a Capture."*

4 *C and D.* The two types of passwords that you can set on Network Monitor are display passwords and capture passwords. The display password allows you to examine only previously captured data. The capture password allows you to both examine previously captured data and create new captures. Setting these passwords is an essential piece of protecting your network from unauthorized use of Network Monitor. *Refer to "Password Protection."*

5 *C.* You not only can detect other people running Network Monitor, but you also can detect whether they even have the driver installed on their computer. Just choose Tools⇨Identify Network Monitor Users. *Refer to "Network Monitor Installations: Detecting Others."*

6 *D.* To reduce CPU load on the server running Network Monitor, you can set the program to run in Dedicated Capture mode. If you later need to view session statistics, you can press the Normal mode button. When you finish looking at the statistics, you can again select Dedicated Capture mode from the Capture menu. *Refer to "Manually Executing a Capture."*

7 *D.* Save the data as a CAP (capture file) and then create a display filter to select the data that you want to examine. A display filter gives you a great deal of control over the way Network Monitor displays the data. You can select certain protocols, certain computers, or any combination of protocols and computers. *Refer to "Saving Captured Data."*

8 *D.* Nothing. To bring up Task Manager via keystrokes, press Ctrl+Shift+Esc. You also can press Control+Alt+Del to bring up the Windows NT Security dialog box, then click the button for Task Manager. *Refer to "Task Manager."*

9 *C.* You have the New Task option. In addition to starting applications via the File menu, you can start them by right-clicking anywhere in the open space for currently running tasks on the Applications tab. *Refer to "Task Manager."*

Chapter 20

Troubleshooting, Assigning Blame, and Covering Your Tracks

Exam Objectives

▶ Understanding and troubleshooting problems with hardware configurations

▶ Understanding the troubleshooting process for NT networks

▶ Understanding and troubleshooting problems with NT permissions

▶ Understanding and troubleshooting the Windows NT boot process

▶ Finding additional help for troubleshooting NT

*M*any NT administrators I know refer to troubleshooting as an art. I guess that means they see themselves as the great artists of our time, working on the IT equivalents of the *Mona Lisa*. I am sorry, but I just don't see it. Most of these folks are no more artists than I am a race car driver. Rather, troubleshooting is a science that leverages a person's knowledge about a topic to solve a particular set of problems related to that topic. The hard part about troubleshooting isn't finding which brush to use, it is knowing whether you have the necessary knowledge to solve the problem, and if not, knowing what knowledge you lack. That is where experience and intuition comes in.

The assumptions you must make for this exam are that you are working on a homogeneous network located at a single site using a single domain. Once you make these assumptions, troubleshooting questions on the NT Server exam become pretty easy.

So how do you prepare for the troubleshooting scenarios on the exam? Well, the short answer is arm yourself with the knowledge covered in the last 20 or so chapters. If you know the details of WINS, DHCP, domains, and the other topics covered here, you will be fine. You don't need to be Michelangelo to be able to Isolate the Problem, Analyze the Situation, and Fix the Problems as discussed in this chapter.

Quick Assessment

Understanding and Trouble-shooting the Windows NT Boot Process

1 (True/False). A Windows NT boot disk contains all the files you need to run Windows NT in System mode.

2 _____ is a required file for dual-booting Windows NT with a non-NT operating system.

3 (True/False). To create emergency repair disks (ERDs), you use Windows NT Fault-Tolerant Repair Disk Creation Tool (Fdisk.exe).

4 _____ is a symptom of an Ntldr failure.

Finding Additional Help for Trouble-shooting NT

5 (True/False). OSLOADER performs the same role on RISC computers as Ntldr performs on Intel-based computers.

6 (True/False). The Last Known Good control set is created by the WinLogon process immediately prior to shutting down the workstation.

7 (True/False). Microsoft recommends that you delete all of the HLP files after you install Windows NT, because they only contain information on installing and configuring Windows NT.

Understanding and Trouble-shooting Problems with Hardware Configurations

8 The _____ is the component of Windows NT that provides a program-matic boundary layer between hardware device drivers and the operating system.

9 (True/False). The Ntdetect.com utility that is automatically run during the NT boot process will automatically identify and configure your network adapter and protocol settings.

10 Prior to the initialization of the operating system, computers first execute a series of BIOS programs referred to as the POST routine. POST stands for P_____ O_____ S_____ T_____ .

Answers

1   *False.* Refer to "Making an NT boot disk."

2   *Bootsec.dos.* Refer to "Troubleshooting the Boot Process."

3   *False.* Refer to "Creating the emergency repair disk (ERD)."

4   *Error loading operating system.* Refer to "Troubleshooting the Boot Process."

5   *False.* Refer to "Troubleshooting the Boot Process."

6   *False.* Refer to "Troubleshooting the Boot Process."

7   *False.* Refer to "Get Yourself Some Help: Other Resources to Check Out."

8   *Hal.dll.* Refer to "Troubleshooting the Boot Process."

9   *False.* Refer to "Troubleshooting the Boot Process."

10   *Power On Self Test.* Refer to "Troubleshooting the Boot Process."

Troubleshooting Principles

Every administrator has a preferred routine for approaching the troubleshooting and support process, but nearly all such routines boil down to a few fundamental principles. I generally approach any problem by taking the following five basic steps. The first and last steps aren't relevant to the exam, but if you memorize the three middle steps, you should be in good shape to attack any troubleshooting question:

1. **Identify the problem:** Know the difference between "normal" operation and trouble. Listen to your environment and listen to your users. (On the exam, you already know you have a problem — the question identifies it for you.)

2. **Isolate the problem area:** Eliminate as much extraneous data and systems as possible from the situation. Stop the problem from affecting other systems if possible. When reading the question while taking the exam, look for the information that relates to the root cause of the problem and set aside the rest.

3. **Analyze the problem:** Study the problem. Separate the symptoms from the disease. Find the root cause of the problem and identify the most efficient way to fix it. Get additional help if you need it and don't forget to refer to that manual if it can help. On the exam, this step translates to considering each answer individually. Does it solve the problem? Is one of the other answers a better solution?

4. **Fix the problem:** Implement the solution that you identified in the preceding step and verify that it works. If the solution doesn't work, you need to go back to the drawing board and reevaluate the problem. Check out TechNet or the Knowledge Base for any known bugs. For the exam, pick the answer you are most comfortable with and move on. If you are running out of time, take a guess and mark the question for review if you have time at the end.

5. **Monitor the area:** After you fix the problem, ensure that it doesn't resurface. Notify others in your area so they know what to look for. Set up monitoring routines to make sure that the problem doesn't flare up again as soon as you turn your back.

You only need to remember the Isolate, Analyze, and Fix (IAF) steps for the exam. The question tells you the problem and you move on to the next question before you can set up a monitoring system. To ace these questions, read them *carefully,* and discard any unneeded information the author includes. Study the remaining answers and choose the best one. If you still can't figure it out, eliminate the obviously wrong answers, take a guess, and mark it for later review.

Outbreak of the dreaded blue green toe fungus

The Centers for Disease Control (CDC) in Atlanta receives a phone call from a doctor in Philadelphia regarding an outbreak of blue-green toe fungus (BGTF) among a small number of people in the area. They have received no other reports, so work continues as normal.

Identify problem: The next day, a doctor in Baltimore reports 10 more cases and then later that week, another doctor reports a half-dozen more cases in Washington, D.C. The CDC realize they have a problem that appears to be moving south along the east coast.

Isolate the problem: After speaking to the doctors again and obtaining a patient history, the only link between the patients is the fact that all have attended the East Coast Shoe-Expo that was recently in each of their towns. CDC moves quickly and stop the Expo before it enters Charleston, South Carolina.

Analyze problem: Understanding that BGTF spreads only through physical contact with the source, CDC first examines every vendor's toes to see if they're infected. Finding no one infected, starts going through the display shoes.

Fix the problem: It doesn't take long before they find a set of brown therapeutic loafers that are infected with BGTF. A good blast of foot spray neutralizes the fungus. CDC distributes samples of the spray and instructs each vendor to spray all shoes before any customer tries them on. All shoes should be sprayed again at the end of each day.

Monitor area: After verifying that the spray does, in fact, kill the fungus, the CDC issues a nationwide bulletin for BGTF to tell doctors what to look for and how to solve the problem.

Troubleshooting Networks

Troubleshooting Windows NT network problems easily fits into the IAF model, but figuring out where to start isolating is sometimes difficult. The network is based on the OSI model, though, so the OSI model is probably as good a place as any to begin.

Some typical client/server problems

The number of communication problems you can have between the server and the client is far too great for me to address all of them here. The big-ticket items, however, are finding and accessing the server from the network.

Finding the server

On a Windows NT network, finding the server usually involves navigating the Windows NT browse list or using Network Neighborhood's Find Computer feature. Either way, you search the local name space and retrieve a computer name. If you already know the name of the resource you want to connect to, your next step is resolving the name into a reference the network understands. (On TCP/IP networks, this reference is the computer's IP address.) The service for doing this type of resolution involves either looking it up from a NetBIOS Name Server like WINS or broadcasting the name and hoping the machine replies with its address. If you cannot find the resource's address, look into the following questions:

- ✔ Are the client and server running the same protocols? If not, install a common protocol on either the client or server.

- ✔ Are the client and server using the same naming server? Can the client resolve the server's address given its name?

- ✔ Are the client and server configured for the right NetBIOS node-type? If the client and the server are installed on different subnets, or if either the client or the server is configured to use b-node, they will never query a WINS to resolve the computer name!

Accessing the server

After you find the address, you need to connect to the server from the client. In order to connect to the server, you need the following security rights:

- ✔ Access to the server from the network. Set via User Manager.

- ✔ Access to Network Share. Set via the Permissions button when setting up the share.

- ✔ Access to the NTFS file system. Set via Explorer or File Manager.

If your account has the rights to access the server from the network, access the share, and access to the file system, you can access the data. If you cannot connect to the share despite properly configured security settings, you should verify the address by attempting to connect to it via some other means. In a TCP/IP environment, you could use the ping or tracert utilities to verify the file server is accessible on the network.

Some typical protocol problems

Most protocol problems stem from a single cause: administrative error. Today's operating system and network peripheral vendors have the network piece down pretty well. TCP/IP, IPX/SPX, and NetBEUI are all firmly entrenched protocols, and they're all implemented in a relatively straightforward manner. If you have trouble with a network protocol, you probably have made a mistake in configuring it for your environment. If so, no problem; everybody does it now and again. The following list describes some of the most common mistakes, by protocol. Each can affect either the client or the server and fixing them is usually as easy as correcting the typo you made.

✔ **TCP/IP:**

- **Incorrect or invalid subnet mask:** Can result in some machines not being able to contact one other. Usually does not work across a router.

- **Incorrect gateway/router:** Cannot connect to machines on different subnets.

- **Incorrect or missing name server (DNS or WINS):** Cannot resolve computer names into addresses.

- **Incorrect entry in HOST or LMHOST file:** Incorrectly resolve computer names into addresses.

- **Improper firewall configuration:** Unable to connect to hosts on the other side of the firewall.

- **Duplicate IP address:** One machine is denied service (TCP/IP protocol does not initialize).

✔ **IPX/SPX:**

- **Incorrect frame type:** Cannot see machines configured to different frame types, even those on the same subnet.

- **Improperly configured router:** Cannot connect to machines on different subnets.

- **Duplicate or zero internal network number:** Cannot connect to machines on affected subnets.

✔ **NetBEUI:**

- **Attempting to use it across a router:** NetBIOS is not a routable protocol.

- **Duplicate machine name on network:** One machine is denied service (NetBEUI protocol does not initialize).

Troubleshooting Hardware

Back in the days of DOS running on 8088 XTs, many people I knew could recite the meaning of the beeps heard during the POST process from memory. Today, most people simply take for granted that the machines will boot and run properly. Hardware, however, still operates under the same principles it did all those years ago — and hardware problems can still jump up and bite you if you're not prepared.

IRQ conflicts: Can't we all just get along?

The most common type of hardware problem on NT networks is the IRQ conflict. Usually, IRQ conflicts manifest as a failure of the system to boot, a blue screen, or a system hang. IRQ settings are visible via the WinMSD utility that ships with NT 4.0, as shown in Figure 20-1.

An *interrupt request* (IRQ) is a signal assigned to a peripheral that permits that peripheral to communicate with the CPU. On most systems, the respective IRQ is dedicated to a single device. Most Intel hardware provides a total of 16 possible IRQs, numbered 0 to 15. Many IRQs are already assigned to built-in devices, such as the system clock, the keyboard, and the communication and parallel ports, but IRQs 5, 9, 10, 11, 12, 13, and 15 usually are available for additional components.

Fixing IRQ conflict problems is usually a process of trial and error. If you have NT running, you can use utilities like WinMSD to view the IRQs assigned to installed devices but changing them is done either in the machine's BIOS, via the use of a utility that shipped with the device or by physically moving jumpers on the device. Fixing an IRQ conflict is mostly trial and error. You have to keep changing the interrupts on a device-by-device basis until you resolve the conflict.

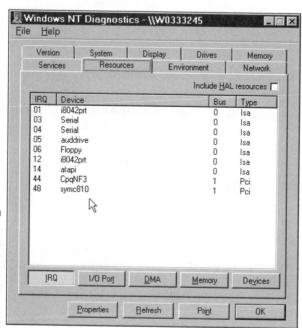

Figure 20-1:
The
Windows NT
Diagnostics
(WinMSD)
utility.

Don't forget your memory

Windows NT requires lots of memory. If you notice your machine running slow or your disk grinding away, you can usually fix it by simply adding RAM. The easiest way to identify whether you need more RAM is to run Performance Monitor and look at pages/sec, page faults/sec, and cache faults/sec under the memory counter (see Figure 20-2). If pages/sec is above 10 and page faults/sec is more than cache faults/sec, you need to add more memory.

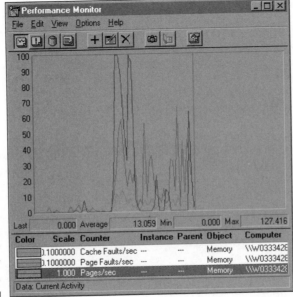

Figure 20-2:
Performance
Monitor
can help
identify
memory
constraints.

Troubleshooting the Boot Process

By far the most frustrating of all NT troubleshooting scenarios is debugging boot problems. You can draw on a wealth of tools for identifying and solving problems on running systems, but only a few actually can help you with a box that just doesn't want to run. Fortunately, only a limited number of things can go wrong to prevent NT from booting, so troubleshooting the boot process is reasonably systematic.

You can expect two or three questions on troubleshooting the boot process. One may concern the boot process on RISC machines, but most relate to Intel hardware. Oddly enough, even though we all must go through this process every time we reboot our systems, these are the questions most people get wrong if they aren't prepared for the test.

Power on: All systems are go . . .

On an Intel system, when you turn on the power, you first hear a gentle hum (that's the fan) and you probably see a few lights blinking. While these sensory delights transpire, a routine known as POST (Power On Self Test) takes place within the guts of the computer.

Every adapter that has a BIOS on your system runs its own POST routine, checking whatever the manufacturers have determined that the adapters must check before startup. On the motherboard, the POST generally verifies the presence of required peripherals, such as the keyboard, as well as the amount of RAM installed.

If no keyboard is connected to the machine, or if a portion of the RAM fails the POST, the system generally displays an error code. If the failure affects a core component, such as video, you may experience a series of beeps. These beeps are hardware specific and translating them in to something meaningful is not an exam question. Any errors identified during POST must be corrected before continuing with the boot.

After the various systems complete their POST routines, the *system BIOS* on your computer's motherboard is executed. The system BIOS is a small program that is responsible for governing the hardware configuration, identifying the startup devices, and executing the Master Boot Record (MBR) to execute the disk's *boot sector* to load the operating system.

If the MBR fails to locate the *boot sector* on the first hard disk, you may receive one of the following errors:

- Missing Operating System
- Error Loading Operating System
- Non-System Disk or Disk Error
  Replace and Press Any Key When Ready

Several problems can cause these errors, the most common of which are

- Setting the wrong partition active via DOS FDISK
- Booting from a non-bootable floppy
- Sustaining a virus infection

You should try using the NT boot disk (or the emergency repair disk, which I discuss in the "Diskus Repairus" section, later in this chapter) to address these problems. If that tactic still fails to resolve the problem, or if you suspect a virus infection, use the DOS utility, FDISK, with the /MBR switch (FDISK /MBR), to reset the Master Boot Record. If all else fails, reinstall NT and restore your data from a backup tape.

Starting the OS: Initiating countdown . . .

The *boot sector* is an operating-system-specific area of the disk that contains the executable code that runs the Ntldr program. After Ntldr executes, the display clears and you see "NT Loader 4.0." NTLDR then reads the file allocation table (if the partition is FAT) or the master file table (if the partition is NTFS) and instructs the processor to use a flat 32-bit memory model before reading the Boot.ini.

The only difference on a RISC computer is that instead of the MBR launching Ntldr, the system's BIOS reads the system's nonvolatile RAM (NVRAM) to select the boot disk and then runs the program OSLOADER. The OSLOADER program functions in much the same way as Ntldr, but uses the NVRAM file instead of Boot.ini to establish the location of the system files.

Back on the Intel platform, Ntldr reads the Boot.ini file and displays a menu that calls on the user to select the operating system to load. If you have only installed Windows NT once and have no other operating systems installed, this menu contains two options:

- ✔ Windows NT Server 4.0
- ✔ Windows NT Server 4.0 (VGA Mode)

If you get an exam question about how to fix a video failure caused by installing the incorrect video drivers, don't forget about the VGA mode of the Boot.ini file. Running NT in VGA mode enables you to access the system running in 640 x 480 x 16 colors and is the answer of choice when an invalid video setting locks you out of your system. After you log on, you can install the proper drivers without losing any other data or configuration settings.

The format of the Boot.ini file is critical to successfully loading the correct operating system. The file contains two sections:

- ✔ **[Boot Loader]:** Identifies the default operating system and the countdown timer.

- ✔ **[Operating Systems]:** Identifies the path to each installed operating system. You can expect questions regarding the [Operating Systems] section of the Boot.ini file on the exam. They generally come in two flavors:

    - Questions relating to multi( ) verse scsi( ) formats
    - Questions concerning the path to the operating system files

If your system is configured to use the scsi( ) setting, you must have Ntbootdd.sys on the root of your boot partition (C:\) to enable proper identification of devices!

You may encounter a troubleshooting scenario that calls on you to know what happens when you install an additional disk controller or configure an additional partition that affects the order of the ARC path in the Boot.ini. If the Boot.ini file doesn't point to the proper disk, partition, and path to launch NT, you will receive the error message "Can't Find NTOSKRNL.EXE." You will also get this error when you have a failure while using the Windows NT software-based mirroring. You can fix Boot.ini ARC path problems by creating an NT boot disk and modifying the ARC path on the disk.

If you reconfigure your partitions and modify the number of the boot partition, you must manually edit the Boot.ini. NT doesn't modify the Boot.ini automatically!

Looking at the hardware: We have ignition . . .

When you select the operating system, Ntldr runs Ntdetect.com. Ntdetect writes the message "NTDETECT v1.0 Checking Hardware" to the screen and begins to interrogate your system's components. Currently, Ntdetect.com can detect the following components:

- ✔ Bus type
- ✔ Video adapter
- ✔ Keyboard type
- ✔ Serial and parallel ports
- ✔ Floppy drives
- ✔ Pointing devices

Ntdetect.com does not configure your network adapter. After Ntdetect detects your hardware, it returns execution to Ntldr.

To identify whether Ntdetect.com is not functioning properly, rename Ntdetect.com to Ntdetect.bak and copy Ntdetect.chk from the \Support\Debug\I386 directory on the server CD to Ntdetect.com on the root of the boot drive. This debug version of Ntdetect.com presents a list of all the components that it identifies during execution. You must acknowledge each screen by pressing Enter, so you probably don't want to leave the feature enabled.

If Ntdetect fails to identify a component, re-seat it to make sure that it's operating properly. If it still doesn't work, contact the vendor.

If you decide to boot an operating system other than NT, Ntldr executes the contents of Bootsect.dos (a file required to run Windows 95 or DOS on NT dual-booted systems). If you opt to run Windows NT, Ntldr presents a choice:

- Load a different hardware profile
- Load the Last Known Good configuration

As Ntldr loads the kernel (Ntoskrnl.exe), the hardware abstraction layer (HAL), and a few other required device drivers, a few dots appear on-screen. At this point, the Ntldr program creates the *control set,* the Last Known Good control set and passes control back to Ntoskrnl.exe.

After Ntoskrnl.exe initializes, the screen turns blue and Ntoskrn displays several important pieces of information:

- Version of the operating system
- Number of processors found
- Type of HAL loaded
- Amount of memory identified

Ntoskrnl then displays a series of dots as it loads and initializes the required boot-time device drives specified in the control set. If required, Ntoskrnl runs a Chkdsk to verify the integrity of the disks before it runs the NT subsystems.

Failures during this period of startup usually result in a blue screen. If you get a blue screen, first attempt to determine whether the failure is video- or system-related. Chances are, if you have just recently installed a new component or piece of software, that new goodie is the culprit behind the blue screen. If the problem is video-related, try booting the system by selecting "Windows NT Server 4.0 (VGA Mode)" when prompted by Ntldr. If the problem is system-related, try booting with a Last Known Good selection. If all of these fail, try the emergency repair disk (ERD). If nothing else works, reinstall the operating system and restore your data from backup tape.

Boot okay: Liftoff . . .

After Ntoskrnl finishes starting all of the required subsystems and all seems well, it prompts you with a logon screen. After you successfully log on to the machine, the control set used to initialize NT is considered good, and becomes the Last Known Good configuration for your next reboot.

Diskus Repairus: ERDs and the NT Boot Disk

So now you have identified the problem and need to fix it. Although these aren't the two tools you use as an MCSE to fix problems on NT systems, you need to know about these two for the exam. You can expect to encounter the NT boot disk during the fault tolerance troubleshooting questions. You can expect to encounter the ERD during a number of different troubleshooting questions. Personally, I am not a big fan of the ERD. Unless you update them after each modification to the system, they can cause as many problems as they solve. The exams, however, view the ERD as an integral part of the repair process, so you need to know how to use one as well as when *Microsoft* wants you to use it.

Making an NT boot disk

Having a Windows NT boot disk around is absolutely critical if you use the Windows NT fault tolerant solution (discussed in Chapter 5) and experience a failure on your primary mirrored partition. Granted, the boot disk does not contain the entire Windows NT operating system; it does, however, contain the files required to start the operating system before returning control to the remaining NT system files located on a fixed disk.

To create a Windows NT boot disk, follow the steps in Lab 20-1.

Lab 20-1	Creating a Windows NT Boot Disk

1. **Insert a blank floppy disk into the floppy drive and format it, using Windows File Manager or Microsoft Explorer.**

2. **From Explorer, select Boot.ini, Ntldr, Bootsec.dos (if present), Ntdetect.com, and Ntbootdd.sys (if present) from the root of your drive and then choose File⇨Properties.**

3. **From the Attributes section, deselect Hidden, System, and Read-Only.**

4. **Copy these files to the root of your floppy drive.**

5. **If you use the software mirroring fault tolerance configuration that ships with Windows NT, edit the Boot.ini file (shown in Figure 20-3).**

   Copy the ARC path that points to the primary Windows NT installation. Paste the line into the end of the file. Edit the disk( ) and/or the partition( ) entries to point to the mirrored copy of NT.

6. **Label the disk with the machine name and store it in a safe place.**

To use the Windows NT boot disk, insert it into a bootable floppy drive on your computer and reboot. When prompted, use the Ntldr menu to select the appropriate version of the operating system to install.

The Windows NT boot disk is specific to your machine configuration. It works only on machines built with the same disk configuration as the one from which you create the disk.

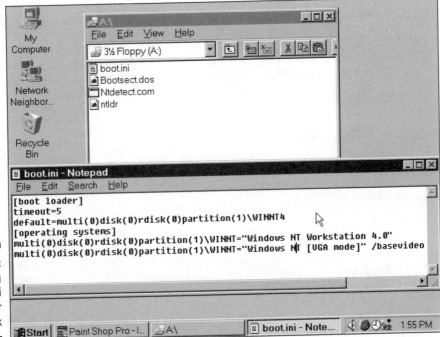

Figure 20-3:
Modifying
the Boot.ini
file on your
boot disk

The emergency repair disk (ERD)

In the *Windows NT 4.0 Setup Troubleshooting Guide,* Microsoft describes the Emergency Repair Disk (ERD) as one of ". . . your primary tools for disaster recovery." They also warn that if you fail to create your ERD, you "are greatly diminishing the chances of recovering your Windows NT installation in the event of hardware or software failure." Whether you agree with this statement is not important in terms of the exam, because the people who made up the test do believe it. That means you need to understand that the ERD is as important as a tape backup or RAID when you tackle your disaster recovery questions.

Creating the emergency repair disk (ERD)

You can create the Windows NT emergency repair disk via one of two different methods:

- Windows NT Setup
- Windows NT RDISK.EXE utility

When you install Windows NT, you are prompted about whether you want to create an ERD after setup. If you choose to do so, you are prompted to insert a blank, $3^1/_2$-inch disk into the floppy drive. If you want to create an ERD after setup, or if you need to update the information on an existing disk, you run the Repair Disk utility (Rdisk.exe), shown in Figure 20-4, and select either the Create Repair Disk button or the Update Repair Info button, as the situation demands.

ERD functions

The ERD contains several important pieces, including:

- A copy of the Windows NT user (SAM) and security policies database
- HKLM\Software and HKLM\System Registry keys
- A checksum list of all Windows NT system files

Because this information is only a snapshot of your system, you need to update your ERD with every major change to your system's configuration or user database.

Creating an ERD is relatively simple. If you run a manual setup, Windows NT prompts you to create one. If you already have NT installed, you can create or update your ERD via the Rdisk.exe utility. This utility enables you to extract all the relevant data into the Winnt\Repair directory and then copy it to the ERD. You also can use Rdisk.exe to format the disk before writing the ERD data to the disk.

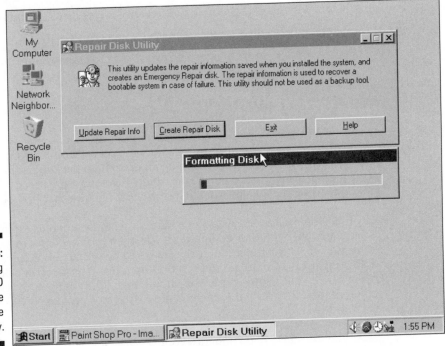

Figure 20-4:
Creating
the ERD
using the
Rdisk.exe
utility.

Using the ERD

If you experience a file corruption or have a configuration setting that prevents Windows NT from booting, you can use your ERD to return NT to a bootable state.

If you don't have your Windows NT Setup Disks, you can create them from the CD by another machine by executing either Winnt /ox or Winnt32 /ox at the command prompt. Follow the on-screen instructions to create the disks.

To use your ERD, break out your Windows NT CD and Windows NT Setup disks and follow these steps:

1. Boot your system using Windows NT Setup Disk 1 and follow the prompts.

2. When prompted, select "Repair an NT Installation" from the menu.

3. Select the following options:

   Inspect Registry Files

   Inspect Startup Environment

   Verify Windows NT System Files

   Inspect Boot Sector

4. Insert Windows NT Setup Disk 2 and any driver disks if required.

5. Insert the ERD disk for the computer when required.

6. Acknowledge each change and restart your system when complete.

Restoring Windows NT

In the event of a catastrophic hardware or software failure that you cannot fix via other means, you need to recover your server from backup tape. That's when you're glad that you keep an up-to-date backup regime and have proper disaster recovery plans, right? If you haven't already done so, do it now, or at least some time before you get hit with that first failure.

Any time you fix the root cause of a hardware failure, such as replacing the failed hard drive or other component, you need to run a basic installation of Windows NT. The installation doesn't have to be perfect because you're only doing the installation to get to your backup tapes. The directory doesn't really matter, but all the same, you should install this version of NT into a different directory from the one you are restoring. I personally like C:\Winnt.bak.

After you install NT and configure your tape device, you need to install your backup software. If you are using the built-in Windows NT backup engine, you can skip this step. After you install the backup software, insert your last full backup tape and restore the data. Repeat this process for any differential or incremental tapes to assure that you have the most recent information possible. Restart your server when complete.

If your servers often contain a large amount of data, you want to keep your operating system on a different partition as your data, so that you can quickly restore the operating system and get the server back online. When you have the server up and running, you can start the longer data restore.

Troubleshooting Security Problems

One of the more interesting troubleshooting topics in the NT environment, and on the exams, is the use of NT's security model. Troubleshooting security problems is relatively straightforward, as long as you know what to look for. The exam includes only four types of security-related troubleshooting questions, as follows:

✔ **User does not have permission to access the computer from the network.**

The user has not been the system right on the remote computer to "Access this computer from the network." By default, the special group Everyone has this right. If the user does not have this right and the special group Everyone no longer has the right, the user gets an "Access Denied" in reply to any attempts to list the shares in Network Neighborhood. You can fix this problem by adding the user or the Everyone group to the right "Access this computer from the network," via User Manager.

✔ **User does not have sufficient permission to the network share.**

By default, the group Everyone has the Full Control right to newly created shares; however, whoever creates the share can set this as they want. If the user has no access to the share, they receive an "Access Denied" message when attempting to connect to the resource.

✔ **User does not have the permission required to traverse the remote directory structure or access the files.**

On NTFS drives, an administrator can set local file system security that restricts access even if the computer and the share permit it. If the user needs to navigate through the directories, they require permissions in the directory in addition to the file they want to access. If the user has no access to the file system, they get the "Access Denied" message after mounting the share.

✔ **Remote computer has disabled the Guest account.**

If a user attempts to access a computer on which he has no rights, Windows NT attempts to use the built-in Guest account to authenticate the user. The Guest account is disabled by default on Windows NT Server 4.0 computers.

For more information, refer to Chapter 15.

Get Yourself Some Help: Other Resources to Check Out

We are not alone. The truth, or in this case, the help, is out there. You simply cannot know all that you need to know in order to troubleshoot properly. The *knowledge* part that I mentioned at the beginning of the chapter always gets in the way. But you don't need to *have* all the answers, you just need to know where to *get* all the answers. The following sections describe a few of the more common answer sources.

- The Windows NT Hardware Compatibility List (HCL)
- Windows Help Files
- Microsoft TechNET
- Microsoft Knowledge Base
- Fine technical manuals like this one!

Prep Test

1 Which of the following do you not need in order to create a Windows NT boot disk?

A ○ Ntldr

B ○ Ntdetect.com

C ○ Ntoskrnl.exe

D ○ Bootsect.dos

2 What does the acronym MBR stand for?

A ○ Master Boot Record

B ○ Multiple Browse Record

C ○ Master Browse Record

D ○ Multiple Boot Record

3 What is the difference between booting a RISC-based PC and an Intel-based PC?

A ○ An Intel-based PC uses the Power On Self-Test (POST), but a RISC-based computer does not.

B ○ The NVRAM loads the operating system on a RISC-based PC, but the boot.ini file loads the operating system on an Intel-based PC.

C ○ The OSLOADER loads the boot.ini file on a RISC-based PC, but the OSLOADER loads Ntoskrnl.exe on an Intel-based PC.

D ○ Ntoskrnl.exe loads after Bootsect.dos on a RISC-based PC, but Bootsect.dos doesn't need to load on an Intel-based PC.

4 If you receive the error, "Can't find NTOSKRNL," what could be the cause?

A ○ The OSLOADER cannot be found.

B ○ The NTLOADER cannot be found.

C ○ The Boot.ini file may be missing.

D ○ Bootsec.dos is missing.

5 What does the Emergency Repair Disk (ERD) contain a list of?

A ○ All files that have been created since the last update.

B ○ Only the files in the WINNT directory.

C ○ All files needed for booting.

D ○ Only files regarding the hard disks and user security.

6 You only need an emergency repair disk (ERD) in which of the following situations?

A ○ When user security changes often.

B ○ If you change your disk configuration often.

C ○ If you need a spare startup disk for diagnostics.

D ○ You should always have an emergency repair disk (ERD).

7 If two machines on the network are configured duplicate IP address, what happens if the second machine attempts to join the network?

A ○ The Windows NT Network dialog box appears, prompting the user to select a different IP address.

B ○ Both machines are notified of the duplicate and the second machine then does not initialize TCP/IP on that adapter.

C ○ The client automatically switches from Static to Dynamic addressing and obtains the IP information from DHCP.

D ○ The machine catches fire and explodes.

8 Which of the following is a required file for SCSI systems only?

A ○ Ntbootdd.sys

B ○ Bootsec.dos

C ○ OSLOADER

D ○ Ntboot.sys

9 By default, the group Everyone receives what permissions to a share?

A ○ No Access

B ○ Read

C ○ Full Control

D ○ Write

10 Which of the following is *not* an option in the Windows NT repair process?

A ○ Inspect Registry Files

B ○ Reset the Local Administrator Password to NUL

C ○ Verify Windows NT System Files

D ○ Inspect Startup Environment

E ○ Inspect the Boot Sector

Answers

1 *D.* You need Bootsec.dos only when dual-booting with a non-NT operating system, such as DOS or Windows 95. *See "Troubleshooting the Boot Process."*

2 *A.* MBR stands for Master Boot Record and identifies the disk as bootable. *See "Troubleshooting the Boot Process."*

3 *B.* The NVRAM loads the operating system on a RISC-based PC, but the boot.ini loads the operating system on an Intel-based PC. The OSLOADER is what you use for the RISC-based PCs but do not need for Intel-based PCs. *See "Troubleshooting the Boot Process."*

4 *C.* The most likely cause for the "Can't find NTOSKRNL" message is that the Boot.ini file is corrupt or missing. *See "Troubleshooting the Boot Process."*

5 *B.* The emergency repair disk (ERD) contains a list of the files in the C:\Winnt directory only. The list also includes checksums for these files so that you can identify different versions. *See "The emergency repair disk (ERD)."*

6 *D.* Microsoft strongly recommends creating the ERD. The ERD contains a copy of the Windows NT user (SAM) and security policies database, HKLM\Software and HKLM\System Registry keys, and a checksum list of all Windows NT system files. *See "The emergency repair disk (ERD)."*

7 *B.* TCP/IP requires a unique IP address to initialize the protocol. If a duplicate IP address is encountered, the protocol does not initialize. Both machines are presented with a dialog box citing the MAC address of the other machine. *See "Some typical protocol problems."*

8 *A.* Ntbootdd.sys is a required file for SCSI systems only. *Refer to "Looking at the hardware: We have ignition . . ."*

9 *C.* By default, the group Everyone has Full Control permissions to a share. You can further limit their access by adjusting the permissions to the files or folders being shared. *Refer to "Troubleshooting Security Problems."*

10 *E.* The option that is missing is to Inspect the Boot Sector. It is not possible to clear the local administrator password using any built-in Windows NT utilities. For more information refer to the section on *"Using the ERD."*

Part VIII
The Part of Tens

The 5th Wave   By Rich Tennant

MCSE CERTIFICATION STEPS

"Can't I just give you riches or something?"

In this part . . .

I present a couple of top ten lists to help you pass the exam. I include a list of top ten resources that I guarantee will help you pass the exam and become an MCSE. I also include my best attempts at advice giving, which I have gathered from test takers, to make your studying and testing experience more enjoyable, and of course, successful.

Chapter 21
Test Day Tips

. . . .

In This Chapter
▶ Preparing for the exam
▶ Taking the exam

. . . .

As any seasoned athlete will tell you, it helps to have a good game plan before entering a contest. Here are some tips that will help you score higher on test day.

Schedule the Exam Carefully

Schedule the exam for a time and date that accommodates your studying needs.

✔ Take the exam on the weekend if possible. This helps you avoid the hassle of having to take a day off work — and you don't have to use a vacation day!

If weekend exams are unavailable, then take the day off! You don't want to deal with crises at work right before you take the exam. Even better, take the exam on a Monday or a Friday. If you take it on Monday, you have the weekend before to prepare and relax. If you take it on a Friday, you have the weekend for post-exam deprogramming.

✔ Schedule your exam in the afternoon. This gives you the entire morning to review.

Review Before Taking the Exam

If you are having difficulty with certain areas that are vitally important for you to understand, review those sections shortly before taking the exam. Having these key ideas fresh in your mind increases the likelihood of you being able to recall them during the exam.

Cramming for the NT Server exam at the last minute without prior study is a strategy that is likely to fail. If you have prepared well, a last-minute review simply helps your recollection.

Choose Your Test Station Wisely

If possible, find a test station that is out of the way. Avoid high traffic areas, such as doorways and hallways. Nearby activity can be very distracting. If the room is not full, choose a seat away from others. This lessens your chances of being annoyed by someone with a distracting habit. Stay away from windows — they make it too easy to daydream! Also, sunlight may cause a glare on the display that makes the screen difficult to read. Finally, make sure that your test station is functioning properly. For example, check the monitor for proper brightness and clarity before beginning.

Review Your Answers

Conventional wisdom cautions against changing your answers. This doesn't mean, however, that you should not review your work. If you complete the MCSE exam and still have some time remaining, use it. First of all, check to be sure that you answered all the questions. You may have skipped over some problems and forgot to mark them for review. When you're certain that you've chosen answers for all the questions, go back and reread the answers that you marked as questionable. Sometimes, you have a new insight the second time that you analyze a problem. After you've looked at these questions, skim through as many of the remaining questions on the exam as time allows, focusing your attention on any areas you may have rushed through. Make sure that you have not marked the wrong answer by mistake or misread the questions or the answers.

Answer Easy Questions First

The MCSE exam allows you to skip questions and come back to them later. Utilize this feature to answer all the easy questions first. Doing so serves three purposes. First of all, it ensures that you secure all the easy points. All too often, MCSE test-takers get hung up on a few difficult problems and end up running out of time with easier problems left unanswered. Secondly, it provides you with a psychological boost. If you start off with a string of successes, your confidence increases, and you can more easily tackle the tougher problems. Finally, answering the easy questions first helps you with time management. After finishing that initial pass through the exam, you have a better idea of how to pace yourself to successfully finish the exam within the allotted time.

Prepare for the Exam Environment

Don't wait until the last minute to make your trip to the testing center. You don't want to have to deal with the stress of trying to beat the clock before you even arrive at the test site. (You get to play that game when you take the exam.) Arriving early gives you the opportunity to familiarize yourself with your surroundings and the test equipment.

Before you begin the exam, make sure that you are taking the correct exam. I once was well into an exam before I realized that it was the wrong one.

Read Questions and Answers Carefully

Some of the situational problem-solving questions on the NT Server exam are very long. However, do not make the mistake of skimming the questions. One or two strategically placed words can change the whole meaning of a question. It is well worth the effort to read each question thoroughly. You should also read each answer thoroughly.

For most questions, at least two answers can be correct, with one being "more" correct.

Watch for Questions with Multiple Answers

Be sure to determine whether a question has multiple answers. A common mistake is to choose the first correct answer in a multiple-answer question then move on before realizing that other answers are correct as well. Fortunately, you can distinguish a question type by the shape of the answer selector. Round radio buttons precede the answers to questions with exactly one answer and square check boxes precede the answers to questions with multiple answers. Questions with multiple answers are also followed by a statement such as "Choose all that apply" or "Choose three." Remember that you don't get partial credit for a partially correct answer on an MCSE exam!

Answer All Questions

You are not penalized for guessing on an MCSE exam. Unanswered questions are counted as incorrect. Therefore, you should attempt to answer all the questions on the exam, even the ones that you are unsure of. If you find that you are approaching the end of the time limit and you have more than a few questions left, use the remaining time to randomly mark answers to them. This strategy gives you a chance of adding a few points to your score. Leaving the rest of the test blank eliminates this chance. However, if you have only a couple of questions left to answer, use your remaining time to answer the next question. One correct answer is likely to earn you more points than a few random guesses.

Use Your Scratch Paper

Many of the problem-solving questions on the NT Server exam require you to visualize a scenario containing multiple objects and mechanisms. Don't try to draw it in your head; sketch out the scenario on your Official MCSE Exam Scratch Paper.

Sketching out the scenario allows you to

✔ Track all of the items in the scenario
✔ See relationships between items

Some scenarios are used in more than one question. Your sketch may allow you to answer other questions without having to reconstruct the scenario.

Chapter 22

Ten Great Resources

In This Chapter

▶ Utilizing Internet-based MCSE resources

▶ Employing other MCSE resources

From MCSE-focused Web sites to MCSE study groups, a vast array of resources can assist you in your pursuit of MCSE certification. That's what this chapter is about.

Internet-based MCSE Resources

Dozens of Internet-based resources are devoted to MCSE certification. These resources offer several advantages over more traditional resources:

✔ They're timely and up-to-date

✔ They're interactive, facilitating idea exchange

✔ They allow you to network with MCSE candidates from all over the world

The following sections describe some of the most popular Internet-based MCSE resources.

MCSE mailing list

A couple guys named Scott Armstrong and Dean Klug maintain the MCSE mailing list. If you subscribe to this mailing list, you get 50 or more messages about the MCSE certification process daily. Fortunately, you can use a *digest* option that allows you to filter out all but the types of messages that you want to receive. To subscribe to the MCSE mailing list, send a message to majordomo@saluki.com. Include the following line as the body of the message:

```
subscribe mcse <your name>
```

NT Server newsgroups

Newsgroups host publicly accessible discussion threads. You can read what others have posted, respond to someone else's post, or start your own discussion thread by posting a new topic.

Newsgroups are a great place to ask others for information and advice, as well as to share your MCSE experiences with others. A number of Microsoft-hosted public newsgroups focus on NT Server-related topics. Most of the newsgroups that focus on NT-related topics begin with microsoft.public.windowsnt, such as microsoft.public.windowsnt.setup and microsoft.public.windowsnt.domain. For a complete list of Microsoft-hosted newsgroups, browse the Microsoft Web site:

```
http://www.microsoft.com/support/news
```

MCSE chat rooms

Internet Relay Chat (IRC) rooms allow you to interact with other people on the Internet in real time. The participants in a chat room converse by typing messages to each other simultaneously. You can use chat rooms with an MCSE focus to hold live conversations with other MCSE candidates around the world. The liveliest MCSE-focused chat room is the MCSE/MCT Resource Page:

```
http://www.geocities.com/~mcse_mct
```

Web sites

Dozens of Web sites on the Internet focus on MCSE certification. Each site has its own focus and its own strengths. The following table lists the best MCSE-focused Web sites and the features that they offer:

Site and Address	Features
MCSE and MCT Resource Page www.geocities.com/~mcse_mct/	Chat room, online meetings, message board, newsfeed, links to other MCSE sites
MCSE MCSD Braindump Heaven www.bnla.baynet.de/bnla01/ members/robsch19/	Observations about the MCSE exams made by people who just took them
How Prepared Are You? www.mcs.net/~hammond/exam/	Online practice exam
Steve Topley's Self Study MCSE Page www.geocities.com/ SiliconValley/9909/	Exam tips, online study groups, MCSE product reviews, links to other MCSE sites

Other MCSE Resources

Any number of MCSE resources are not strictly Internet-based. The following sections describe the best ones.

Periodicals

Two NT Server focused magazines are worth a subscription.

BackOffice Magazine provides extensive coverage of all the Microsoft BackOffice products, including NT Server. It is published monthly free for qualified professionals. To subscribe, visit the BackOffice site:

```
http://www.backoffice.com
```

Windows NT Magazine offers in-depth coverage of the NT operating system and its supporting market. It is also published monthly. To subscribe, go to the site:

```
http://www.winntmag.com
```

NT user groups

Joining an NT user group is a wonderful way to learn more about NT Server, as well as to network (in the social sense). Many NT user groups offer free technical training sessions, executive briefings, and seminars to their members. Some host MCSE study groups, which are a great way to meet other certification candidates like yourself and to add some structure to your study habits.

To find the NT user group chapter that is nearest to you, contact the NT Professional User Group:

```
http://www.ntpro.org
```

Or, visit the Worldwide Association of Windows NT User Groups:

```
http://www.wantug.org
```

Better yet, pay both of 'em visits.

Test software

The goal of test simulation software is to accurately emulate the software and the questions you get on the real MCSE exams. They offer you the most realistic idea of what taking the actual MCSE exam is like.

Windows NT Resource Kit

The *Windows NT Resource Kit* CD contains plenty of useful documentation for studying for the NT Server exam. The *Resource Kit* documentation has more technical depth than the standard NT help documents. It targets NT-knowledgeable people who want to become true NT experts, which makes it ideally suited for MCSE candidates.

Three of the books in the *NT Resource Kit's* "Online Docs" folder contain information that appears on the NT Server exam:

- *Windows NT Server Resource Guide*
- *Windows NT Server Networking Guide*
- *Windows NT Server Internet Guide*

Microsoft assessment exams

If you do not want to buy commercial test simulation software, but still want to sample the structure and style of the MCSE exams, download the Microsoft Assessment exams. They're on the Microsoft Web site:

```
http://microsoft.com/Train_Cert/download/downld.htm
```

Click the three hyperlinks entitled "Assessment Exam" to download them. Be sure to obtain all three files (asm1.exe, asm2.exe, and asm3.exe) before installing them.

These exams contain material from a number of certification areas, so they are not the best source of information for any one exam.

Microsoft course outlines

Most of the MCSE exams have corresponding Microsoft training courses. You can find outlines for each of these courses at Microsoft's Web site:

```
http://microsoft.com/mcp/certstep/mcse.htm
```

Part IX
Appendixes

The 5th Wave — By Rich Tennant

©RICHTENNANT

"It's part of my employer tuition assistance agreement with the 'Pizza Bob' corporation."

In this part . . .

Appendixes are just appendixes, right? Well, not always. These are some great appendixes — extremely useful! Practice exams in Appendixes A and B let you get a peek at what the real thing's like. And you want to get a handle on Microsoft's certification guidelines? Those are here, too. And, of course, you can peruse Appendix D to see what goodies are on the CD-ROM. (Oh! Did I forget to mention that the CD-ROM contains hundreds of practice questions? Well, you probably already knew that, didn't you?)

Appendix A
Sample Test 1

Practice Exam Rules

▶ 90 minutes

▶ 36 correct answers to pass

▶ 44 questions

*T*he actual MCSE exam does not let you bring in any notes, so try to answer the questions without looking through the book, then you can review the questions that you miss.

Prep Test

1 You have an administrator in domain1. Domain2 trusts domain1. What do you have to do to allow the domain1 administrator to be an administrator in domain2?

A ○ Create a local group in domain1.

B ○ Create a local group in domain2.

C ○ Create a global group in domain1.

D ○ Add the administrator account to the domain2 local administrator group.

2 How does a Windows NT Server communicate with a UPS?

A ○ Comm port

B ○ Parallel port

C ○ Ethernet port

D ○ Infrared port

3 Which application would you use to view the roles of all computers in a domain?

A ○ User Manager for Domains

B ○ Network Manager

C ○ Server Manager

D ○ Server Administrator

4 You have received an updated printer driver and would like to install it on all of your client workstations. What should you do?

A ○ Install the driver on every workstation using the setup program provided by the manufacturer.

B ○ Install the driver on the print server.

C ○ Place the driver in a shared folder on the server for users to install.

D ○ Update the driver in the printer configuration on the print server.

5 You are concerned that your system has started paging too much. What can you do to reduce the amount of paging?

A ○ Increase the size of the paging file

B ○ Decrease the size of the paging file

C ○ Increase the amount of RAM

D ○ Install another hard drive

6 Balanced Books accounting has a group of accountants who work at customer sites. These users need to be able to connect back to the office for mail and to submit reports. All of the users are running Windows NT and RAS. Because of the highly sensitive nature of the data, you want to protect all aspects of the communications between the user and the home office.

> **Required Results:**
> All remote users must be able to access the office via RAS. All data transmitted between the client computers and the server should be encrypted.
>
> **Optional Results:**
> All passwords between the client and the server must be encrypted.
>
> The server must authenticate the number the client is calling from before allowing the connection.
>
> **Proposed Solution:**
> Create a group containing all of the field representatives and grant them access to dial-in via RAS. Configure the RAS server to accept any authentication including clear text. Configure the RAS server with callback security.
>
> What results does the proposed solution produce?

A ○ The proposed solution produces the required results and all optional results.

B ○ The proposed solution produces the required result and one of the optional results.

C ○ The proposed solution produces the required result and none of the optional results.

D ○ The proposed solution fails to produce the required result.

7 You have a folder on the file, myfile.doc, on your Windows NT Server with READ permissions for the Everyone group. You copy the file to a folder where Everyone has No Access on the same drive. What is the current permission for the Everyone group on the file, myfile.doc?

A ○ Read

B ○ No Access

C ○ Change

D ○ Full Control

8 How does the binding order of network protocols affect the system performance?

A ○ There is no affect on system performance.

B ○ You should move the least frequently used protocols to the top of the binding order to improve performance.

C ○ You should move the fastest protocols to the top of the binding order to improve performance.

D ○ You should move the most frequently used protocols to the top of the binding order to improve performance.

9 Your Windows NT server has started generating a lot of STOP errors. Where can you go to find out more information on the STOP errors?

A ○ Event Viewer

B ○ Server Manager

C ○ Log Viewer

D ○ Dr. Watson

10 You are configuring TCP/IP on your NT Server on a routed Network. You have configured the server with a statically assign IP address. What other parameters must you configure so that the machine can communicate with other devices on the network? (Choose all that apply.)

A ❑ Subnet Mask

B ❑ WINS Server

C ❑ DNS Server

D ❑ Default Gateway

11 Joe has forgotten his password, and has asked you to reset his domain password. You make the changes from the BDC, but Joe is unable to log on. Why?

A ○ You should have made the changes on the PDC.

B ○ Joe is validating against a BDC that has not been synchronized yet.

C ○ Joe has his Caps Lock key down.

D ○ You need to change the password on all BDCs and PDCs in the domain.

12 You are configuring a new laser printer on your Windows NT 4.0 print server. You want to ensure that users on Windows 95, NT 3.51, and NT 4.0 can get the drivers from the server and print. Which driver should you install?

A ○ Windows NT 4.0 drivers only

B ○ Windows 95 drivers only

C ○ Windows 95 and Windows NT 3.51 drivers only

D ○ All drivers for all platforms

13 The finance department generates large print jobs every day detailing all the financial activity of Widget Inc. This ties up the printer for several hours at a time. The sales department needs to get their print jobs out as quickly as possible using the same printer. What should you do?

A ○ Tell the accounting department to only print at night.

B ○ Create two print spoolers, accounting and sales. Set permissions so that only people from the respective departments can access the printer spoolers. Set the priority on the sales spooler to 1. Set the priority on the accounting spooler to 99. Set printer hours on the accounting spooler.

C ○ Create two print spoolers, accounting and sales. Set permissions so that only people from the respective departments can access the printer spoolers. Set the priority on the sales spooler to 99. Set the priority on the accounting spooler to 1.

D ○ Create a printer pool, and assign the sales group higher priority than the accounting group.

14 Which tools require TCP/IP? (Choose all that apply.)

A ❑ Browsing Services

B ❑ FTP

C ❑ Telnet

D ❑ IPX/SPX

15 Your boss has asked you to provide a report of server performance over the next 30 days. Which option do you choose from the View menu in Performance Monitor?

A ○ Report

B ○ Chart

C ○ Log

D ○ Alert

16 You are experiencing problems with your RAS server, and have turned on Device logging. Where would you look to find the Device.log file?

A ○ In the \Winnt_root directory

B ○ In the \Winnt_root\system32 directory

C ○ In the \winnt_root\system32\RAS directory

D ○ In the \winnt_root\logs directory

17 You have assigned all of your users in the Corp domain a mandatory profile, which is stored on your PDC. Unfortunately, your PDC has gone down because of a bad disk. What happens to those users who have NOT logged on to the domain previously?

A ○ The user receives the default profile on their workstation.

B ○ The user is supplied with a default profile from the BDC.

C ○ The BDC provides a cached profile.

D ○ The user cannot log on.

18 Which tool do you use to create accounts in a domain?

A ○ User Manager

B ○ Server Manager

C ○ Account Manager

D ○ User Manager for Domains

19 The system administrator, Susan, must create dozens of accounts every day. Each account must be a member of several groups based on their department. How can Susan best manage this responsibility?

A ○ Create a template for new users, and assign the groups based on their department.

B ○ Assign the task to her understudy.

C ○ Create a template for each department with the appropriate groups already set and copy this template to create new users.

D ○ Put all users in every group by default.

20 Susan wants to delegate the administration of user accounts to Bob. What special group can she place Bob in that would grant him privilege to do this?

A ○ Server Operators

B ○ Administrators

C ○ Account Operators

D ○ User Administrators

21 If Joe enables file auditing on his server, where can he go to view the audit logs?

A ○ Log file in the WinNT directory

B ○ Security Control Panel

C ○ Event Viewer

D ○ Audit Viewer

22 You want to use one of your computers as an export server using the Directory Replicator Service. Which of the following types of computers could you use? (Choose all that apply.)

A ❑ Windows NT member server

B ❑ Primary domain controller

C ❑ Backup domain controller

D ❑ Windows NT workstation

23 Balanced Books Accounting has a NetWare server that has several resources that their Windows 95 users need to access. What must they install to allow the Windows 95 users access to these resources through their Windows NT server? (Choose all that apply.)

A ❑ Client Services for NetWare on the server

B ❑ Client Services for NetWare on the Windows 95 systems

C ❑ Gateway Services for NetWare on the server

D ❑ NWLink

24 What must you install to allow Macintosh users access to resources on your Windows NT server?

A ○ Service For Macintosh

B ○ Microsoft client on each Macintosh

C ○ SNMP

D ○ TCP/IP

25 The sales group is complaining that the server is not as responsive as it was in the past. What tools can you use to determine the problem with the server?

A ○ Server Monitor

B ○ Network Analyst

C ○ System Diagnostics

D ○ Performance Monitor

26 The accounting department is complaining that their print jobs are not coming out. The jobs appear to be getting to the server, but the server is not processing them. What should you try?

A ○ Reinstall all your print spoolers.

B ○ Reinstall Windows NT Server.

C ○ Cancel all the print jobs.

D ○ Stop and Start the Spooler Service in the Services Control Panel.

27 Don has five hard drives on his server. He needs to ensure that if one fails that the data on the server is still accessible. Which RAID level should he implement?

A ○ RAID 0

B ○ RAID 1

C ○ RAID 5

D ○ RAID 7

28 To restore a disk that failed in a mirrored set, which steps would you follow?

A ○ Break the mirror, install a new drive, and re-create the mirror in Disk Administrator.

B ○ Install a new drive and select Regenerate in Disk Administrator.

C ○ Install a new drive and select Restore in Disk Administrator.

D ○ Install a new drive and restore the data from backup.

29 You have a server with 7 drives configured as a stripe set with parity. Two of the drives have failed. What is the best way to proceed with the restore?

A ○ Replace the drives and select Regenerate in Disk Administrator.

B ○ Replace the drives and do nothing. Windows NT will repair the disks automatically.

C ○ Replace the drives and use Windows NT backup to regenerate the striped set with parity.

D ○ Replace the drives and recreate the striped set with parity in Disk Administrator. Restore the data from backups.

30 You just purchased a new client/server accounting application that you want to install. The clients are all NetWare clients. You want to use your new Windows NT server as the server. What do you need to install on the server?

A ○ NWLink

B ○ Gateway Service For NetWare

C ○ TCP/IP

D ○ Client Services For NetWare

31 You just installed a new Ethernet card in the server, and now it will not boot properly. How should you begin the troubleshooting process?

A ○ Remove the card and restart

B ○ Re-install Windows NT Server

C ○ Boot from a CD-ROM

D ○ Boot from the Last Known Good Hardware Configuration

32 What happens if you move a file from one folder to another on the same partition?

A ○ The file inherits the permissions of its new parent folder.

B ○ The file retains its current permissions.

C ○ The file inherits a default set of permissions.

D ○ All file permissions are lost.

33 You have managed to restore your crashed server using the emergency repair disks, but you cannot log on and users cannot access network resources. What has happened?

A ○ The repair was unsuccessful; you need to reinstall.

B ○ You have restored an old version of the Registry. The administrator account or password is different and no user accounts were in the ERD backup.

C ○ Everyone has the Caps Lock key pressed down.

D ○ All passwords are reset to a default value of "NEW2DAY."

34 You have several NetWare clients and servers currently installed on your network. You are installing a new NT server, on which you plan to run a NETBIOS application. What must you install on the NT server so that the NetWare clients can access the application?

A ○ Gateway Service For NetWare

B ○ Client Services For NetWare

C ○ NWLink

D ○ RIP

35 You have installed the Server Tools on your Windows 95 machine. What tool can you use to manage the security of the printers on your NT Servers?

A ○ Server Manager

B ○ Explorer

C ○ User Manager

D ○ Printer Manager

36 You have lost your setup disks and need to make new ones to boot your server from in case of an emergency. What tool can you use to make these disks?

A ○ Winnt32.exe on the installation CD-ROM

B ○ Rdisk /s

C ○ The administrative Wizards in Windows NT Server

D ○ Server Manager

37 You have lost your emergency repair disks. How can you create a new set of ERDs?

A ○ Run Setup from the CD-ROM.

B ○ Use Rdisk /s.

C ○ Format a floppy and copy the main Win NT systems files to it.

D ○ Order a replacement set from Microsoft.

38 You are concerned that someone is accessing your server without authorization. Where can you set audit policies to monitor the server?

A ○ User Manager for Domains

B ○ Server Manager

C ○ Security Manager

D ○ Event Viewer

39 You have decided you want everyone to have a Home Directory on the PDC in the Corp domain. How do you configure their accounts to support the home directory?

A ○ In User Manager for Domains, specify the UNC Path to the Home Directory.

B ○ In User Manager for Domains, specify domain, server, and directory name for the home directory.

C ○ In Explorer, create the home directory on the BDC and assign take ownership to the user.

D ○ In Explorer, create the home directory on the BDC and assign Full Control to the user.

40 Several users have asked to have the same desktop appear no matter where they log on. How can you accomplish this feat?

A ○ On a domain controller, in system properties, copy a user profile to the user's account.

B ○ On a domain controller, in system properties, copy a user profile to the profiles directory.

C ○ In User manager for Domains, assign a UNC path to the profile.

D ○ In User manager for domains, assign a home directory to the user. A roaming profile will be automatically created the next time the user logs on.

41 You are installing a new SQL Server and need to define the server's role. Which role do you select?

A ○ Balanced

B ○ Maximize Throughput for File Sharing

C ○ Maximize Throughput for Network Access

D ○ None; the server automatically defines its optimal role.

42 You have configured a server/printer with the DLC protocol. After you reboot, you can't print. Why?

A ○ Your network does not support DLC.

B ○ Another user has captured the printer with DLC in continuous mode.

C ○ The printer is no longer on the network.

D ○ DLC only works with HP printers.

43 You run performance monitor to determine why your hard drives are performing so slowly. When you bring up the counters they all have values of zero. Why?

A ○ The disk is too busy to report performance data.

B ○ You need to use Disk Administrator to monitor disk performance.

C ○ You need to run diskperf -y.

D ○ You can only monitor disk performance from a remote machine.

44 Your network has three NT servers. You want to change the role of the BDC to PDC. You are working from a Windows NT workstation with network admin tools installed. What is the best process to use to promote the BDC?

A ○ Shut down the existing PDC and use Server Manager to promote the BDC. Restart PDC and it is demoted.

B ○ Shut down both the PDC and BDC. Restart the BDC and it automatically demotes the PDC.

C ○ Use Server Manager to stop the NetLogon service on both servers. Promote the BDC to PDC and demote the PDC to BDC. Restart Logon service.

D ○ Use Server Manager to promote the BDC to PDC and the existing PDC demotes automatically.

Answers

1 *D.* Since Domain2 trusts Domain1, you only need to add the administrator from Domain1 to the administrators group in Domain2. This will grant the administrator in Domain1 full access. *Objective: Managing User Accounts (Chapter 14).*

2 *A.* The Windows NT Server communicates with the UPS via the Comm Port. *Objective: Configure Peripherals and Devices (Chapter 8).*

3 *C.* Server Manager is the administrator tool you can run from either the PDC or BDC to view the roles of all servers in the domain. *Objective: Managing Server Accounts (Chapter 15).*

4 *D.* You only need to update the drivers for the configured printers on the NT Server. The clients will automatically download the new versions of the drivers. *Objective: Configuring Printers (Chapter 12).*

5 *C.* When the system starts paging that means that physical RAM has been exhausted. To correct this problem you should install more RAM on the server. You can also increase the size of the paging file, or spread it across multiple disks to improve paging performance. *Objective: Memory optimization (Chapter 19).*

6 *C.* You have configured the server to accept clear text passwords instead of encrypted password. You have also failed to implement a dial back security function. *Objective: Configuring RAS (Chapter 16).*

7 *B.* When you copy a file to a new folder on the same partition the file inherits the permissions of its new parent folder. When you move a file on the same partition it keeps its original permissions. *Objective: Copying and Moving Files (Chapter 15).*

8 *D.* To get the best performance on client machines move the most frequently used protocols to the top of the binding order. *Objective: Network optimization (Chapter 19).*

9 *A.* The event viewer is where all logging information and error messages are written. *Objective: Troubleshooting (Chapter 20).*

10 *A, D.* On a routed TCP/IP network, you need to configure both the subnet mask and the default gateway. The subnet mask defines which networks are local, and the gateway tells the computer how to communicate across the router. *Objective: Configuring Protocols (Chapter 9).*

11 *B.* When you make account changes in a domain, you are always editing the copy of the SAM database on the PDC. The default behavior in Windows NT is to have the BDCs synchronize every five minutes. You can as an administrator, force synchronization. *Objective: Manage User Accounts (Chapter 13).*

12 *C.* The Windows NT 4.0 drivers are installed when you create the printer. You will also need to specify and load the Windows 95 and NT 3.51 drivers. Windows NT 3.51 drivers are different than Windows NT 4.0 drivers. *Objective: Configuring A Printer (Chapter 8).*

13 *C.* Creating separate spoolers to the same printers allows you to configure it so the sales group can get their jobs out as quickly as possible, and the accounting group can batch their jobs to print at night. *Objective: Setting Printer Priorities (Chapter 8).*

14 *B, C.* FTP and Telnet are two services built on top of TCP/IP. IPX/SPX is another network protocol, and Browsing services will work over TCP/IP, IPX, or NetBEUI. It does not require TCP/IP in order to function though. *Objective: Choosing A Protocol (Chapter 9).*

15 *A.* A Report allows you to look at the performance trend between any two data points. *Objective: Monitor Performance (Chapter 18).*

16 *C.* You turn on the RAS Device by making a registry modification. Once turned on you will find a device.log file in the \winnt_root\system32\RAS directory. *Objective: Resolving RAS Problems (Chapter 16).*

17 *A.* The users will receive a default profile. Those users who have logged in will receive a cached profile. *Objective: Create and manage profiles (Chapter 13).*

18 *D.* User Manager for Domains is the domain version of the normal User Manager utility in Windows NT. *Objective: Managing User Accounts (Chapter 13).*

19 *C.* While it would be great to assign it to the understudy, we all know that as system administrators we are expected to do everything. The best bet here is to create a set of templates, one for each department, with the group information already set. Just copy to create new users for that department. *Objective: Managing User Accounts (Chapter 13).*

20 *C.* The account operators special group has the ability to create and manage user/group accounts. *Objective: Managing Groups (Chapter 14).*

21 *C.* All audit, security, system, and application logs can be viewed from the Event Viewer. *Objective: Establishing File Auditing (Chapter 15).*

22 *A, B, C.* Any Windows NT Server can act as an export server. An NT Workstation cannot act as an export server. *Objective: Configuring Directory Replicator (Chapter 10).*

23 *C, D.* Gateway Service for NetWare allows an NT server to act as an intermediate between the client and NetWare server. NWLink is the protocol used to communicate between the NT and NetWare server. *Objective: Configure for NetWare (Chapter 17).*

24 *A.* Service For Macintosh (SFM) is what allows Macintosh users to connect to an NT server. *Objective: Configuring Network Services (Chapter 10).*

25 *D.* Performance monitor can be used to monitor a multitude of objects and counters relating to server performance. In this case you would probably monitor disk utilization, network utilization, and CPU performance objects. *Objective: Monitoring Server Performance (Chapter 8).*

26 *D.* Occasionally, the print spoolers will get stuck. Advice from Microsoft is to first try to Stop and Start the spooler service to see if it clears the problem. *Objective: Troubleshooting Printers (Chapter 8).*

27 *C.* RAID 5 is a striped set with parity. If one drive fails the data is still accessible because of the parity information. *Objective: Choosing Fault-Tolerance (Chapter 5).*

28 *A.* There is no need to restore or regenerate the data because the other drive in the mirror has a complete copy. Just break the old mirror set, install a new drive, and create a new mirror set. Windows NT will begin the process of synchronizing the two drives. *Objective: Troubleshooting Fault-Tolerance failure (Chapter 5).*

29 *D.* If two drives fail you are forced to restore the data from backup. Striped set with parity can only survive the loss of one drive. *Objective: Choosing Fault-Tolerance (Chapter 5).*

30 *A.* You only need to install the protocol for the server to communicate with the clients. The client/server application handles the rest. *Objective: Interoperability with NetWare (Chapter 17).*

31 *D.* Go back to the Last Known Good Configuration, and begin checking things like IRQ conflicts, driver conflicts, new drivers needed, and so on. *Objective: Troubleshooting Configuration Problems (Chapter 20).*

32 *A.* When moving a file on the same partition it will inherit the permissions of its new parent folder. When copying it will retain its original permissions. *Objective: Moving and copying files (Chapter 15).*

33 *B.* This is why you should keep your ERD up to date. There is nothing worse than a successful restore back to a state where you don't remember the Administrator password. *Objective: Troubleshooting Configuration Problems (Chapter 20).*

34 *C.* You only need to install NWLink on the NT Server. Since the application is a client/server application, NetWare clients will access it directly via NWLink. *Objective: Interoperability with NetWare (Chapter 17).*

35 B. To manage printer permissions you will use the Windows 95 Explorer. *Objective: Administering Remote Servers (Chapter 15).*

36 A. To recreate the three setup floppies that came with your CD-ROM, you can run setup. *Objective: Installing Windows NT Server (Chapter 7).*

37 B. To recreate the ERD disks use rdisk from the command line. The /s option makes a copy of all the system files onto the floppy also. *Objective: Troubleshooting Configuration Problems (Chapter 20).*

38 A. User Manager for Domains is where you define the Audit policies for your domain or server. You can view the audit record in the Event Viewer. *Objective: Establishing Auditing (Chapter 15).*

39 A. In User Manager for Domains, as part of an account profile, you can specify a home directory. You can also specify a drive for it to be mapped to. *Objective: Managing User Accounts (Chapter 13).*

40 C. For each user account you can specify a specific profile to be used. This is configured in User Manager for Domains. *Objective: Managing Profiles (Chapter 13).*

41 C. SQL server is a network application. You want to optimize for Network access. Windows NT Server will NOT set this automatically. *Objective: Configuring For Optimal Performance (Chapter 19).*

42 B. DLC has a continuous capture mode. Once captured in this mode, no other machine can talk to the printer. *Objective: Troubleshooting Printer Problems (Chapter 8).*

43 C. By default, disk performance counters are off because there is a slight performance overhead to running them. If your counters are at zero, it is probably because they are off. Run diskperf -y to turn them on. *Objective: Performance Monitoring (Chapter 18).*

44 D. Using Server Manager from any supported platform allows you to reconfigure the PDC and BDC servers for a domain. When you promote a BDC to PDC, it will communicate with the existing PDC and cause it to demote itself. You cannot promote a member server to either BDC or PDC status without reinstalling. *Objective: Remote Server Management (Chapter 15).*

Appendix B
Sample Test 2

Practice Exam Rules

▶ 90 minutes
▶ 44 correct answers to pass
▶ 54 questions

*T*he actual MCSE exam does not let you bring in any notes, so try to answer the questions without looking through the book.

Prep Test

1 You are installing NT Server 4 on a computer with no preexisting server software. You want to skip the process of creating setup disks. Which command would you use to do a floppyless installation of Windows NT?

A ○ WINNT.EXE /ox

B ○ WINNT32.EXE /ox

C ○ WINNT.EXE /b

D ○ WINNT32.EXE /b

2 You are configuring a computer that has the following operating systems installed in the following order: Windows NT 4.0, Windows 95, Windows NT Workstation 4.0. You go into the system properties, and click the Startup/ Shutdown tab. Which operating system is configured to start as the default operating system?

A ○ Windows NT 4.0

B ○ Windows NT Workstation 4.0

C ○ Windows 95

D ○ None of the above

3 Your network has 50 Windows NT clients that access a laser printer. You have just obtained an updated printer driver. What is the best way to get all computers that access this printer to use the updated driver?

A ○ Update the server, then instruct each person who uses the printer to download and install the driver on their computer.

B ○ Update the driver on each computer that accesses the print server. There is no need to update the driver on the print server.

C ○ Create a new printer that uses this driver, and instruct everyone to now use the new printer.

D ○ Update the driver only on the print server.

4 Julie has left her position in the finance department. Jennifer will be taking her place. What is the best and easiest way to remove Julie's access to the system, and give Jennifer an account with the same access to network resources that Julie had?

A ○ From Server Manager, rename Julie's account and have Jennifer change her password the first time she logs on.

B ○ From User Manager for Domains, rename Julie's account and have Jennifer change her password the first time she logs on.

C ○ From Server Manager, use Julie's account as a template for creating Jennifer's account. Delete Julie's account.

D ○ From User Manager for Domains, use Julie's account as a template for creating Jennifer's account. Delete Julie's account.

5 You are upgrading a previous version of Windows NT to NT Server 4, and want to take advantage of file system security features offered in this version. Which file system will you choose?

A ○ FAT

B ○ FAT32

C ○ NTFS

D ○ 3rd Party File System

6 You are required to promote a BDC on your network to a PDC. Which application would you use?

A ○ Server Manager

B ○ Network Administrator

C ○ Windows NT Explorer

D ○ User Manager for Domains

7 After installing NT Server, you're told that Services for Macintosh will need to be installed. Which would you use to install this?

A ○ Server Manager

B ○ Control Panel / Network / Services

C ○ Service Manager

D ○ User Manager for Domains

8 You move a file from an uncompressed folder on an NTFS partition to a folder on another NTFS partition that is compressed. Will this file compress once it's moved to the target folder?

A ○ The file will retain its attributes as being uncompressed

B ○ The file will inherit the attributes of the target folder, and become compressed.

C ○ An error message will occur.

D ○ A dialog box will appear asking if you want the file to be compressed or not.

9 Your network has 30 NT Workstations accessing an HP LaserJet printer. You have just been told that 10 Macintosh computers are to now have access to this same printer. There are no Macintosh services installed on the print server. Which services will you need to install on the server so that the Mac users can access the printer?

A ○ Print Services for Macintosh

B ○ Client Services for Macintosh

C ○ Services for Macintosh

D ○ Nothing. Print Manager already has the ability to service Mac clients.

10 You are required to incorporate fault tolerance into your server. Which level of RAID should you use?

A ○ RAID Level 0
B ○ RAID Level 1
C ○ RAID Level 3
D ○ RAID Level 4

11 Your server has slowed down tremendously during peak hours, and the hard drive seems to be working at a feverish pace. You believe disk thrashing may be occurring. Which application can you use to prove your suspicions?

A ○ Disk Administrator
B ○ Server Manager
C ○ Performance Monitor
D ○ Network Administrator

12 The World Wide Web is based on which protocol?

A ○ HTTP
B ○ FTP
C ○ Gopher
D ○ NetBEUI

13 You have decided to implement disk striping with parity on your server. How many physical hard disks are required on the server to perform this action?

A ○ One
B ○ Two
C ○ Three
D ○ Four

14 A company merger requires you to connect your existing NT Workstations to a UNIX Server. Which is the best protocol to install on your NT Workstations for these two systems to communicate?

A ○ NWLink
B ○ TCP/IP
C ○ NetBEUI
D ○ IPX/SPX

15 You have a Windows NT Server with 50MB of RAM. What is the recommended initial size of the paging file?

A ○ 62MB
B ○ 74MB
C ○ 38MB
D ○ 46MB

16 Suppose the following situation exists: A recent company merger requires you to add Macintosh clients to your existing network. Before adding these new clients, your network has consisted of 40 NT workstations, and one NT Server. Before the merger, security and fault tolerance has never been an issue. For this reason, the server uses a FAT file system, and has only done regular backups to protect themselves from a problem. In addition, your boss has told you that these Macs constantly use the Internet and are prone to viruses! Required Result: *The clients must be able to access the server and save files to it's disk drives.* Optional Desired Result: *Protect the system from viruses. Implement fault tolerance.* Proposed Solution: *Install AppleTalk and Services for Macintosh on the server. Install a reliable virus scanner and do regular virus scans. Install user disk striping with parity on the servers disk drives.*

Which results does the proposed solution produce?

A ○ The solution produces the required result and both of the optional desired results.

B ○ The solution produces the required result, but only one of the optional desire results.

C ○ The solution produces the required result, and none of the optional desired results.

D ○ The solution does not produce the required result.

17 You have installed RAS on your Windows NT Server. A computer user using SLIP complains of not being able to connect. How can you fix the problem?

A ○ Tell the user to change his or her script, so it selects SLIP when logging on to the RAS Server.

B ○ Set the user as using SLIP in User Manager for Domains.

C ○ Select "Allow Remote SLIP clients to access" in RAS Server configuration

D ○ Tell the user to use PPP instead.

18 You have decided to install IIS. Of the following protocols, which does Internet Information Server serve?

A ○ HTTP, Gopher, POP

B ○ HTTP, SMTP, FTP

C ○ HTTP, Gopher, FTP

D ○ POP, SMTP, FTP

19 Of the following, what best describes what DNS does?

A ○ Resolves Fully Qualified Internet names to IP addresses

B ○ Resolves NetBIOS names to IP addresses

C ○ Resolves SIDs to IP addresses

D ○ Resolves SIDs to NetBIOS names

20 Which of the following would an emergency repair disk be used to restore?

A ○ Registry Information
B ○ System backups
C ○ Missing system files
D ○ None of the above

21 A user complains that she can view all the logs in Event Viewer, except the Security log. What is most likely the problem?

A ○ The user doesn't have permissions for the directory that the security log is stored in.
B ○ The user doesn't realize that the security log is a hidden file.
C ○ The user isn't a local administrator.
D ○ The user doesn't have the "View Security Log" setting enabled in their user account.

22 Which of the following contains a copy of the directory database?

A ○ Stand Alone Server and Master Browser
B ○ Primary Domain Controller and Member Server
C ○ Backup Domain Controller and Member Server
D ○ Primary Domain Controller and Backup Domain Controller

23 What are the two licensing modes offered by Windows NT Server?

A ○ Per Server and Per Computer
B ○ Per Domain and Per Computer
C ○ Per Server and Per Seat
D ○ Per System and Per Seat

24 You get an "Access Denied" error showing that the Directory Replicator is unable to replicate! What would you check to solve this problem?

A ○ Event Viewer and User Manager for Domains
B ○ Event View and Network Monitor
C ○ User Manager for Domains and Network Monitor
D ○ Server Manager and User Manager for Domains

25 Jennifer has just tried booting the Server and received this error: NTDETECT V1.0 Checking Hardware .... NTDETECT failed.

What are you going to tell Jennifer to reinstall for NT Server to boot correctly?

A ○ NTLDR
B ○ Ntdetect.com
C ○ Ntoskrnl.exe
D ○ Bootsect.dos

26 You are running a network with a single server that supports all workstations. Which licensing mode should you choose?

A ○ Per Server

B ○ Per Seat

C ○ Per Seat on the Server and Per Server on the workstations

D ○ None of the above

27 Complaints are coming in from users across your network who are attempting to print to a shared printer. No one can print to it, and when you attempt deleting the jobs, it won't let you. What is the most likely problem?

A ○ Incorrect printer driver

B ○ Stalled print spooler

C ○ Spooler priority is set too high

D ○ Spooler priority isn't set high enough

28 A Windows NT RAS client has attempted a connection, but failed in making the connection. Which application would you use to troubleshoot the problem?

A ○ User Manager for Domains

B ○ Server Manager

C ○ RAS Administrator

D ○ Event Viewer

29 Which of the following collects and maintains a list of the available network servers on its subnet?

A ○ Domain Master Browser

B ○ Master Browser

C ○ Backup Browser

D ○ Potential Browser

30 Windows NT allows a one time, one way switch of licensing modes. What kind of switch is this?

A ○ From Per Server to Per Seat

B ○ From Per Seat to Per Server

C ○ None of the above. NT doesn't allow such a switch.

31 You have decided not to use DHCP, and instead manually configure TCP/IP. When specifying an IP address, what information must you supply?

A ○ IP address

B ○ Subnet Mask

C ○ Default Gateway

D ○ All of the above

32 Which of the following enables Windows NT to bind one or more protocols to a network adapter?

A ○ File System Drivers

B ○ NDIS

C ○ NIC

D ○ DLC

33 Which of the following displays data about current processes?

A ○ Network Administrator

B ○ Resource Manager

C ○ Task Manager

D ○ Power Tools for Windows NT

34 You want to boost the foreground application's priority by one level. In Application Performance, on the Performance tab of System Properties, what would you set the slider bar to?

A ○ None

B ○ One

C ○ Middle

D ○ Maximum

35 During installation, on which partition does Windows NT store the operating system files? Choose the best answer.

A ○ Primary partition

B ○ Extended partition

C ○ Boot partition

D ○ System partition

36 Your server has 2 SCSI drives, each of which has its own disk controller. You have decided to implement fault tolerance, and want to be able to continue using one of the drives if one fails. Which type of fault tolerance will you choose?

A ○ Stripe set with parity

B ○ Strip set

C ○ Volume set

D ○ Disk duplexing

37 You have installed several new protocols on workstations in your network. Now users are complaining that it is slower connecting to the network. What can you do to the binding order to increase performance?

A ○ Move less frequently used protocols to the top of the binding order.

B ○ Move most frequently used protocols to the top of the binding order.

C ○ Binding order of protocols have no effect on performance. The answer to this problem lies elsewhere.

D ○ Slower protocols should be moved to the bottom of the binding order.

38 Your company recently merged with a company that has only used NetWare. Previous to this you only used NT Server, Workstation, and 95. Now, you need to allow your Windows 95 and NT Workstation computers to access files on the NetWare server. Without installing NetWare on the NT and 95 machines, what do you need to install to do this?

A ○ Gateway Service for NetWare on the NT Server

B ○ Gateway Service for NetWare on the NetWare Server

C ○ Gateway Service for NetWare on the Windows 95 and NT Workstations

D ○ NWLink on the NetWare Server

39 You attempt to place a local group within a global group. NT Server won't let you. What is the most likely reason?

A ○ You don't have the proper permissions.

B ○ Global groups can only contain global groups.

C ○ Global groups cannot contain local groups.

D ○ Global groups can only contain domain local groups.

40 You decide to monitor the disk usage on your server. You open Performance Monitor, but can't find any disk counters. What is the most likely reason?

A ○ You must run Disk Administrator to view the counters.

B ○ You must run DISKPERF.EXE for the counters to appear.

C ○ You must run Disk Administrator for the counters to appear.

D ○ Counters for disk drives are not available until future versions of NT.

41 You have used RAID level 0 on your NT Server, and one disk fails. How can you retrieve the data using a fault tolerance method?

A ○ Replace the failed disk, and regenerate the data.

B ○ Replace the failed disk, break the mirror, and then reestablish the mirror.

C ○ Replace the hard disk controller card, then reboot the system.

D ○ You can't. All data is lost.

42 You have just installed a new printer onto your network. Now, users are complaining that only illegible gibberish is printing out! What is the likely cause of this problem?

A ○ Print spooler has stalled

B ○ Print spooler is corrupt

C ○ Incorrect printer driver

D ○ DLC has not been installed

43 You want to implement fault tolerance on your server, and put the system and boot partitions on the new drive set. Which of the following will allow you to do this?

A ○ Stripe set with parity
B ○ Stripe set
C ○ Volume set
D ○ Disk Mirroring

44 During installation, on which partition does Windows NT store the files it requires to boot with? Choose the best answer.

A ○ Primary partition
B ○ Extended partition
C ○ Boot partition
D ○ System partition

45 You are running a network with multiple servers supporting 30 workstations. Which licensing mode should you choose?

A ○ Per Server
B ○ Per Seat
C ○ Per Seat on the Server and Per Server on the workstations
D ○ None of the above

46 You are running a network that has just installed a new Hewlett-Packard printer. You want to use the HP Print Monitor. Which protocol must you install?

A ○ DLC
B ○ TCP/IP
C ○ NetBEUI
D ○ NetBIOS

47 Which of the following validates user logons?

A ○ Stand Alone Server, Member Server, and Master Browser
B ○ Primary Domain Controller, Server, and Member Server
C ○ Primary Domain Controller and Backup Domain Controller
D ○ Primary Domain Controller, Backup Domain Controller, and Member Server

48 Of the following, what best describes what WINS does?

A ○ Resolves Fully Qualified Internet names to IP addresses
B ○ Resolves SIDs to NetBIOS names
C ○ Resolves SIDs to IP addresses
D ○ Resolves NetBIOS names to IP addresses

49 DHCP stands for:

A ○ Dynamic Host Connection Protocol
B ○ Dynamic Host Configuration Protocol
C ○ Domain Host Connection Protocol
D ○ Domain Host Configuration Protocol

50 You suspect a problem with a user, and have decided to enable the audit policy. Which application should you use to do this?

A ○ Server Manager
B ○ Windows NT Explorer
C ○ Security Manager
D ○ User Manager for Domains

51 You have decided to have your server dual boot between Windows 95 and Windows NT Server. Which file system is the best choice for this situation?

A ○ FAT
B ○ FAT32
C ○ NTFS
D ○ CDFS

52 A company merger requires you to connect your existing NT Workstations to a NetWare Server. Which is the best protocol to install on your NT Workstations for these two systems to communicate?

A ○ NWLink
B ○ DLC
C ○ NetBEUI
D ○ AppleTalk

53 You decide to monitor your network to see how close the network is to maximum utilization. You open Performance Monitor, but can't find the % Network Utilization counter. What must you install for this counter to appear?

A ○ Network Monitor Agent
B ○ Diskperf
C ○ Simple Network Management Service
D ○ TCP/IP

54 You are required to incorporate fault tolerance on your server. After deciding which level of RAID to use, which application would you use to implement it on your system?

A ○ Network Administrator
B ○ Server Manager
C ○ Windows NT Explorer
D ○ Disk Administrator

Prep Test Answers

1 *C. WINNT.EXE /b.* Winnt32.exe is used only for upgrading earlier versions of Windows NT. The switch /ox is used to only create the boot disks. Therefore, the only way to do a new installation, and skip the creation of the three setup disks, is with the command Winnt.exe /b. *Objective: Install Windows NT Server on Intel-based platforms (Chapter 7).*

2 *B. Windows NT Workstation 4.0.* The default setting is to use the last operating system installed as the default operating system. With this particular system, it would be set to boot up in Windows NT Workstation 4.0. *Objective: Install Windows NT Server by using various methods (Chapter 7).*

3 *D. Update the driver only on the print server.* There is no need to update each computer manually, or create a new printer. When users attempt to use the printer with the updated driver, the server will automatically copy the updated driver to that computer. *Objective: Configure printers (Chapter 8).*

4 *B. From User Manager for Domains, rename Julie's account and have Jennifer change her password the first time she logs on.* Server Manager is not used for creating, deleting and managing accounts. User Manager for Domains is used for these functions. When accounts are copied, they lose account descriptions and permissions. Therefore, in situations like this, it is always better to rename an account and have the password changed, then to use another account as a template. *Objective: Manage user and group accounts (Chapter 13).*

5 *C. NTFS.* NTFS takes advantage of Windows NT's file security features. FAT does not. FAT32 is an enhanced version of FAT designed for Windows 95, and is not supported under NT 4.0. *Objective: Plan the disk drive configuration for various requirements (Chapter 5).*

6 *A. Server Manager.* Server Manager is the application used to promote BDCs to PDCs. *Objective: Configure Windows NT Server core services (Chapter 15).*

7 *B. Control Panel / Network / Services.* To install Services for Macintosh on an NT Server after it has been installed, use the Services tab of the Network applet in the Control Panel. *Objective: Choose the appropriate course of action to take to resolve connectivity problems (Chapter 10).*

8 *B. The file will inherit the attributes of the target folder, and become compressed.* A file moved or copied to a compressed folder on a different partition will inherit the attributes of that folder. However, if the file is moved or copied to a folder on the same partition, the file retains its own attributes. *Objective: Manage disk resources (Chapter 15).*

9 *C. Services for Macintosh.* Installing Services for Macintosh on a server installs software for Mac printer sharing, file sharing, and the application extension map. *Objective: Choose the appropriate course of action to take to resolve connectivity problems (Chapter 10).*

10 B. *RAID Level 1.* Windows NT only supports RAID levels 0, 1 and 5. RAID level 1 doesn't provide fault tolerance. Since RAID level 5 wasn't an option, the answer can only be RAID level 1 (which is disk mirroring). *Objective: Plan the disk drive configuration for various requirements (Chapter 5).*

11 C. *Performance Monitor.* If disk thrashing is suspected, Performance Monitor can be used to check memory, disk usage, and number of page faults. *Objective: Monitor performance of various functions by using Performance Monitor (Chapter 19).*

12 A. *HTTP.* The World Wide Web is based on the HyperText Transfer Protocol (HTTP). *Objective: Choose a protocol for various situations (Chapter 9).*

13 C. *Three.* Disk striping with parity requires three physical hard disks to implement. *Objective: Plan the disk drive configuration for various requirements (Chapter 5).*

14 B. *TCP/IP.* TCP/IP is the protocol of choice when communicating with UNIX computers. It is the protocol of the Internet, which is predominantly UNIX systems. It is a standard, routable protocol that is also the protocol of the Internet (the servers of which are predominantly UNIX). *Objective: Choose a protocol for various situations (Chapter 9).*

15 A. *62.* The recommended initial paging file size is the amount of RAM plus 12MB. *Objective: Configure Windows NT Server core services (Chapter 15).*

16 D. *The proposed solution does not produce the required result.* Because the file system on the server is FAT, the Mac clients will not be able to store files on the server. NTFS must be used if the Macintosh computers are to use the servers disk drives. This is because only NTFS can understand the method Macintosh uses to save files. *Objective: Configure hard disks to meet various requirements (Chapter 5).*

17 D. *Tell the user to use PPP instead.* While you can configure RAS to dial out to another computer using SLIP, it cannot be configured to accept a connection that is using SLIP. As such, the user would have to use PPP to connect to the RAS. *Objective: Choose the appropriate course of action to take to resolve RAS problems (Chapter 16).*

18 C. *HTTP, Gopher, and FTP.* Internet Information Server offers services for Gopher, HTTP, and FTP protocols. *Objective: Install and Configure Remote Access Services (RAS) (Chapter 16).*

19 A. *Resolves Fully Qualified Internet names to IP addresses.* DNS resolves IP addresses to NetBIOS computer names. *Objective: Choose a protocol for various situations (Chapter 9).*

20 C. *Missing system files.* Emergency Repair Disks are used to restore missing or corrupt system files. *Objective: Choose the appropriate course of action to take to resolve boot failures (Chapter 20).*

21 *C. The user isn't a local administrator.* By default, everyone can view all logs in event viewer except for the security log. Only local administrators have access to this log. *Objective: Choose the appropriate course of action to take to resolve resource access and permission problems (Chapter 20).*

22 *D. Primary Domain Controller and Backup Domain Controller.* Only the Primary Domain Controller and Backup Domain Controller contain copies of the directory database. *Objective: Install Windows NT Server on Intel-based platforms (Chapter 7).*

23 *C. Per Server and Per Seat.* Windows NT Server offers Per Server and Per Seat licensing modes. *Objective: Install Windows NT Server on Intel-based platforms (Chapter 7).*

24 *A. Event Viewer and User Manager for Domains.* If an access denied error occurs during directory replication, check the event view to see that the Directory Replicator is configured to log on using a specific account, and use User Manager for Domains to check permissions. *Objective: Choose the appropriate course of action to take to resolve RAS problems (Chapter 16).*

25 *B. NTDETECT.COM.* Ntdetect.com needs to be reinstalled. This error occurs when this file is missing. *Objective: Choose the appropriate course of action to take to resolve boot failures (Chapter 20).*

26 *A. Per Server.* If there is only one server, the best choice of licensing is Per Server. *Objective: Install Windows NT Server on Intel-based platforms (Chapter 7).*

27 *B. Stalled print spooler.* This situation has all the indicators of a stalled print spooler. To correct this, open Services in the Control Panel and then stop and restart the spooler service. *Objective: Choose the appropriate course of action to take to resolve printer problems (Chapter 8).*

28 *D. Event Viewer.* RAS events are logged to the system log, and can be viewed with Event Viewer. *Objective: Install and configure Remote Access Services (RAS) (Chapter 16).*

29 *B. Master Browser.* The master browser collects and maintains a list of all available browsers on its subnet. *Objective: Install Windows NT Server to perform various server roles (Chapter 10).*

30 *A. From Per Server to Per Seat.* Windows NT allows a one time, one way change of licensing from Per Server to Per Seat. *Objective: Install Windows NT Server using various methods (Chapter 7).*

31 *D. All of the Above.* When specifying an IP address, you must input the IP address, Subnet Mask, and Default Gateway. *Objective: Configure protocols and protocol bindings (Chapter 9).*

32 *B. NDIS.* NDIS allows multiple protocols to be bound to a network adapter. *Objective: Configure protocols and protocol bindings (Chapter 9).*

33 *C. Task Manager.* Task Manager provides data about current processes. *Objective: Identify Performance Bottlenecks (Chapter 18).*

34 *C. Middle.* To increase the foreground's priority by one level, set the Application Performance boost to the middle. *Objective: Identify Performance Bottlenecks (Chapter 19).*

35 *C. Boot partition.* Windows NT stores the operating system files on the boot partition. *Objective: Install Windows NT Server on Intel-based platforms (Chapter 7).*

36 *D. Disk duplexing.* Disk duplexing is the same as disk mirroring, except that each physical disk has it's own controller card. Therefore, even if one controller card fails, the network can continue using the other disk! *Objective: Plan the disk drive configuration for various requirements (Chapter 5).*

37 *B. Move the most frequently used protocols to the top of the binding order.* Move the most frequently used protocols to the top of the binding order. The higher a protocol is on the list, the faster it's accessed. *Objective: Configure protocols and protocol bindings (Chapter 9).*

38 *A. Gateway Service for NetWare on the NT Server.* For the Windows 95 and NT Workstations to access files on a NetWare server, you would need to install Gateway Services for NetWare on your NT Server. *Objective: Configure Windows NT Server for interoperability with NetWare servers by using various tools (Chapter 17).*

39 *C. Global groups cannot contain local groups.* Global groups cannot contain local groups. *Objective: Manage user and group accounts (Chapter 14).*

40 *B. You must run DISKPERF.EXE for the counters to appear.* For Performance Monitor to view disk counters, you must run DISKPERF.EXE first. *Objective: Monitor performance of various functions by using Performance Monitor (Chapter 18).*

41 *A. Replace the failed disk, and regenerate the data.* RAID level 0 is disk striping without parity. If a disk fails, all data is lost. You must replace the disk, create a new set, and restore data from a backup. *Objective: Choose the appropriate course of action to take to resolve fault-tolerance failures (Chapter 5).*

42 *C. Incorrect Printer Driver.* Illegible printouts are usually the result of an incorrect printer driver being used. *Objective: Choose the appropriate course of action to take to resolve printer problems (Chapter 18).*

43 *D. Disk Mirroring.* You cannot put the system or boot partitions on a stripe or volume set. You can however put them on a mirrored set. *Objective: Plan the disk drive configuration for various requirements (Chapter 5).*

44 *D. System Partition.* Windows NT stores the files it requires to boot with on the system partition. *Objective: Install Windows NT Server on Intel-based platforms (Chapter 7).*

45 *B. Per Seat.* If there are multiple servers, the best choice of licensing is Per Seat. *Objective: Install Windows NT Server using various methods (Chapter 7).*

46 *A. DLC.* The Hewlett-Packard Print Monitor requires the DLC protocol. *Objective: Configure printers (Chapter 12).*

47 *C. Primary Domain Controller and Backup Domain Controller.* PDCs and BDCs validate user logons. *Objective: Install Windows NT Server to perform various server roles (Chapter 7).*

48 *D. Resolves NetBIOS names to IP addresses.* WINS resolves NetBIOS names to IP addresses. *Objective: Choose a protocol for various situations (Chapter 9).*

49 *B. Dynamic Host Configuration Protocol.* DHCP stands for Dynamic Host Configuration Protocol. *Objective: Choose a protocol for various situations (Chapter 9).*

50 *D. User Manager for Domains.* User Manager for Domains is used to enable auditing of a user. *Objective: Manage user and group accounts (Chapter 13).*

51 *A. FAT.* FAT is the only file system that both Windows 95 and NT Server can support. FAT32 is an enhanced version of FAT that isn't supported by NT Server, while NTFS is not supported by Windows 95. CDFS isn't used for hard disks. It is the CD-ROM File System. *Objective: Plan the disk drive configuration for various requirements (Chapter 5).*

52 *A. NWLink.* NWLink is Microsoft's implementation of the IPX/SPX protocol used by NetWare and the best choice when connecting these two systems. *Objective: Choose a protocol for various situations (Chapter 9).*

53 *A. Network Monitor Agent.* Network Monitor Agent installs the network performance counters that you can then use in Performance Monitor. Diskperf allows you to view the hard drive counters, while Simple Network Management Agent (SNMP) allows you to use TCP/IP related counters. *Objective: Monitor performance of various functions by using Performance Monitor (Chapter 18).*

54 *D. Disk Administrator.* Disk Administrator is used to create, extend, stripe, and make volume sets. *Objective: Configure hard disks to meet various requirements (Chapter 5).*

Appendix C

About the CD

∙ ∙

On the CD-ROM

▶ The QuickLearn game, a fun way to study for the test

▶ Practice with Self-Assessment tests, to make sure that you're ready for the real thing

▶ Practice test demos from Transcender, QuickCert, and EndeavorX

∙ ∙

System Requirements

Make sure that your computer meets the minimum system requirements listed next. If your computer doesn't match up to most of these requirements, you may have problems using the contents of the CD.

- ✔ A PC with a 486 or faster processor.
- ✔ Microsoft Windows 95 or later.
- ✔ At least 16MB of total RAM installed on your computer.
- ✔ At least 32MB of hard drive space available to install all the software from this CD. (You need less space if you don't install every program.)
- ✔ A CD-ROM drive — double-speed (2x) or faster.
- ✔ A sound card for PCs.
- ✔ A monitor capable of displaying at least 256 colors or grayscale.
- ✔ A modem with a speed of at least 14,400 bps.

Using the CD with Microsoft Windows

To install the items from the CD to your hard drive, follow these steps:

1. **Insert the CD into your computer's CD-ROM drive.**
2. **Click Start➪Run.**
3. **In the dialog box that appears, type** D:\SETUP.EXE.

   Replace *D* with the proper drive letter if your CD-ROM drive uses a different letter.

4. **Click OK.**

   A license agreement window appears.

5. **Read through the license agreement, nod your head, and then click the Accept button if you want to use the CD — after you click Accept, you'll never be bothered by the License Agreement window again.**

   The CD interface Welcome screen appears. The interface is a little program that shows you what's on the CD and coordinates installing the programs and running the demos. The interface basically enables you to click a button or two to make things happen.

6. **Click anywhere on the Welcome screen to enter the interface.**

   Now you're getting to the action. The next screen lists categories for the software on the CD.

7. **To view the items within a category, just click the category's name.**

   A list of programs in the category appears.

8. **For more information about a program, click the program's name.**

   Be sure to read the information that appears. Sometimes a program has its own system requirements or requires you to do a few tricks on your computer before you can install or run the program, and this screen tells you what you may need to do, if necessary.

9. **If you don't want to install the program, click the Go Back button to return to the previous screen.**

   You can always return to the previous screen by clicking the Go Back button. This feature enables you to browse the different categories and products and decide what you want to install.

10. **To install a program, click the appropriate Install button.**

    The CD interface drops to the background while the CD installs the program you chose.

11. **To install other items, repeat Steps 7 through 10.**

12. **When you finish installing programs, click the Quit button to close the interface.**

    You can eject the CD now. Carefully place it back in the plastic jacket of the book for safekeeping.

In order to run some of the programs on the *MCSE Windows NT Server 4 For Dummies* CD, you may need to keep the CD inside your CD-ROM drive. This is a Good Thing. Otherwise, the installed program would require you to install a very large chunk of the program to your hard drive, which may keep you from installing other software.

What You'll Find

Here's a summary of the software on this CD.

Dummies test prep tools

This CD contains questions related to **NT Server.** Most of the questions are networking topics that you can expect to be on the test. We've also included some questions on other **NT Server** topics that may or may not be on the current test or covered in the book, but that you will need to perform your job.

QuickLearn Game

The QuickLearn Game is the *...For Dummies* way of making studying for the Certification exam fun. Well, okay, less painful. OutPost is a DirectX, high-resolution, fast-paced arcade game.

Answer questions to defuse dimensional disrupters and save the universe from a rift in space-time. (The questions come from the same set of questions that the Self-Assessment and Practice Test use, but isn't this way more fun?) Missing a few questions on the real exam almost never results in a rip in the fabric of the universe, so just think how easy it'll be when you get there!

The QuickLearn game requires Microsoft DirectX 5.0 or later. If you have Windows 95 or Windows 98 without DirectX, you can download DirectX at www.microsoft.com/directx/resources/dx5end.htm. DirectX 5.0 does not run on Windows NT 4.0. When Windows NT 5 is released, it will run DirectX 6.0.

Practice Test

The Practice Test is designed to help you get comfortable with the MCSE testing situation and pinpoint your strengths and weaknesses on the topic. You can accept the default setting of 60 questions in 60 minutes, or you can customize the settings. You can pick the number of questions, the amount of time, and even decide which objectives you want to focus on.

After you answer the questions, the Practice Test gives you plenty of feedback. You can find out which questions you got right or wrong and get statistics on how you did, broken down by objective. Then you can review the questions — all of them, all the ones you missed, all the ones you marked, or a combination of the ones you marked and the ones you missed.

Self-Assessment Test

The Self-Assessment Test is designed to simulate the actual MCSE testing situation. You must answer 60 questions in 60 minutes. After you answer all the questions, you find out your score and whether you pass or fail — but that's all the feedback you get. If you can pass the Self-Assessment Test fairly regularly, you're ready to tackle the real thing.

Links Page

This is a handy starting place for accessing the huge amounts of information on the Internet about the MCSE tests. You can find the page, Links.htm, at the root of the CD.

Commercial demos

Transcender Certification Sampler, from Transcender Corporation

Transcender's demo tests are some of the most popular practice tests available. The Certification Sampler offers demos of all the exams that Transcender offers.

QuickCert, from Specialized Solutions

This package from Specialized Solutions offers QuickCert practice tests for several Certification exams. Run the QuickCert IDG Demo to choose the practice test you want to work on.

EndeavorX, from VFX Technologies

EndeavorX is a powerful new knowledge assessment application, with four different testing modes and a wide variety of question filters.

The first time you run EndeavorX, you need to import the exam set:

1. **Choose File⇨Import/Export to open the Administration dialog box.**

2. **Navigate to the file** Microsoft Evaluation Exams for Import.mdb **and enter it in the Import Data From text box.**

3. **Click the Import button and select exactly what elements you want to import.**

   VFX also provides the file Novell Evaluation Exams for Import.mdb as a bonus.

4. **After you import the exams, use the Control Panel to select the test or the categories you want to work with and to set the other test parameters.**

When you install EndeavorX, I advise you to accept the default installation location and use the Typical installation option. If you choose to install the software on a drive or in a directory other than the default, EndeavorX can't find the question database.

If the physical installation and the registry settings don't match, one or more error messages may appear. If you get an error message, try the following steps to straighten things out:

1. **When the File Open dialog box opens looking for** EndeavorX.mdb, **navigate to the directory/drive where the software is installed.**

2. **Double-click the** EndeavorX.mdb **file.**

   To update all the registry settings, proceed immediately to the EndeavorX Control Panel.

3. **Review all the settings, make any changes needed, and then click the OK button to close the Control Panel and save these settings.**

4. **If any tests have been imported, select a test and some combination of categories.**

5. **Select a default printing device.**

6. **Set the Font to any font installed on your system.**

   All font characteristics should be listed, as well as a sample of the font.

7. **Carefully examine the colors to ensure that the foreground and background colors contrast (for example, black on white).**

   Typically, the explanation text is offset as a different color than the question/answer text.

8. **For environmental settings, "uncheck" login, tips, and so on.**

   By default, only the Splash Screen and the Auto Advance are checked.

9. **Click OK to exit the EndeavorX Control Panel.**

If You've Got Problems (Of the CD Kind)

I tried my best to compile programs that work on most computers with the minimum system requirements. Alas, your computer may differ, and some programs may not work properly for some reason.

The two most likely problems are that you don't have enough memory (RAM) for the programs you want to use, or that you have other programs running that are affecting installation or running of a program. If you get error messages like Not enough memory or Setup cannot continue, try one or more of these methods and then try using the software again:

✔ **Turn off any antivirus software that you have on your computer.**
Installers sometimes mimic virus activity and may make your computer
incorrectly believe that it is being infected by a virus.

✔ **Close all running programs.** The more programs you're running, the
less memory is available to other programs. Installers also typically
update files and programs; if you keep other programs running, installation may not work properly.

✔ **In Windows, close the CD interface and run demos or installations
directly from Windows Explorer.** The interface itself can tie up system
memory or even conflict with certain kinds of interactive demos. Use
Windows Explorer to browse the files on the CD and launch installers or
demos.

✔ **Have your local computer store add more RAM to your computer.**
This is, admittedly, a drastic and somewhat expensive step. However, if
you have a Windows 95 PC or a Mac OS computer with a PowerPC chip,
adding more memory can really help the speed of your computer and
enable more programs to run at the same time.

If you still have trouble installing the items from the CD, please call the IDG
Books Worldwide Customer Service phone number: 800-762-2974 (outside
the U.S.: 317-596-5430).

Index

(continued)

(continued)

(continued)

Notes

IDG Books Worldwide, Inc., End-User License Agreement

• •

5. **Limited Warranty.**

   (a) IDGB warrants that the Software and Software Media are free from defects in materials and workmanship under normal use for a period of sixty (60) days from the date of purchase of this Book. If IDGB receives notification within the warranty period of defects in materials or workmanship, IDGB will replace the defective Software Media.

   (b) **IDGB AND THE AUTHOR OF THE BOOK DISCLAIM ALL OTHER WARRANTIES, EXPRESS OR IMPLIED, INCLUDING WITHOUT LIMITATION IMPLIED WARRANTIES OF MERCHANTABILITY AND FITNESS FOR A PARTICULAR PURPOSE, WITH RESPECT TO THE SOFTWARE, THE PROGRAMS, THE SOURCE CODE CONTAINED THEREIN, AND/OR THE TECHNIQUES DESCRIBED IN THIS BOOK. IDGB DOES NOT WARRANT THAT THE FUNCTIONS CONTAINED IN THE SOFTWARE WILL MEET YOUR REQUIREMENTS OR THAT THE OPERATION OF THE SOFTWARE WILL BE ERROR FREE.**

   (c) This limited warranty gives you specific legal rights, and you may have other rights that vary from jurisdiction to jurisdiction.

6. **Remedies.**

   (a) IDGB's entire liability and your exclusive remedy for defects in materials and work-manship shall be limited to replacement of the Software Media, which may be re-turned to IDGB with a copy of your receipt at the following address: Software Media Fulfillment Department, Attn.: *MCSE Windows NT Server 4 For Dummies,* IDG Books Worldwide, Inc., 7260 Shadeland Station, Ste. 100, Indianapolis, IN 46256, or call 800-762-2974. Please allow three to four weeks for delivery. This Limited Warranty is void if failure of the Software Media has resulted from accident, abuse, or misapplication. Any replacement Software Media will be warranted for the remainder of the original warranty period or thirty (30) days, whichever is longer.

   (b) In no event shall IDGB or the author be liable for any damages whatsoever (including without limitation damages for loss of business profits, business interruption, loss of business information, or any other pecuniary loss) arising from the use of or inability to use the Book or the Software, even if IDGB has been advised of the possibility of such damages.

   (c) Because some jurisdictions do not allow the exclusion or limitation of liability for consequential or incidental damages, the above limitation or exclusion may not apply to you.

7. **U.S. Government Restricted Rights.** Use, duplication, or disclosure of the Software by the U.S. Government is subject to restrictions stated in paragraph (c)(1)(ii) of the Rights in Technical Data and Computer Software clause of DFARS 252.227-7013, and in subpara-graphs (a) through (d) of the Commercial Computer–Restricted Rights clause at FAR 52.227-19, and in similar clauses in the NASA FAR supplement, when applicable.

8. **General.** This Agreement constitutes the entire understanding of the parties and revokes and supersedes all prior agreements, oral or written, between them and may not be modified or amended except in a writing signed by both parties hereto that specifically refers to this Agreement. This Agreement shall take precedence over any other documents that may be in conflict herewith. If any one or more provisions contained in this Agreement are held by any court or tribunal to be invalid, illegal, or otherwise unenforceable, each and every other provision shall remain in full force and effect.

Installation Instructions

*H*ere's what you can find on the *MCSE Windows NT Server 4 For Dummies* CD-ROM:

- ✔ The QuickLearn Game, a fun way to study for the test
- ✔ Practice and Self-Assessment Tests, to make sure that you're ready for the real thing
- ✔ Practice test demos from Transcender, QuickCert, and EndeavorX

To install the items from the CD to your hard drive, follow these steps:

1. **Insert the CD into your computer's CD-ROM drive.**
2. **Click Start➪Run.**
3. **In the dialog box that appears, type** D:\SETUP.EXE.

   Replace *D* with the proper drive letter if your CD-ROM drive uses a different letter.
4. **Click OK.**

   A license agreement window appears.
5. **Read through the license agreement, and then click Accept. You'll never see the License Agreement window again.**

   The CD interface Welcome screen appears. The interface shows you what's on the CD and coordinates installing the programs and running the demos.
6. **Click anywhere on the Welcome screen to enter the interface.**

   You see a list of categories for the software on the CD.
7. **To view the items within a category, click the category's name.**

   A list of programs in the category appears.
8. **To install a program, click the appropriate Install button.**

   The CD interface drops to the background while the CD installs the program you chose.
9. **When you finish installing programs, click Quit.**

   The CD interface closes, and you can eject the CD. Carefully place it back in the plastic jacket of the book for safekeeping.

To run some of the programs on the *MCSE Windows NT Server 4 For Dummies* CD, you may need to keep the CD inside your CD-ROM drive.

For details about the contents of the CD-ROM and instructions for installing the software from the CD-ROM, see the "About the CD" appendix in this book.

IDG BOOKS WORLDWIDE BOOK REGISTRATION

We want to hear from you!

Register This Book and Win!

Visit **http://my2cents.dummies.com** to register this book and tell us how you liked it!

- ✔ Get entered in our monthly prize giveaway.

- ✔ Give us feedback about this book — tell us what you like best, what you like least, or maybe what you'd like to ask the author and us to change!

- ✔ Let us know any other *...For Dummies*® topics that interest you.

Your feedback helps us determine what books to publish, tells us what coverage to add as we revise our books, and lets us know whether we're meeting your needs as a *...For Dummies* reader. You're our most valuable resource, and what you have to say is important to us!

Not on the Web yet? It's easy to get started with *Dummies 101*®: *The Internet For Windows*® *95* or *The Internet For Dummies*,® 5th Edition, at local retailers everywhere.

Or let us know what you think by sending us a letter at the following address:

...For Dummies Book Registration
Dummies Press
7260 Shadeland Station, Suite 100
Indianapolis, IN 46256-3945
Fax 317-596-5498

BUSINESS AND
**GENERAL
REFERENCE
BOOK SERIES
FROM IDG**

**COMPUTER
BOOK SERIES
FROM IDG**